Phonics for Pupils with Special Educational Needs

Book 3: Sound by Sound Part 1

Phonics for Pupils with Special Educational Needs is a complete, structured, multisensory programme for teaching reading and spelling, making it fun and accessible for all. This fantastic seven-part resource offers a refreshingly simple approach to the teaching of phonics, alongside activities to develop auditory and visual perceptual skills. Specifically designed to meet the needs of pupils with special educational needs of any age, the books break down phonics into manageable core elements and provide a huge wealth of resources to support teachers in teaching reading and spelling.

Book 3: Sound by Sound Part 1 focuses on discovering complex sounds and their relationship with letters and letter combinations. Each chapter explores a key sound (sh/ th/ ng/ ch/ k/ qu/ f/ l/ s) and contains over 40 engaging activities, including: sound exchange, word scramble, spot the spelling, word detective and writing challenge. Thorough guidance is provided on how to deliver each activity, as well a lesson planner template, a handy list of high frequency words and posters for teachers and teaching assistants to use to support learning.

Each book in the series gradually builds on children's understanding of sounds and letters and provides scaffolded support for children to learn about every sound in the English language. Offering tried and tested material which can be photocopied for each use, this is an invaluable resource to simplify phonics teaching for teachers and teaching assistants and provide fun new ways of learning phonics for all children.

Ann Sullivan is an educational consultant and trainer. Having gained experience of teaching in mainstream primary classrooms and in secondary learning support departments, she went on to become a high school SENCO. The move to specialist education seemed natural and for nine years she worked as an outreach/advisory teacher based at a specialist support school, providing advice, support and training to staff in mainstream schools to enable them to meet the needs of their pupils with SEND. She became a Specialist Leader in Education in 2017. Ann has made it her career's work to explore the best ways of teaching young people to read, spell and write effectively, leading her to develop these resources, which she has tested in a variety of mainstream and special schools.

Phonics for Pupils with Special Educational Needs

This fantastic seven-part resource offers an innovative and refreshingly simple approach to the teaching of phonics that is specifically designed to meet the needs of pupils with special educational needs. The books strip phonics down into manageable core elements and provide a wealth of resources to support teachers in teaching reading and spelling. They systematically take the pupil through incremental steps and help them to learn about and thoroughly understand all of the sounds in the English language.

Other resources in *Phonics for Pupils with Special Educational Needs*

Book 1: Building Basics	**Introducing Sounds and Letters**	
Book 2: Building Words	**Working on Word Structure with Basic Sounds**	
Book 3: Sound by Sound Part 1	**Discovering the Sounds**	
Book 4: Sound by Sound Part 2	**Investigating the Sounds**	
Book 5: Sound by Sound Part 3	**Exploring the Sounds**	
Book 6: Sound by Sound Part 4	**Surveying the Sounds**	
Book 7: Multisyllable Magic	**Revising the Main Sounds and Working on 2, 3 and 4 Syllable Words**	

Phonics for Pupils with Special Educational Needs

Book 3: Sound by Sound Part 1

Discovering the Sounds

Ann Sullivan

LONDON AND NEW YORK

First published 2019
by Routledge
2 Park Square, Milton Park, Abingdon, Oxon OX14 4RN

and by Routledge
711 Third Avenue, New York, NY 10017

Routledge is an imprint of the Taylor & Francis Group, an informa business

British Library Cataloguing-in-Publication Data
A catalogue record for this book is available from the British Library

Library of Congress Cataloging-in-Publication Data
Names: Sullivan, Ann (Educational consultant) author.
Title: Phonics for pupils with special educational needs / Ann Sullivan.
Description: Abingdon, Oxon ; New York, NY : Routledge, 2019–
Identifiers: LCCN 2018015561 (print) | LCCN 2018033657 (ebook) | ISBN 9781351040303 (ebook) | ISBN 9781138488373 (book 1) | ISBN 9781351040303 (book 1 : ebk) | ISBN 9781138488434 (book 3) | ISBN 9781351040181 (book 3 : ebk) | ISBN 9781138313583 (book 5) | ISBN 9780429457555 (book 5 : ebk) | ISBN 9781138313637 (book 6) | ISBN 9780429457517 (book 6 : ebk) | ISBN 9781138313682 (book 7) | ISBN 9780429457487 (book 7 : ebk)
Subjects: LCSH: Reading—Phonetic method. | Reading disability. | Special education.
Classification: LCC LB1573.3 (ebook) | LCC LB1573.3 .S85 2019 (print) | DDC 372.46/5—dc23
LC record available at https://lccn.loc.gov/2018015561

ISBN: 978-1-138-48843-4 (pbk)
ISBN: 978-1-351-04018-1 (ebk)

Typeset in VAG Rounded
by Apex CoVantage, LLC

To Matthew, Ruth and Tom

Contents

Introduction

Phonics is the established method for teaching reading and spelling in schools, but many pupils with special educational needs find conventional phonics programmes and schemes difficult to access and so struggle to find success.

Pupils with special educational needs require a clear and consistent, multisensory approach to phonics and the teaching of reading and spelling. A programme should give them the opportunity to systematically and thoroughly explore all sounds and letters, gradually building up their understanding and knowledge of how the written English language works so that they are able to apply these when reading and spelling words. They also require specific instructional techniques to develop and master key reading and spelling skills and be given the opportunity to work at a pace appropriate to their individual needs.

Phonics for Pupils with Special Educational Needs is a complete programme, made up of seven books, which simplifies the way written language is presented to the child, demystifying phonics to make it accessible and fun. The programme is multisensory, systematic, logical, thorough and cumulative in its approach, taking the child from their first encounter with sounds and letters through to managing and using multisyllable words.

Many pupils with special educational needs have underlying difficulties with auditory and visual perception and processing, which often goes unrecognised. Difficulties processing auditory and visual information will have a direct impact on reading and spelling acquisition, as written English is essentially a cipher or code that converts speech sounds into visual figures for spelling and vice versa for reading. The cipher is dependent on an individual being able to work with and interpret sounds and symbols; yet processing auditory and visual information may be the very things that a pupil finds difficult to do. Pupils with perceptual difficulties require access to materials that work to develop and improve these auditory and visual skills in the context of the sounds and letters they are learning. Built into the *Phonics for Pupils with Special Educational Needs* programme are worksheets, resources and activities which support the development of underlying auditory and visual skills.

Difficulties with visual perception and processing will also impact on the child's ability to easily access teaching materials presented to them. For this reason, the worksheets, resources and activities in *Phonics for Pupils with Special Educational Needs* are simple in format, uncluttered and with a simple to follow linear progression.

Book 3 Sound by Sound Part 1: Discovering the Sounds

This book introduces the pupil to the complex **sounds** (speech sounds or phonemes) in words and explores the relationship between each sound and **letters or groups of letters** (sound spellings). The book focuses on the following sounds: 'sh' 'th' 'ng' 'ch' 'k' 'qu' 'f' 'l' and 's', with subsequent books ensuring coverage of all sounds.

In Book 3, the pupil:

- learns and explores the important concepts or ideas about the English language; that letters are ***symbols*** or ***pictures*** that ***represent*** speech sounds in spoken words; that some of the symbols are made up of one letter but some have two, three or even four letters; that some sounds are represented by more than one symbol;
- revises the basic sounds and the single letters that represent them;
- learns to manage these sounds in words of a variety of structures: VC, CVC, VCC, CVCC, CCVC and CCVCC+ words (V = vowel, C = consonant);
- gradually discovers complex sounds and the letters or groups of letters (sound spellings) that represent them;
- continues to practise the key reading and spelling skills of blending, segmenting and phoneme manipulation;
- reinforces understanding and application of a dynamic blending strategy for reading words;
- reinforces understanding and application of a sequential segmenting strategy for spelling words;
- continues to develop auditory perceptual and processing skills in relation to the sounds introduced;
- continues to develop visual perceptual and processing skills in relation to the letters and groups of letters (sound spellings) introduced;
- experiences reading and spelling words at single word and sentence level and
- experiences reading at text level.

Book 1 introduced the pupil to the basic sounds and the single letters that represent them. Book 2 developed the pupil's ability to work with these sounds in words with a more complex structure: VCC, CVCC, CCVC and CCVCC+ words. Books 3–6 introduce and systematically explore the more complex sounds in the English language and Book 7 revises and explores all the sounds in the context of 2, 3 and 4 syllable words and works on suffixes.

Working through the programme

It is strongly recommended that anyone delivering the programme reads through the teaching notes in the 'Working through the programme' section of this book, where the programme is explained in detail and specific techniques are described and explained.

Teaching materials

Most of the resources in the programme have instructions on delivery of the activity or worksheet on the sheet itself to provide a helpful prompt for teachers and teaching assistants. A few activities only have instructions written in the 'Working through the programme' section of this book and teachers and teaching assistants should make themselves familiar with the details of these.

All the resources in the programme are designed to have a simple format and presentation to support access for pupils with visual perceptual difficulties. As a result, they are age neutral and so are suitable for pupils of a wide age range; primary, secondary and post 16.

Phonics for Pupils with Special Educational Needs is suitable for pupils in mainstream and specialist school settings.

Planning and delivery

A simple to use planning sheet enables teachers and teaching assistants to plan teaching sessions by selecting from the menu of available programme activities, ensuring an overall even and complete coverage of skills, concepts and knowledge. The planning sheet also enables staff to track pupil progression thorough the programme.

A child or group of children can work through the programme at a pace that is appropriate for them or their peer group.

Working through the programme

Starting out

Before beginning to work through the programme with a child or a group of children, it is important for teachers and teaching assistants to read through this introductory section to familiarise themselves with the programme's structure and how it works, as well as the specific instructional techniques, resources and activities.

It is assumed that a child starting on the activities in this book has worked through Books 1 and 2, Building Basics, or that the child has knowledge of the basic sounds and letters (sound spellings), key skills and concepts equivalent to having worked through Books 1 and 2 of this programme.

This section covers **the things you need to know about and understand before you start**:

- the ideas or concepts which underpin the structure of written English;
- the skills that children need to master to be able to work with sounds and letters / letter combinations (sound spellings): blending, segmenting and phoneme manipulation;
- the body of knowledge children need to know, remember and recall and
- visual and auditory perception and processing related to working with sounds and letters.

It covers **how to teach the programme** at Book 3 level:

- the teaching order of sounds,
- introducing sounds and letters / letter combinations (sound spellings),
- working in a multisensory way,
- teaching the concepts to the child,
- teaching the skills to the child and
- building up the child's knowledge of sounds and letters / letter combinations (sound spellings).

It also covers **how to organise delivery of the programme**:

- structuring a teaching session and
- planning and progression.

Note that in the explanations which follow, sounds are always written in speech marks, e.g. 's' 'l' 'ch', and letters / letter combinations (sound spellings) are always written in bold, e.g. ***s l ch tch*** *etc.*

The written English language – an overview

Written language developed hundreds of years ago because people realised they needed to fix information in a form that remained constant over time. In this way information could be passed on easily, without people having to speak directly to each other. Writing developed as a way of storing information, carrying messages and sharing news and stories.

Experiments in drawing pictures to represent information proved ineffective as pictures can be interpreted in so many ways and are open to an individual's interpretation. However, people soon realised that there is one characteristic of the spoken word that could be exploited to create a permanent and fixed visual representation of the information.

The spoken word is made up of speech sounds (or phonemes). When we say any word, we must be consistent with the sounds we use and the order we say them for us to convey the intended meaning.

If I say the sounds 'c' 'a' 't' together to make a word, then you think of a furry pet. If I change the first sound to 'h' then the meaning changes and you think of something quite different.

Written English capitalises on this consistency and uses letters as ***symbols*** to, one by one, represent ***individual speech sounds***. In other words, letters are a written form of spoken sounds.

This is the first of four ideas or concepts that children need to understand to be able to read and spell but there are three more; all are explained below.

The concepts – how the written word is put together

1. **Letters represent sounds**

   In the written word the letters represent the speech sounds of the spoken word.

   For example, the word dog has three sounds in it, 'd' 'o' 'g', which are represented by the three letters:

   d o g.

   This concept is introduced in Book 1 of the programme.

   In *Phonics for Pupils with Special Educational Needs*, letters are referred to as '***sound spellings***'. This label describes letters in terms of their function, i.e. that a ***sound*** is represented in a written form when we ***spell*** / write words. It gives the teacher a simple term that describes single letters and, more importantly, also describes combinations of letters which appear in this part of the programme. This term also reinforces the sound to symbol relationship, '***sound*** > ***spelling***' and the term is easy for children to understand and remember.

2. **Sound spellings can be one letter or more**

   Some of the sound spellings we use are made up of just one letter, like those in dog, but many are made up of several letters which, in combination, act as a single unit within the word, together representing one sound.

   For example, **sh** is the sound spelling for the sound 'sh' in the word **sh**op and **th** is the sound spelling for the sound 'th' in the word mo**th**. **sh** and **th** are sound spellings that are made up two letters, but some sound spellings are made up of three or even four letters, e.g. **igh** representing 'i-e' and **ough** representing 'o-e'.

   This concept is introduced in this book, Book 3 of the programme.

3. **Sounds can be represented by more than just one sound spelling**

   Many sounds can be represented in more than just one way, i.e. by more than one sound spelling.

   For example: b**oa**t t**oe** s**o** gr**ow** c**o**d**e** th**ough**

   These all have an 'o-e' sound, but it is written differently in each word, using the sound spellings:

   oa, oe, o, ow, o-e and **ough**, respectively.

   This concept is touched upon in Book 1, but is fully explored in this book, Book 3.

   Phonics for Pupils with Special Educational Needs focuses on working on only **one sound at a time** and enabling the child to discover ***all*** the ways of representing it. Time is given to experience and explore all the sound spellings at word and sentence level before moving on to the next sound in the book.

4. **Some sound spellings can represent more than one sound**

   Certain sound spellings can be used to represent one sound in one word but a different sound in another word.

   For example: gr**ow** br**ow**n

   The sound spelling **ow** is in both words, but in the first it represents an 'o-e' sound and in the second it represents an 'ow' sound.

   This concept is introduced in Book 4 of the programme.

Phonics for Pupils with Special Educational Needs addresses this at appropriate points in the programme for key sound spellings, giving the child the opportunity to explore all the sounds that these sound spellings can represent.

To be able to read and spell effectively, children need to understand these four concepts. *Phonics for Pupils with Special Educational Needs* presents children with the opportunity to explore them for each sound in English over the seven books in the programme.

At this point it is important to understand that the child's understanding of these concepts will be implicit rather than explicit. This means that they will have processed their experiences of sounds, sound spellings and words and reached an unconscious understanding about the concepts. The programme does not demand that the child talks about or explains the concepts but instead they demonstrate their understanding by the way they respond to sounds, sounds spellings and words during teaching sessions and whenever they are reading and writing.

The skills – what we do with the sounds and sound spellings

As well as understanding these four concepts, children also need to be able to ***work with*** the sounds and sound spellings to read or spell words. Like all skills, these need to be taught and practised to achieve mastery. The skills needed to be able to read and spell are:

1. **Blending** – to be able to push speech sounds together to make a meaningful word. This skill relates directly to reading.
2. **Segmenting** – to be able to break up words into all the separate speech sounds that make up that word, in the right order. This skill relates directly to spelling.
3. **Phoneme manipulation** – to be able to slide speech sounds in and out of words. This skill relates to both reading and spelling.

Developing an understanding of how the English language is put together and practising these important skills starts on day one of the programme and continues right the way through to mastery.

The knowledge – what we need to know, remember and recall

Skills and concepts are not the only things children need to learn to be able to read and spell effectively. They also need a good working knowledge of the sounds and sound spellings. Specifically, they need to know the relationship between the two and this is something that is gradually and cumulatively built up as the child works through this programme.

There are around 140 sound spellings representing the 40 *or so* sounds we use (*regional differences influence exactly how many sounds we perceive in words with variation from 40–42*). At the end of this section there are two posters that show all the sounds and their main sound spellings which you may find helpful.

Step by step and sound by sound, *Phonics for Pupils with Special Educational Needs* works through all the sounds and all their sound spellings, guides the child to understand how written language is put together and supports them to master the skills needed to become fluent readers and spellers.

Automaticity

At first, reading may be a slow process of working through a word, sound spelling by sound spelling, but with experience, repetition and practice the child achieves 'automaticity'. Automaticity happens when all the things the child has experienced and learned come together to enable them to look at a written word, process it rapidly and without apparent effort simply say the word. As competent adult readers we have achieved this automaticity and can no longer remember just how we learned to read.

The activities and techniques in *Phonics for Pupils with Special Educational Needs* are designed to provide the child with this experience, repetition and practice with the aim of children achieving reading and spelling automaticity.

Books 3–6 The *Sound by Sound* books

In Book 3 the sound to sound spelling relationship is explored for the sounds: 'sh' 'th' 'ng' 'ch' 'k' 'qu' 'f' 'l' and 's' and more are investigated in Books 4, 5 and 6 to ensure coverage of all sounds. The teaching order of sounds is shown in Table 1.

From Book 3 onwards the sounds that the child studies can be described as being more complex in that the child needs to deal with not just the first of those four important concepts but also the second and third.

The complex sounds have:

- sound spellings made up of more than one letter and
- more than one sound spelling to represent them.

Table 1 The teaching order of sounds in *Phonics for Pupils with Special Educational Needs*

<table>
<tr><th colspan="4">Phonics for Pupils with Special Educational Needs teaching order</th></tr>
<tr><th>Book</th><th>Sounds</th><th>Word structure</th><th>Skills</th></tr>
<tr><td rowspan="7">1 Building Basics: Introducing Sounds and Letters
Focus: Basic sounds and their relationship with letters</td><td>s a t p</td><td rowspan="7">VC and CVC words</td><td rowspan="42">Blending, segmenting & phoneme manipulation

Teaching to mastery</td></tr>
<tr><td>i n m d</td></tr>
<tr><td>g o c k</td></tr>
<tr><td>e u r</td></tr>
<tr><td>h b f l</td></tr>
<tr><td>j v w x</td></tr>
<tr><td>y z</td></tr>
<tr><td rowspan="5">2 Building Words: Working on Word Structure with Basic Sounds
Focus: Increasingly complex word structure</td><td rowspan="5">All the sounds from Book 1</td><td>VCC words</td></tr>
<tr><td>CVCC words</td></tr>
<tr><td>CCVC words</td></tr>
<tr><td>CCVCC+ words</td></tr>
<tr><td>CAPITALS</td></tr>
<tr><td rowspan="9">3 Sound by Sound Part 1: Discovering the Sounds
Focus: Complex sounds and their relationship with letters and letter combinations</td><td>sh</td><td rowspan="30">Mixed
VC
CVC
VCC
CVCC
CCVC
CCVCC+
words</td></tr>
<tr><td>th</td></tr>
<tr><td>ch</td></tr>
<tr><td>k</td></tr>
<tr><td>qu</td></tr>
<tr><td>ng</td></tr>
<tr><td>f</td></tr>
<tr><td>l</td></tr>
<tr><td>s</td></tr>
<tr><td rowspan="7">4 Sound by Sound Part 2: Investigating the Sounds
Focus: Complex sounds and their relationship with letters and letter combinations</td><td>o-e</td></tr>
<tr><td>z</td></tr>
<tr><td>ee</td></tr>
<tr><td>a-e</td></tr>
<tr><td>er</td></tr>
<tr><td>e</td></tr>
<tr><td>ow</td></tr>
<tr><td rowspan="7">5 Sound by Sound Part 3: Exploring the Sounds
Focus: Complex sounds and their relationship with letters and letter combinations</td><td>oy</td></tr>
<tr><td>oo</td></tr>
<tr><td>u</td></tr>
<tr><td>i-e</td></tr>
<tr><td>aw</td></tr>
<tr><td>air</td></tr>
<tr><td>ar</td></tr>
<tr><td rowspan="7">6 Sound by Sound Part 4: Surveying the Sounds
Focus: Complex sounds and their relationship with letters and letter combinations</td><td>s (advanced)</td></tr>
<tr><td>l (advanced)</td></tr>
<tr><td>b and d (advanced)</td></tr>
<tr><td>o</td></tr>
<tr><td>i</td></tr>
<tr><td>u-e</td></tr>
<tr><td>Miscellaneous consonants</td></tr>
</table>

***Phonics for Pupils with Special Educational Needs* teaching order**			
Book	**Sounds**	**Word structure**	**Skills**
7 Multisyllable Magic: Revising the Main Sounds and Working on 2, 3 and 4 Syllable Words Focus: Reading and spelling 2 syllable words and revising the main sounds. Reading and spelling 3 and 4 syllable words and words with key suffixes.	Revision of o-e	2 syllable words	
	Revision of ee		
	Revision of a-e		
	Revision of er		
	Revision of e		
	Revision of ow		
	Revision of oy		
	Revision of oo		
	Revision of u		
	Revision of i-e		
	Revision of aw		
	Revision of air		
	Revision of ar		
	Revision of o	3 and 4 syllable words	
	Revision of i		
	Revision of u-e		
	Suffixes		

The final of the four concepts is introduced from Book 4 onwards when key sound spellings are targeted and explored to identify all the sounds they represent, as shown in Table 2.

In this way the child discovers all four concepts related to written language as they work through the programme.

Table 2 Key sound spelling focus in *Phonics for Pupils with Special Educational Needs*

Book	**Focus sound**	**Key sounds spelling focus**
4 Sound by Sound Part 2: Investigating the Sounds	o-e	**o** representing the sounds: 'o' and 'o-e'
	z	**s** representing the sounds: 's' and 'z'
	ee	
	a-e	
	er	
	e	**ea** representing the sounds: 'ee', 'a-e' and 'e'
	ow	**ow** representing the sounds: 'o-e' and 'ow'
5 Sound by Sound Part 3: Exploring the Sounds	oy	
	oo	
	u	**oo** representing the sounds: 'oo' and 'u' **ou** representing the sounds: 'oo', 'ou' and 'ow'
	i-e	**ie** representing the sounds: 'i-e' and 'ee'
	aw	**ough** representing the sounds: 'aw', 'o-e', 'ow' and 'oo'
	air	
	ar	**ear** representing the sounds: 'er', 'air' and 'ar'

Book	Focus sound	Key sounds spelling focus
6 Sound by Sound Part 4: Surveying the Sounds	s (advanced)	**c** representing the sounds: 'c' and 's'
	l (advanced)	**al** representing the sounds: 'aw', 'ar' and 'l'
	b and d (advanced)	
	o	**o-e** representing the sounds: 'o-e', 'u', 'o' and 'oo' **o** (revisited) representing the sounds: 'o', 'o-e', 'oo' and 'u' **a** representing the sounds: 'a', 'a'-e', 'o', 'u' and 'ar'
	i	**y** representing the sounds: 'y', 'I' and 'ee'
	u-e	**u** representing the sounds: 'u', 'u-e' and 'oo'

Working with sounds

When working with a child on any reading and spelling activity it is important to be aware of the need to be careful about our personal articulation of the sounds as we are modelling our pronunciation for the child to copy and learn. When we say individual sounds to children it is easy to fall into the trap of saying them inaccurately or 'untidily'. Indeed, many of us were taught to say the sound that way when we were at school; but things have changed.

For example, the sound 'm' is often mispronounced as a 'muh' sound rather than a pure 'mmm'. This is unhelpful for the child who needs to hear the precise sound in order to be able to deal with it when reading and spelling words. The apparent addition of an 'uh' sound after the 'm' can easily result in confusion and lead to reading and spelling errors. So, we must make a conscious effort to say the sounds clearly and accurately. We also need to support the child to always say 'tidy' sounds themselves and gently correct them if necessary.

Be aware that we are not trying to change the way pupils speak. We are giving them as good a chance as possible to hear and access sounds in words (whatever their natural regional variations are) to increase their success with reading and spelling.

Table 3, below, goes some way to explain some of the pitfalls encountered when working with sounds, but it may be helpful to access an audio or video file of correct 'phonics' pronunciation, many of which are readily available on the internet.

Table 3 Simple speech sounds and strategies for accurate articulation

Sounds	Strategy	Difficulties
b c/k d g j t ch	Be aware of the need to *gently* 'clip' these sounds when speaking and avoid the 'uh' on the end. When reading a word, it is more difficult to blend from these sounds into the next so make sure you encourage the child to say the sound and rapidly move on to the next sound.	Short, clipped sounds – very easy to add an untidy 'uh' sound at the end, e.g. 'buh' rather than 'b'.

Sounds	Strategy	Difficulties
f l m n r s v z sh th ng	Wonderful sounds that can go on for a long time, e.g. 'mmmmmmmmm'. Make the most of these sounds when playing the blending games with the child.	
h p	Practise saying these sounds in a breathy way rather than 'huh' and 'puh'.	Breathy sounds – very easy to add an untidy 'uh' sound at the end, e.g. 'huh' rather than 'h'.
a e i o u a-e ee i-e o-e u-e er ow oy oo aw air ar	These are vowel sounds and are quite flexible and can be spoken for an extended time for emphasis.	If overextended, these can become distorted, e.g. with the sound 'ee' there is a tendency to add a 'y' sound at the end.
y z	Practise saying them clearly. A good strategy is to start to say a word containing the sound, e.g. yes. Start to say it but stop without saying the 'e' 's' part of the word. In this way you say the pure 'y' sound.	Treat very carefully. These are always followed by another sound in words, e.g. yes, wet. When we say them on their own we tend to say 'yuh' and 'wuh'.

Developing sensory perception and processing skills

An aspect of learning to read and spell which is frequently overlooked is the role of the child's sensory perceptual and processing abilities.

We are surrounded by things in our environment that stimulate our senses. We notice and respond to things we see, hear, touch, taste and smell. How our body and brain receive this information is termed perception, and how the brain interprets, organises, stores and responds to these stimuli is termed processing.

One way we perceive the world is through the things we hear; this is termed auditory perception and processing. Auditory perception does not relate to 'how well our ears work' but how we perceive and respond to the things we hear. Individuals with auditory perceptual difficulties may appear to 'hear things differently' from others and this may affect their ability to process verbal information. Indeed, children with these difficulties are likely to struggle with attention and listening, following verbal instructions and keeping up with teacher explanations. Auditory perception and processing can be separated into different aspects which include: auditory discrimination, auditory fusion, auditory memory, auditory sequential memory and auditory tracking, all of which are explored in activities within this programme. More specifically there is an aspect of auditory processing that relates to the processing of speech sounds or phonemes within words. This is called phonological processing, and children with difficulties in this area are likely to struggle with acquiring age appropriate reading and spelling skills.

In the *Phonics for Pupils with Special Educational Needs* programme there are activities and worksheets which work on and develop the child's auditory perception and processing of speech sounds. These are **Activities 1–7 Sound target story, Tongue twister fun, Odd one out, What sound am I? Same or different? How many did you hear? What comes next?** with learning objectives, as follows:

Activity	Learning objectives
1 Sound target story	**Auditory attention and tracking**: Actively listen to and follow to the end auditory information in the form of a story. **Phonological discrimination**: Discriminate between different sounds and identify words that start with a target sound.
2 Tongue twister fun	**Auditory attention and tracking**: Actively listen to and follow to the end auditory information in the form of a tongue twister. **Auditory sequential memory**: Remember and recall verbally a sequence of words heard.
3 Odd one out	**Auditory attention and tracking**: Actively listen to and follow to the end auditory information in the form of a list of words. **Phonological discrimination**: Discriminate between different sounds, identify the starting sound of words and identify which is word has a different target sound.
4 What sound am I?	**Auditory attention and tracking**: Actively listen to and follow to the end auditory information in the form of a list of words. **Phonological discrimination**: Discriminate between different sounds and identify the starting sound of words. **Auditory recall memory**: remember and recall verbally a word heard.
5 Same or different?	**Auditory attention and tracking**: Actively listen to and follow to the end auditory information in the form of word pairs. **Phonological discrimination**: discriminate between different sounds, identify the starting sound of words and identify whether they are the same or different.
6 How many did you hear?	**Phonological and auditory fusion**: Recognise gaps between sounds and words.
7 What comes next?	**Auditory attention and tracking**: Actively listen to and follow to the end auditory information in the form of a sequence of sounds. **Phonological sequential memory**: Remember and recall a sequence of sounds heard. **Phonological and auditory processing**: Identify patterns within the sounds and identify the sound which would come next in the sequence.

Children can work on these auditory activities **before, as well as after**, they are introduced to the sound spellings that represent them, as these activities are purely oral.

Another way we perceive the world is visually, using our eyes to see; this is termed visual perception. Visual perception does not relate to 'how well our eyes work' but how we perceive and respond to the things we see. Individuals with visual perceptual difficulties may appear to 'see the world differently' from others and this may affect their ability to process visual figures, shapes and forms in their environment. Since letters are visual figures, children with underlying visual perceptual and processing difficulties are likely to struggle to get to grips with letters and words for reading and spelling. Visual perception can be separated into different aspects which include: visual discrimination, spatial relationships, visual memory, visual sequential memory, visual closure, form constancy and visual tracking, all of which are explored within the programme.

In the *Phonics for Pupils with Special Educational Needs* programme there are activities and worksheets for all of the sounds in this book, which work on and improve the child's visual perception and processing of sound spellings. These are **Activities 11–18 Sound spelling tracker, Remembering sound spellings, Spot the sound spelling, Which is the same? Bits missing, Busy sound spellings, Where am I? Remembering lots of sound spellings** with learning objectives, as follows:

Activity	Learning objectives
11 Sound spelling tracker	**Tracking**: Visually track, left to right, through a list of sound spellings. **Visual discrimination**: Discriminate between visually similar sound spellings to identify a target sound spelling.
12 Remembering sound spellings	**Visual memory**: Recall and identify a single sound spelling from memory.
13 Spot the sound spelling	**Visual discrimination**: Discriminate between visually similar sounds spellings to identify a target sound spelling.
14 Which is the same?	**Form constancy**: Generalise the form of sound spellings. Recognise sound spellings when not in a typical presentation.
15 Bits missing	**Visual closure**: Identify sound spellings from a visually incomplete picture.
16 Busy sound spellings	**Figure ground**: Identify sound spellings from a visually complex presentation.
17 Where am I?	**Spatial relations**: Perceive the position / spatial orientation of sound spellings on the page. Accurately reproduce sound spellings on the page to match a given position / spatial orientation.
18 Remembering lots of sound spellings	**Visual sequential memory**: Remember and recall a sequence of sound spellings. Complete a sequence of sound spellings.

Children should work on these visual activities **after** the sounds and sound spellings have been introduced, as described later in this chapter.

A third way we perceive the world is through the movements we make to interact with our environment. This is our kinaesthetic sense and in relation to reading and spelling refers to the fine movements of our fingers, hand, arm and shoulder to form the letters in written words.

Activity 19 Writing sound spellings works specifically on conventional 'pen and paper' sound spelling formation, with learning objectives below. Instructions are given at the top of the individual sheet.

Activity	Learning objectives
19 Writing sound spellings	**Letter formation**: Form letters that make up a sound spelling with: accuracy, size consistency size and spatial awareness of the line.
	Kinaesthetic awareness: Develop the 'muscle memory' associated with formation of target sound spellings.

Multisensory writing strategy

Phonics for Pupils with Special Educational Needs has an overarching multisensory approach to teaching which integrates visual, auditory and kinaesthetic processing while enhancing and supporting learning and acquisition of skills.

From this point on, whenever the child forms or writes a sound spelling, require them to **ALWAYS *say the associated sound at the same time as writing it*.** This applies to when writing single sound spellings or when writing a sequence of sound spellings to make a word.

In this way all the senses are engaged:

- the **visual** sense (seeing the sound spelling form),
- the **auditory** sense (hearing the sound) and
- the **kinaesthetic** sense (feeling the specific movement associated with forming the sound spelling shape).

The three sensory experiences are simultaneously processed, making connections in the brain between the different aspects of the information and maximising the child's chance of remembering it.

Introducing the sounds and their sound spellings

In this book the child focuses on just one sound at a time and explores it in depth.

Investigating the sound (Activity 8) enables the child to discover and understand some new concepts and add to their developing knowledge of sounds and sound spellings.

For the sounds 'sh', 'th' and 'ng', the child discovers that some sounds are represented by sound spellings which contain more than one letter.

For the sounds which follow, the child discovers that some sounds are represented by more than one sound spelling and that some of the sound spellings have two or three letters.

There are instructions on how to explore a sound at the top of the Activity 8 worksheet. In brief, the child encounters a list of words, all of which contain the focus sound, and reads through them. They then identify how the focus sound is represented in each word (find the matching sound spelling) and sort the words into groups or lists which all have the same sound spelling for the focus sound.

For example, investigating the sound 'ch'

ch	tch
chin	*patch*
much	*itch*
champ	*hutch*

It is important for the child to have the experience of working through this sorting process and recording the words in lists, as the act of writing the words provides that important multisensory experience. The child sounds out the word and matches a sound spelling to each sound in sequence, saying the associated sound at the same time as writing each sound spelling.

Word cards – sorting (Activity 9 – see Activity 20 for the cards) requires the child to read through word cards and sort them into groups based on what sound spelling is used to represent the focus sound. Although this is similar to Activity 8, this activity does not include the kinaesthetic element, as the child is not required to write, so should not be used as the only way the child discovers the sound spellings.

There are two types of word cards available for this activity. One set has the focus sound's sound spellings highlighted and the other set does not. The two sets present different challenges to the child as the highlighted set has visual prompts which are more supportive.

Once the child has identified and explored all the sound spellings for the focus sound, the **Activity 10 Sound spelling cards** may be helpful to use as memory prompts at the start of a subsequent teaching session on that sound.

In addition to the sound spelling cards, each sound has a poster which shows all the main sound spellings. This is a helpful prompt and can be displayed once the child has completed Activity 8.

The learning objectives for these activities are as follows:

Activity	Learning objectives
8 Investigating the sound 9 Word cards – sorting	Identify all the sound spellings that represent the target sound.

Describing and working with sound spellings

During a teaching session it is helpful to focus on the sound spellings as a whole, without describing them by using letter names.

Using a sequence of letter names to describe a sound spelling, e.g. referring to **sh** as 'ess' 'aich', places an additional cognitive burden on the child. They have to learn and then recall the letter name and convert that to a visual symbol, requiring the brain to carry out an additional processing task. Additionally, using letter names confuses the child, as letter names do not actually have a part to play in the relationship between sound and symbol, a relationship which we are trying to teach and strengthen. To avoid saying a list of letter names when talking about a sound spelling it is helpful to have the sound spelling cards (Activity 10) from the programme available as a visual reference to use during teaching sessions. For example, if the child is spelling the word **hill** we can say, "In this word we use this sound spelling (showing the card that matches - **ll**) for the 'l' sound." Alternatively have a whiteboard handy and when talking about a specific sound spelling write it on the board so that you can show it to the child as you are talking about it and simply refer to it as 'this way of writing the sound…'.

It is also not advisable to describe sound spellings by basic sounds associated with their component letters, e.g. **sh** as 's' 'h'. Once again this is confusing for the child and actively works against what you are trying to teach, as the focus should be the relationship between the sound 'sh' and the sound spelling **sh**. Having the sound spelling cards or a whiteboard handy, used as described above, supports the child's understanding of the sound to symbol relationship whilst also giving you a way to talk about individual sound spellings.

As well as increasing the child's knowledge of sounds and sound spellings, the programme also teaches and develops the key skills of blending, segmenting and phoneme manipulation. If the child has worked through Books 1 and 2 then they will have experience of activities which support the development of these skills. Some children may have not achieved mastery of these skills and so may need continued practise, so for this reason these skills are also covered in Book 3 onwards.

Skill 1 – blending for reading

If you have worked through Books 1 and 2 with a child or group of children then you will be familiar with the blending technique used in *Phonics for Pupils with Special Educational Needs*, although a refresher is always helpful. If you are starting the child at this point in the programme, then it is important that you read this section.

Blending is the ability to push sounds together to make a word and is a key skill in reading. It is important that blending is taught as an active or ***dynamic*** process – pushing the sounds together as the child moves through the word and listening for the word forming.

The dynamic blending technique

- When the child is reading a word, ask them to say the sounds as you simultaneously move your pen or finger underneath the word so that you are indicating which sound spellings to think about.
- Have the child say the sounds in a ***dynamic*** blended fashion (connecting the sounds and pushing them together).

  So rather than the child saying separate sounds quickly one after the other, e.g. 'f' 'i' 'sh', have the child actively push the sounds into each other without a gap, e.g. 'fffiiish'.

  In this way the child simply has to listen and then say the word they heard forming. It may be helpful to point out to the child that it sounds like we are saying the word very slowly and ask them what the word would be if we speeded it up.

  Be aware of the need to say the sounds clearly and purely. Some sounds are more difficult to blend as they are clipped, e.g. 'b', 'p', 't', 'd' etc. When reading words with these sounds in you will have to make sure the child says the sound and very rapidly moves on to the next sound. This avoids the child distorting the clipped sound; if it takes too long they are forced to artificially stretch it out before blending it into the next.
- Model this dynamic blending technique for the child.
- When working on any task with the child be aware of the need to gently correct their blending technique and encourage them to push the sounds together, modelling the technique if necessary.

Blending activities

Dynamic blending – target sound word cards (Activity 20)

There are two sets of word cards in each section of the book relating to the sounds being explored. One set of these have the sound spelling that matches the focus sound highlighted and the other set does not. Practise dynamic blending, as described above, using cards from either of these sets. Model this process for the child if necessary.

Blending bricks* (Activity 21)

Use some large plastic construction bricks for this activity. The teacher word list at the beginning of each chapter of the book will help you choose words to use. You will need the correct number of bricks – you will need a brick for each sound in the word. Present the bricks separately with a sound spelling written on each using a non-permanent whiteboard pen (this can be wiped off). Note that if a sound spelling has two or more letters in then you write them all on one brick.

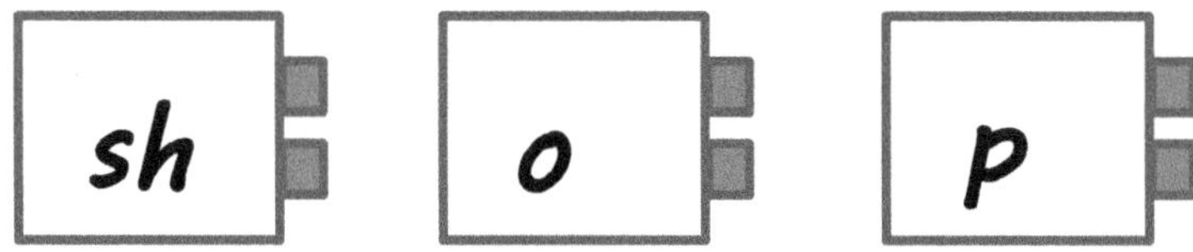

Ask the child to push the bricks together in order and say the sounds, dynamically blending as they go through the word.

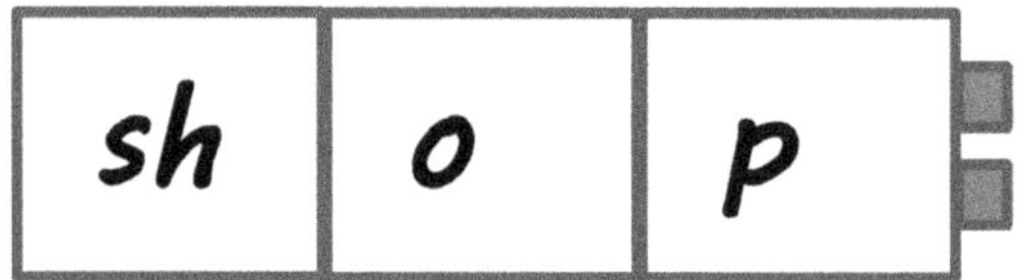

When finished, ask the child to say the word they heard forming. Model this process for the child if necessary. This activity is a concrete way of demonstrating the reading process, e.g. **three** sounds (**three** bricks) are pushed together to make **one** word (**one** solid 'wall' of bricks).

Speed blending* (Activity 22)

Using the Target Sound Word Cards (from Activity 20), present a word to the child. You will require the child to say the sounds, dynamically blending, as you move your pen across the sound spellings and through the word. However, there are some rules the child must follow for this game. The child must say the sound for as long as the pen is under the sound spelling and is not allowed to move to the next sound until you move your pen. In this way you control the child's blending and progression through the word. As soon as the child says the last sound, they are to shout out the word, *but* as soon as they say the last sound *you* shout out the word too. Whoever is first wins.

Reveal and blend* (Activity 23)

Using the Target Sound Word Cards (from Activity 20), present a word to the child. Cover the word with a blank top card. Slowly pull back the top card revealing the sound spellings one by one. Ask the child to say the sounds, dynamically blending, as each sound spelling is revealed. When finished, ask the child to say the word they heard forming. Model this process for the child if necessary.

Flippies (Activity 24)

Flippies are sets of cards that are clipped together so that when the child runs their finger along the sound spellings the individual cards flip up. This provides a kinaesthetic as well as auditory and visual experience for the child when reading the word. Follow the instructions on the sheet to make the flippies out of card.

Present the flippy to the child. Ask the child to move their finger across the cards, saying each sound (in a dynamic, blended fashion) as each sound spelling 'flips up'. When finished, ask the child to say the word they heard forming. Model this process for the child if necessary.

There is a blank template at the end of this section, so you can make your own bespoke flippies.

The learning objectives for these activities are as follows:

Activity	Learning objectives
20 Dynamic blending – target sound word cards	Use the dynamic blending strategy to read words. Read words containing the target sound represented by all possible sound spellings.
21 Blending bricks	Actively push sounds together using the dynamic blending strategy for reading words.
22 Speed blending	Use the dynamic blending strategy to read words. Rapidly say what word can be heard forming when blending.
23 Reveal and blend	Use the dynamic blending strategy to read words.
24 Flippies	Use the dynamic blending strategy to read words.

Skill 2 – sequential segmenting for spelling

Segmenting is the ability to split words up into their component sounds in sequence and is a key skill in spelling. The child needs to isolate each sound and match a sound spelling to that sound to successfully spell a word. It is important that the child is taught to segment sequentially through the word as this is how to access sounds in words to be able to spell them effectively.

The sequential segmenting technique

When supporting a child to spell a word it is helpful to provide visual prompts to indicate where to listen for a sound, e.g. draw lines on a whiteboard or piece of paper.

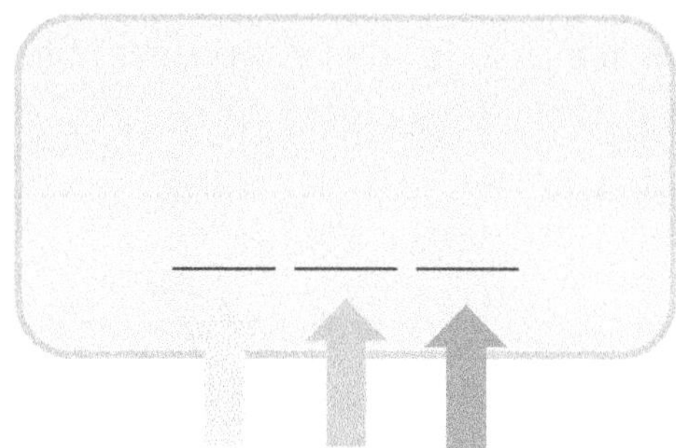

- Pointing to the first line, ask the child, "What sound can you hear ***here*** in the word.......?"
- Repeat the word (saying it in a dynamic blended style and moving your finger along the lines, as above) and then the question. You may need to repeat this several times, especially when this activity is new to the child, and you may need to emphasise the target sound to support the child to identify it.
- Once the child has identified the sound, ask them to write the matching sound spelling on the appropriate line.

  At this stage avoid using language such as 'first', 'initial' and 'beginning' which requires the child to think about the position in the word, as this requires additional cognitive processing. Using this technique, the visual prompts of the lines and your finger to indicate the 'place to listen', removes the burden of this extra cognitive task.
- Once the child has identified the 'initial' sound and written the sound spelling, move on to the 'middle' sound using the same technique and then the 'final' sound. Note that although it is useful for professionals to talk using positional language, take care to avoid labels such as 'medial', 'second', 'middle', 'next', 'final', 'last', 'third' or 'end'. Instead point to the place to listen and ask the child what sound they hear, 'here'.
- By working sequentially through the word, the child has identified the sounds and can then match sound spellings and so successfully spell the word. This simple technique can be used to spell any word.
- At this stage in the programme the child ***may*** be able to cope with use of positional language and indeed it is useful when supporting spelling, particularly in other curriculum areas. However, there is no specific point at which this happens for all children; timing is individual to each child. Teachers and teaching assistants will need to be aware of when this subtle shift occurs and choose appropriate strategies to support spelling.

Segmenting activities

Sound boxes (Activity 25) and How many sounds? (Activity 26)

These activities are worksheet based and instructions are written at the top of the sheet.

Segmenting bricks* (Activity 27)

Use some large plastic construction bricks for this activity. The teacher word list for each chapter of the book will help you choose words to use. Present the bricks already pushed together, a brick for each sound with a sound spelling written on each using a non-permanent whiteboard pen (this can be wiped off). Note that if a sound spelling has two or more letters then you write them all on one brick. Ask the child to pull the bricks apart in order and say the sounds one by one as they go through the word, removing a brick at a time. Model this process for the child if necessary.

Alternatively present the child with unmarked bricks already pushed together such that there is a brick for each sound. Say a word to the child and ask them to pull apart the bricks, one by one in order and say the sounds that make up the word. Then ask the child to write the corresponding sound spelling on each brick.

Phoneme frame* (Activity 28)

There are four phoneme frames, with three, four, five and six boxes, available at the end of the chapter. Copy these on to card and place them in individual transparent file pocket-wallets (you can now write on these using non-permanent whiteboard pens and it will wipe off). Use the three-box frame when working on two and three sound words, the four-box frame when working on two, three and four sound words and so on. The teacher word list for each chapter of the book will help you choose words to use. Work through the activity in this way:

- Place the appropriate frame in front of the child and place a counter underneath each box.
- Present the chosen word orally.
- Say the word in a dynamic blended style and at the same time move your finger across the frame across all the boxes. Your finger should be pointing to the box that corresponds to the sound in the word as you say it.
- Ask the child to tell you all the sounds in the word, one by one. As the child says each sound they push a counter into the box.
- If the child needs support, use the sequential segmenting technique described earlier.

An extension activity could be to ask the child to match a sound spelling to each sound and write it under the box.

The learning objectives for these activities are as follows:

Activity	Learning objectives
25 Sound boxes	Identify all the sounds in a word. Use the sequential segmenting strategy to spell words.

Activity	Learning objectives
26 How many sounds?	Identify all the sounds in a word. Use the sequential segmenting strategy to spell words.
27 Segmenting bricks	Identify all the sounds in a word. Use the sequential segmenting strategy to spell words.
28 Phoneme frame	Identify all the sounds in a word. Use the sequential segmenting strategy to spell words.

Spelling, spelling choices and the 'accepted' spelling

In Books 1 and 2 the majority of the sounds investigated were represented by one sound spelling made up of one letter. The child learned a simple sequential segmenting strategy for identifying the sounds and then matching a sound spelling to spell the word. At this basic level this is an easy strategy which brings a high level of success for the child.

However, in this and subsequent books, the child learns that the relationships between sounds and their sound spellings are more complex than previously understood. This impacts on how the pupil can use the sequential spelling strategy for spelling and some additions are required, as follows:

- Identify all the sounds in the word one by one, in order.
- For each sound match a sound spelling.
- For some sounds the pupil now knows that there may be a choice of sound spellings available, any one of which could be used.
- For these sounds encourage the child to try a sound spelling and write it.
- On finishing the word, encourage the child to look over it and think whether it 'looks right' or 'feels right'. The most difficult part of the word will be where there are a number of possible sound spellings for a sound.
- If the child doesn't think it looks right, ask them to try a different sound spelling and then reflect on the word again.

For example, the child wants to write the word **brown** which is made up of four sounds and so four sound spellings:

4 sounds	'b'	'r'	'ow'	'n'
4 sound spellings	**b**	**r**	**ow / ou / ough**	**n**

There are three possible sound spellings for the 'ow' sound.

ow, ou and **ough** *all* represent the sound 'ow' so any one of them is ***technically correct***.

If the child writes **broun** or **broughn** then they have written a 'correct' spelling for the word brown.

If the child has previously struggled with spelling, then this is a really encouraging discovery; they might not be as 'wrong' as they thought they were!

The key point to make is that unfortunately it isn't helpful for us all to spell words with any 'correct' sound spelling we fancy. Everyone would get very mixed up and it would take much longer to work things out and read messages and stories.

Dictionaries list words and their meanings, but their writers also chose one sound spelling when writing the word and this was set in print. Over time these have become set as the 'agreed' or 'accepted' sound spellings to use in the word. So, when writing the word brown as broun or broughn, the child is correct but hasn't written the 'accepted spelling' and will need to make some changes.

When supporting a child with spelling always have this in mind and support them to use this strategy.

Skill 3 – phoneme manipulation

Phoneme manipulation is the ability to slide sounds in and out of words and is important when reading and spelling.

The *Phonics for Pupils with Special Educational Needs* programme includes activities and worksheets to work on this skill.

Activities 29–31 Sound swap, Sound exchange, Sound sums work on phoneme manipulation, and instructions are written at the top of the worksheet.

When working on phoneme manipulation with a child, remember to use the sequential segmenting and dynamic blending techniques as appropriate.

The learning objectives for these activities are as follows:

Activity	Learning objectives
29 Sound swap	Swap, add or delete sounds in words to make meaningful words.
30 Sound exchange	Swap, add or delete sounds in words to make meaningful words.
31 Sound sums	Swap, add or delete sounds in words to make meaningful words.

Reading and spelling activities

From 32 onwards the activities are designed to give the child the opportunity to overlearn the relationships between sounds and sound spellings and gain experience in applying their skills, knowledge and understanding of sounds and sound spellings to read and spell single words and words in the context of sentences. The programme also incorporates reading at text level by sharing an appropriate book, usually at the end of a teaching session.

Activities 32–37 focus on reading single words.

Reading high frequency words (Activity 32)

In each chapter of the book there is a set of high frequency words relating to the sound being studied. Practise dynamic blending, as described earlier, using the cards. Model this process for the child if necessary.

High frequency words are discussed in greater detail later in this section of the book.

Activities 33–37 Reading race, Word tracker, Remembering words, Word detective, Remembering lots of words have instructions written at the top of the worksheet, with learning objectives as follows:

Activity	Learning objectives
32 Reading high frequency words	Use the dynamic blending strategy to read high frequency words. Read words containing the target sound represented by all possible sound spellings. Develop automaticity of reading high frequency words.
33 Reading race	Use the dynamic blending strategy to read words. Read words containing the target sound represented by all possible sound spellings. Develop reading speed and fluency.
34 Word tracker	Track, left to right, through a list of words. Use the dynamic blending strategy to read words. Discriminate between different sounds and identify words that contain a target sound.
35 Remembering words	Use the dynamic blending strategy to read words. Recall and identify a single word from memory.
36 Word detective	Use the dynamic blending strategy to read words. Read words containing the target sound represented by all possible sound spellings. Recognise and identify real and nonsense words.
37 Remembering lots of words	Use the dynamic blending strategy to read words. Remember and recall a sequence of words. Complete a sequence of words.

Activities 38–42 focus on spelling single words.

Word build (Activity 38)

There is a sheet for the word build activity. Copy the activity onto card and cut out and clip together all the cards for each word. You will need a whiteboard and pen. Work through the activity in this way:

- Present the picture to the child and talk about what word it might represent.
- Place the sound spelling cards on the whiteboard in front of the child but make sure they are mixed up randomly.
- Draw a line for each sound in the word on the whiteboard, e.g. three lines for a word with three sounds, four lines for a word with four sounds etc.
- Using the sequential segmenting technique ask the child what sounds they can hear in the word. When the child has identified a sound correctly they can then choose its matching sound spelling from the cards available and place it on the appropriate line. In this way they build up the word.

For example,

Activities 39 and 40 Word tech, Word scramble have instructions written at the top of the worksheet.

Spelling with sound spelling cards (Activity 41)

Present a range of sound spelling cards to the child and allow them to select and use them to build a given word. Use the teacher word list to help select appropriate words. Support the child to self-correct when errors are made. (Use the basic sound spelling cards from Book 1 earlier in the programme as well as the cards provided for each sound in this book.)

Spelling challenge (Activity 42)

The spelling challenge sheets provide the child with a structured method for practising and learning to spell the high frequency words. Work with the child through the sheets in this way:

much   m u ch   m u ch

- Encourage the child to read the word on the left then look at the same word in the middle.
- Encourage the child to notice the sound spellings that represent each of the sounds, e.g. 'much' 'm' 'u' 'ch' is represented by the sound spellings **m u ch** – the sound spellings are spread out to make this clear.
- Ask the child to write over the grey sound spellings one by one, saying the corresponding sound at the same time as writing each sound spelling.
- Next, notice that there are two sets of lines, one made up of a number of small lines and the other a solid line. The number of small lines corresponds to the number of sounds in the word.
- Ask the child to write the sound spellings one by one on the small lines in the first set of lines, saying the corresponding sound at the same time as writing each sound spelling, e.g. **m u ch**.
- Now ask the child to write the word, sound spelling by sound spelling, on the solid line, once again saying the corresponding sound at the same time as writing each sound spelling, e.g. **m u ch**.

The child has now written the word three times and has made important connections between the sounds in the word and the sound spellings we write. Next time the child wants to write that word they can use the sounds (which they can access from the spoken word using the sequential segmenting technique) as a prompt to write the sound spellings in the right order and so spell the word.

To make the activity more challenging you could cover the words so that the child does not have a visual cue when writing the word on the lines. The child could then check their own work.

The learning objectives for these activities are as follows:

Activity	Learning objectives
38 Word build	Use the sequential segmenting strategy to spell words. Spell words containing the target sound represented by all possible sound spellings.
39 Word tech	Use the sequential segmenting strategy to identify all sounds in a word. Identify all the sound spellings in a given word.
40 Word scramble	Use the sequential segmenting strategy to spell words with the aid of visual prompts.
41 Spelling with sound spelling cards	Use the sequential segmenting strategy to spell words with the aid of visual prompts. Proofread spelling and self-correct as required.
42 Spelling challenge	Use the sequential segmenting strategy to spell words with the aid of visual prompts. Develop automaticity of spelling high frequency words.

Activities 43–46 Oops! Correct the spelling, Spot the spelling, Making better sentences, Writing challenge focus on reading and spelling words in sentences and have instructions written at the top of each sheet.

The learning objectives for these activities are as follows:

Activity	Learning objectives
43 Oops! Correct the spelling	Proofread spelling and identify words that are misspelled. Use the sequential segmenting strategy to spell words.
44 Spot the spelling	Proofread spelling and identify the accepted spelling of words. Use the sequential segmenting strategy to spell words.
45 Making better sentences	Read sentences closely matched to phonic knowledge with fluency and accuracy. Understand the meaning of what has been read. Expand sentences to add detail and interest whilst retaining meaning and context.
46 Writing challenge	Read sentences closely matched to phonic knowledge with fluency and accuracy. Remember and verbally recall a sequence of words read. Recall and write a sequence of words. Use the sequential segmenting strategy to spell words. Spell words containing the target sound represented by all possible sound spellings.

Activities 47 and 48 Investigating a sound spelling and Investigating a sound spelling with word cards focus on specific sound spellings which represent more than one sound and relate to concept 4 discussed at the start of the book.

There is consistency in the activities available across all four parts of the Sound by Sound Books (Books 3–6 of the programme) so that the child develops familiarity with the materials and is able to access the tasks easily. This consistency extends to the planning sheet for this part of the programme which is the same for all four books.

Note that activities 47 and 48 are not relevant to the sounds studied in Book 3, but appear on the planning sheet to maintain the above consistency across all four books.

Overview of activities

Table 4 shows all the activities in Book 3.

Note that some of the activities, indicated by an asterisk*, do not require a corresponding worksheet and these are described and explained in this introductory section. Not all activities are applicable to all sections of the programme and for these worksheets and resources are not available, as indicated by a cross.

Table 4 Overview of *Phonics for Pupils with Special Educational Needs* – activities and resources, Book 3

Activity		Covered in this chapter	sh	th	ng	ch	k	qu	f	l	s
	Sound poster		✓	✓	✓	✓	✓	✓	✓	✓	✓
	Teacher word list		✓	✓	✓	✓	✓	✓	✓	✓	✓
1	Sound target story		✓	✓	×	✓	✓	✓	✓	✓	✓
2	Tongue twister fun		✓	×	×	✓	✓	×	✓	✓	✓
3	Odd one out		✓	✓	✓	✓	✓	×	✓	✓	✓
4	What sound am I?		✓	✓	✓	✓	✓	×	✓	✓	✓
5	Same or different?		✓	✓	×	✓	✓	×	✓	✓	✓
6	How many did you hear?		✓	✓	✓	✓	✓	×	✓	✓	✓
7	What comes next?		✓	✓	✓	✓	✓	×	✓	✓	✓
8	Investigating the sound	✓	✓	✓	✓	✓	✓	✓	✓	✓	✓
9a	Sorting word cards – highlighted words* (see 20a)	✓	✓	✓	✓	✓	✓	✓	✓	✓	✓
9b	Sorting word cards – non-highlighted words* (see 20b)	✓	✓	✓	✓	✓	✓	✓	✓	✓	✓
10	Sound spelling cards*	✓	✓	✓	✓	✓	✓	✓	✓	✓	✓
11	Sound spelling tracker		×	×	×	✓	✓	✓	✓	✓	✓
12	Remembering sound spellings		✓	✓	✓	✓	✓	✓	✓	✓	✓
13	Spot the sound spelling		✓	✓	✓	✓	✓	×	✓	✓	✓
14	Which is the same?		×	×	×	×	✓	✓	✓	×	×
15	Bits missing		×	×	×	×	✓	✓	✓	×	×
16	Busy sound spellings		×	×	×	×	×	✓	×	×	×
17	Where am I?		✓	✓	✓	✓	✓	✓	✓	✓	✓
18	Remembering lots of sound spellings		✓	✓	✓	✓	✓	✓	✓	✓	✓
19	Writing sound spellings		×	×	×	✓	✓	✓	✓	✓	✓
20a	Dynamic blending highlighted word cards	✓	✓	✓	✓	✓	✓	✓	✓	✓	✓
20b	Dynamic blending non-highlighted word cards	✓	✓	✓	✓	✓	✓	✓	✓	✓	✓
21	Blending bricks*	✓									
22	Speed blending*	✓									

Activity		Covered in this chapter	sh	th	ng	ch	k	qu	f	l	s
23	Reveal and blend*	✓									
24	Flippies	✓	✓	✓	✓	✓	✓	✓	✓	✓	✓
25	Sound boxes		✓	✓	✓	✓	✓	✗	✓	✓	✓
26	How many sounds?		✓	✓	✓	✓	✓	✗	✓	✓	✓
27	Segmenting bricks*	✓									
28	Phoneme frame*	✓									
29	Sound swap		✓	✓	✓	✓	✓	✓	✓	✓	✓
30	Sound exchange		✓	✓	✓	✓	✓	✓	✓	✓	✓
31	Sound sums		✓	✓	✓	✓	✓	✓	✓	✓	✓
32	Reading high frequency words*	✓	✓	✓	✓	✓	✓	✓	✓	✓	✓
33	Reading race		✓	✓	✓	✓	✓	✓	✓	✓	✓
34	Word tracker		✓	✓	✓	✓	✓	✓	✓	✓	✓
35	Remembering words		✓	✓	✓	✓	✓	✓	✓	✓	✓
36	Word detective		✓	✓	✓	✓	✓	✓	✓	✓	✓
37	Remembering lots of words		✓	✓	✓	✓	✓	✓	✓	✓	✓
38	Word build		✓	✓	✓	✓	✓	✓	✓	✓	✓
39	Word tech		✓	✓	✓	✓	✓	✓	✓	✓	✓
40	Word scramble		✓	✓	✓	✓	✓	✓	✓	✓	✓
41	Spelling with sound spellings cards*	✓									
42	Spelling challenge	✓	✓	✓	✓	✓	✓	✓	✓	✓	✓
43	Oops! Correct the spelling		✓	✗	✗	✓	✓	✗	✗	✗	✗
44	Spot the spelling		✓	✓	✓	✓	✓	✓	✗	✗	✗
45	Making better sentences		✓	✓	✓	✓	✓	✓	✓	✓	✓
46	Writing challenge		✓	✓	✓	✓	✓	✓	✓	✓	✓
47	Investigating a sound spelling	n/a									
48	Investigating a sound spelling using word cards	n/a									
	Key sound spelling poster	n/a									
49	Reading book	✓									

High frequency words

The high frequency words are the most common words used in written English and many programmes focus heavily on learning these as 'sight words'. This programme does not take this approach. A child with special educational needs is less likely to find success with a 'visual only' strategy than when using a multisensory approach to reading and spelling, and many such children struggle to learn and remember a bank of sight words in this way.

Even if we explore the auditory or phonic aspect of high frequency words early on in the programme, explicitly working on them as a group in their own right would mean we have to carry out focus work on a multitude of key sounds all at the same time, which would be very confusing for the child. Yet, the very point about these words is that they are 'high frequency' and so are likely to appear in even simple text and pupils may encounter them very early in their reading experience. This presents us with a dilemma.

The solution is that the programme takes a gentler approach to high frequency words with a longer-term view of the situation and does not explicitly teach them as a separate group of words requiring their own focus and teaching materials.

The high frequency words are studied when the child works on the appropriate focus sound as they work through the programme. At the end of this section of the book is a list of the high frequency words organised according to the key sounds in the word and the point at which they fit into the programme.

Most importantly, high frequency words are also dealt with as they naturally arise in the context of the child's reading or writing. The same dynamic blending strategy is used for reading and the same sequential segmenting strategy is used for spelling, but the teacher or teaching assistant steps in to support the child with just that little bit of knowledge that they lack.

The strategies for dealing with reading and spelling high frequency words are as follows:

Scaffolding reading high frequency words

A scaffolding approach is taken to support a child to read high frequency words when they naturally crop up when reading. The teacher or teaching assistant uses their knowledge of what the child has learned and understood so far to enable them to support in just the right way and provide only the information that the child lacks.

For example, a child working at the Book 3 level encounters the word **seen** in a story book.

As the teacher or teaching assistant you know that they have worked on the sounds 's' and 'n' and so you can assume that they know them and can work with them. You also know that the child has not yet worked on the 'ee' sound and it is the sound spelling **ee** which will potentially cause them difficulties.

- Encourage the child to start decoding the word and for them to begin by identifying and saying the sound 's'.
- As they move on to the next sound spelling, gently interrupt them and point to the **ee** sound spelling (drawing a ring around or underlining the two letters can help the child to notice the sound spelling).
- Pointing to the **ee** sound spelling say, "This is a picture of the sound 'ee'. You haven't done this sound yet, but you will. This is 'ee.'"
- Support the child to start over and dynamically blend the 's' and 'ee' sounds together.
- The child can then continue on through the word independently, identify the 'n' sound, dynamically blending to get the word 'seen'.

In this way the child has actually decoded 66% of the word, blended 100% of it and concluded what the word is (or 'read' it) themselves.

When supporting reading in this way, there is never a need to simply supply a whole word for the child.

Scaffolding spelling high frequency words

Similarly, a scaffolding approach is taken to support a child to spell high frequency words when they naturally crop up when writing. The teacher or teaching assistant uses their knowledge of what the child has learned and understood so far to enable them to support in just the right way and provide only the information that the child lacks.

For example, a child working at the Book 3 level is doing a writing task and wishes to spell the word 'said'.

As the teacher or teaching assistant you know that they have worked on the sounds 's' and 'd' and so you can assume that they know them and can work with them. You also know that the child has not yet worked on the 'e' sound and it is the sound spelling **ai**, which will potentially cause them difficulties.

- Draw three lines on a whiteboard, one line for each sound in the word.
- Using the sequential segmenting technique encourage the child to identify the first sound they can hear in the word 'said'.

- Invite the child to match a sound spelling for the sound 's'.
- Using the sequential segmenting technique encourage the child to identify the next (middle) sound they can hear in the word 'said'.
- The child will be able to identify the 'e' sound but will not be able to match the appropriate sound spelling. Gently interrupt them, saying, "Yes, there is an 'e' sound here. You haven't investigated this sound fully yet but you will. We use this way of writing 'e' in this word." Write in the **ai** sound spelling on the line for the child.
- The child can then continue on through the word, identify the 'd' sound, and match a sound spelling to the sound.
- If the child then copies the word from the whiteboard into their book require them to say each sound at the same time as writing the appropriate sound spelling.

These gentle approaches to the high frequency words primes the child for the time when they can work on them more fully.

Listening to a child read

Teaching a child to efficiently decode words is only one part of reading. Alongside this, children need to understand what they have read, included in which is the ability to 'read between the lines and beyond the text', and develop an interest and enthusiasm for stories, poetry and writing. All teachers strive to generate in their pupils a 'love of books'.

Although this programme does not address the specifics of reading comprehension it does set a place for developing an interest and enthusiasm for reading at all levels by encouraging pupil and teacher to share a book and talk about what they have read.

Activity 49 Reading book

The last **quarter** of any teaching session should be devoted to reading a book with the child, supporting them to apply their increasing knowledge, skills and understanding to read the text.

This gives you an opportunity to gently correct errors as they read, by highlighting sound spellings, referencing sounds, providing information about sounds they have not yet covered, correcting them when they use the wrong sound, pointing out where they have missed out or added sounds and by supporting and modelling a good dynamic blending technique.

During this activity also take time to enjoy sharing a book with the child and stimulate their interest in the story, poem or text by talking about it. The content of this discussion and the depth to which texts can be explored will depend on the child's age and cognitive abilities but some suggestions about areas of questioning and discussion are given below:

- Identify the general 'topic' of the text
- Identify where a story takes place
- Identify the main character(s)
- Identify what is happening and be aware of the sequence of events
- Identify characters, places and objects in illustrations and pictures
- Be aware of the importance of key events in the text
- Make connections between the text and personal experiences
- Draw conclusions about events in the text
- Make predictions about what might happen next
- Identify cause, effect and consequences within the text
- Make connections between the text and the child's prior knowledge or experience
- Describe the main character
- Express opinions about a character's actions or speech
- Express opinions about their enjoyment of the story or otherwise
- Identify different genres of writing and express preferences

Choosing the right book

There are several book series that take a phonics approach to writing and produce books that focus on a key sound or groups of sounds. These books are really useful if they match the sound that the child is working on from this programme, as the child is likely to experience a higher level of success when reading these, which is a great confidence boost. Be aware that the language in these books can be a little unnatural or stilted as the writers are restricted by which words are available for them to use to write the story.

Other books that do not take this phonics approach are just as accessible, but the child is likely to require much more adult support. The child is also more likely to encounter high frequency words (refer to section on High Frequency Words) that they have not yet worked on within the programme. Since a higher level of adult support may be required, the child may feel less successful when reading these books.

No type of book is better than another. A mixture of books is preferable to balance the child's diet of reading material to make it as rich and interesting as possible whilst allowing the child to experience success and independence.

Pace

When sharing a book with emerging readers the flow and pace of reading may be stalled if the child has to be supported to decode several words in a sentence. This may mean that the child will lose track of the meaning of what they have been reading. If this is the case, at the end of each sentence stop and re-read it for the child so that they can focus on language and meaning. This is a good opportunity to talk about the story, characters and events.

A few more considerations...

By now you should have a good overview of the programme, how it works and how to begin to deliver it, but there are a few other aspects that are worth taking time to consider and reflect on which will help you when working with a child or a group of children.

Regional variations

Earlier in this chapter there was reference to the number of sounds in spoken English and the fact that this varies according to regional differences associated with accent and pronunciation.

For example, in most of the UK the words **book**, **cook** and **look** are pronounced with a 'u' sound in the middle but in some areas an 'oo' sound is used. There is a subtle difference in the pronunciation of the 'u' sound in words like **bus** and **run** in different parts of the UK and of course there is the classic 'castle' and 'bath' debate where the **a** sound spelling represents the sound 'ar' for some people but 'a' for others.

When creating the content of the programme every effort was made to reduce the impact of these differences by careful selection of example words. However, it is important for you as a practitioner to be selective about the words presented to your child or group of children and **always** follow your local pronunciations. In the rare event of you finding in the programme a word is out of place then just avoid it and remember to deal with it in a section appropriate to you and the child.

Terminology

Many phonics programmes use terminology that children with special educational needs find difficult to understand, remember and use. In *Phonics for Pupils with Special Educational Needs* this terminology is kept to a minimum and is made as child friendly as possible. Labels such as phoneme, grapheme, short vowel, long vowel, digraphs, trigraphs, dipthong and spilt-vowel digraph are not used in this programme.

Knowing these terms does not have a direct impact on a child's reading and spelling accuracy and performance. Instead accessible terms such as sound, sound spelling and split sound spelling are used.

Tricky words

Phonics for *Pupils with Special Educational Needs*' view of written language means that nearly all words can be decoded and there are very few 'common exception' or 'tricky' words. Please refer to the list of high frequency words which also shows how these common words are coded.

There are some words that do appear to be truly 'tricky' and difficult to decode. Investigation of their origins and history can be quite revealing. Encountering these words in the course of their reading presents an opportunity to talk about this with the child at a level that is appropriate to their cognitive abilities.

the	When pronounced as 'thee', e.g. before words starting with a vowel or used for emphasis, it is easy to decode as 'th' 'ee'. Otherwise this is often pronounced as 'thuh'. The 'uh' sound is a schwa (which is covered extensively in Book 7). The easiest way to describe this is an 'untidy' or 'sloppy' sound.
one	Originally pronounced using an 'u' sound, like in the phrase 'a good 'un'. The 'wun' pronunciation appeared in the south-west of England in the 14th century and spread rapidly.
once	Its history mirrors that of the word one.
two	From the old English **twa** which contained pronounced consonants and an 'a-e' sound 'tway'. The reason for the shift to the 'too' pronunciation is no longer known.
friend	Decodable but unique – the sound spelling **ie** represents the sound 'e' in this word. This word is investigated when working on the 'e' sound in Book 4.
people	Decodable but unique – the sound spelling **eo** represents the sound 'ee' in this word. This word is investigated when working on the 'ee' sound in Book 4.
minute	Middle English from the Latin **minutus** (meaning small) pronounced with an 'oo' sound. This is another example of a schwa.
hour	From the Latin **hora**. Although the 'h' hasn't been pronounced since Roman times, the **h** has persisted to distinguish it visually from the word **our**.
busy	From the Old English **bisig** originally referring to 'having a care or anxious'. Later it referred to being occupied doing something. Spelling shifted from **i** to **u** in the 15th century for a reason no longer known.
business	Source is the same as above **bisgnes**. The original meaning, referring to **busyness** as 'the state of being busy', has become obsolete and replaced by today's meaning and spelling.
iron	From the Celtic word **isarnon**, which means holy metal (metal made into swords for the Crusades), the Old English word was **iren**.
Mr	A contraction of the word **M**iste**r** – taking just the first and last letter as a short form of the word.
Mrs	A contraction of the word **M**ist**r**e**ss** – taking the first and last letter and the middle letter r as a short from of the word 'missus' (which is in itself a short form of mistress which is an out-dated formal title for a woman).

Planning

At the end of this section there is a lesson planner which can be used to plan teaching sessions and track pupil progression through the programme.

All possible activities are listed on the planner which could be viewed as a menu of activities. Do note that not all activities are appropriate for every stage of the programme, so you may not be able to plan certain activities for all sounds. Table 3 is helpful to identify which activities are available for each sound when lesson planning.

To use the lesson planner, simply date the column and strike through the small box corresponding to each activity you plan to do in the session. ⧅ You can cross check through once completed. ☒

This provides a simple visual map of the pupil(s)' progress through the programme.

There is space to write brief notes and a larger space at the bottom of the planner where dynamic teacher assessment notes can be written on individual pupil responses / errors, teacher reflections and next steps for the pupil or group.

Structuring a session

Teaching sessions can be of any length but should always include as wide a range of activities as possible. The activities are grouped according to the focus of the activity and this is made clear on the planning sheet:

- Auditory (phonological) processing
- Investigating the sounds and discover the sound spellings – a multisensory approach
- Visual processing and sound spellings
- Dynamic blending
- Segmenting
- Phoneme manipulation
- Reading words
- Spelling words
- Working in sentences
- Reading text

Sessions should be planned to ensure that over time there is even coverage of all these aspects and all activities available. As a general rule, all sessions should finish with reading text, a book, either listening to the child read or a shared reading activity in a group.

Note that for each chapter in the book there is a corresponding answer sheet for your information.

The tasks

Children with special educational needs are often easily distracted and find it difficult to concentrate for long periods on the same task. For this reason, it is recommended that the activities are time limited rather than task limited.

For example, if a child starts a worksheet with support but after five minutes has only completed two items then stop there, record that the sheet is incomplete and move on to the next activity. The child can always continue work on the incomplete sheet in a subsequent session. It is better to keep the lesson interesting and varied to maintain a high level of engagement rather than finish a worksheet for the sake of it. Depending on the child, individual activities should only last around five to six minutes.

Progress through the programme

Do not feel that a child or group of children must go through every single activity and worksheet in the programme. If you have introduced a sound and sound spellings and the child is able to reliably and consistently recall the sound when shown a sound spelling and identify the sound spellings when told the sound, then move them on to the next sound. Remember that the child takes all previous sounds and their sound spellings with them into the next section so nothing is ever left behind.

They also work on the key skills at every stage in the programme so if they are still learning and developing their blending, segmenting and phoneme manipulation but are secure in their knowledge of sounds and sound spellings you can safely move them on.

Where to start

Ideally a pupil will have worked through Books 1 and 2 of this programme before starting Book 3. However, some children may start at this point, having had some other previous experience of phonics. For these pupils work out which sounds and sound spellings they can recall reliably and consistently. Then start them on the next sound that is unfamiliar.

Recognise that although these pupils may have knowledge of sounds and sound spellings they may have poor key skills and may need intensive work on blending, segmenting and phoneme manipulation. This programme allows pupils to work on these skills at this level.

And finally...

You now have an overview of the programme, its approach to written language, how to teach the key skills and the important techniques required to support a child or group of children.

You have all the tools necessary to expand the child's knowledge of sounds and sound spellings, teaching them to become readers and spellers.

Lesson planner Book 3

Name(s):			**Date**		**Date**		**Date**		**Date**		**Date**	
Book 3 focus sound:				**Notes**		**Notes**		**Notes**		**Notes**		**Notes**
Auditory processing without visuals	1	Sound target story										
	2	Tongue twister fun										
	3	Odd one out										
	4	What sound am I?										
	5	Same or different?										
	6	How many did you hear?										
	7	What comes next?										
Sound and sound spellings	8	Investigating the sound										
	9	Sorting word cards										
	10	Sound spelling cards										
Visual processing sound spellings	11	Sound spelling tracker										
	12	Remembering sound spellings										
	13	Spot the sound spelling										
	14	Which is the same?										
	15	Bits missing										
	16	Busy sound spellings										

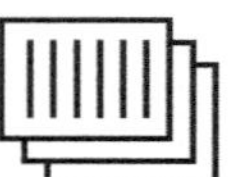

Name(s):		Date		Date		Date		Date		Date	
Book 3 focus sound:			Notes		Notes		Notes		Notes		Notes
	17 Where am I?										
	18 Remembering lots of sound spellings										
	19 Writing the sound spellings										
Dynamic blending	20 Dynamic blending – word cards										
	21 Blending bricks*										
	22 Speed blending*										
	23 Reveal and blend*										
	24 Flippies										
Sequential segmenting	25 Sound boxes										
	26 How Many Sounds?										
	27 Segmenting bricks*										
	28 Phoneme frame*										
Phoneme manipulation	29 Sound swap										
	30 Sound exchange										
	31 Sound sums										
Reading words	32 Reading high frequency Words										
	33 Reading race										
	34 Word tracker										
	35 Remembering words										
	36 Word detective										
	37 Remembering lots of words										

Name(s):		Date		Date		Date		Date		Date	
Book 3 focus sound:			**Notes**		**Notes**		**Notes**		**Notes**		**Notes**
	38 Word build										
Spelling words	39 Word tech										
	40 Word scramble										
	41 Spelling with sound spelling cards*										
	42 Spelling challenge										
Working in sentences	43 Oops! Correct the spelling										
	44 Spot the spelling										
	45 Making better sentences										
	46 Writing challenge										
Focus on target sound spelling	47 Investigating a sound spelling	From Book 4 onwards									
	48 Investigating a sound spelling with word cards										
Reading text level	49 Reading book*										
Observation / assessment notes											

High frequency word list

The following list is the high frequency words organised according to the sounds in the word and in relation to the programme. Each word is explored at an appropriate point in the programme, as indicated. Of course, children are likely to encounter these words at earlier stages in their reading as they share books and will be guided to decode them, with a 'heads up' to sounds not yet studied.

Book	Structure / sound(s)	Top 100 high frequency words	Top 101–200 high frequency words
1	**Set 1 VC** **CVC**	a at sat	
1	**Set 2 VC** **CVC**	in it did	am an dad man
1	**Set 3 VC** **CVC**		on can cat dog got not top
1	**Set 4 VC** **CVC**		up get mum put* ran red run sun
1	**Set 5 VC** **CVC**		if bad bed big but fun had hat him hot let
1	**Set 6** **CVC**		fox
1	**Set 7** **CVC**		yes
2	**All Sets** **VCC**	and ask* it's	end
2	**All Sets** **CVCC**	help just went	best fast* last* lost lots must next wind
2	**All Sets** **CCVC**	from	gran stop
2	**All Sets** **CCVCC+**		didn't grandad plant*
3	**sh**		fish wish

Book	Structure / sound(s)	Top 100 high frequency words	Top 101–200 high frequency words
3	th	that this them then with	bath* path*
3	ng		along king long thing
3	ch		much children
3	k	back	duck
3	f	off	
3	l	will	fell still tell
3	s		across miss
4	o-e	don't go no old so	cold going most told boat grow snow window
4	z	as his is	clothes has us
4	ee	be he me she we see very	began he's been feet green keep need queen sleep three tree each eat sea tea even here these only really
4	a-e	day came made make they	away may play say way gave take great again* baby
4	er	her were	after ever every never over under different first girl word work we're

Book	Structure / sound(s)	Top 100 high frequency words	Top 101–200 high frequency words
4	e	again* said head	any many friend
4	ow		down how now town about found our out round **sh**out
5	oy		boy
5	oo	do into to you look* too	tod**ay** food room took* **th**rough
5	u	put* look looks come love some could	book good look**ing** took some**thing** couldn't would com**ing** ano**ther** mo**ther** o**ther**
5	i-e	by my I I'm like time	fly find I'll inside liked night right
5	aw	for a**ll** ca**ll** saw your	morn**ing** or sma**ll** wat**er** **th**ought before more door
5	air	**th**ere **th**eir	**th**ere's bear air **ch**air

Book	Structure / sound(s)	Top 100 high frequency words	Top 101–200 high frequency words
5	ar	are	after* can't fast* father last* car dark garden hard park
6	s		horse house mouse place
6	l		animals people
6	b		rabbit
6	d	looked called	jumped pulled cried suddenly
6	o	was	want wanted gone
6	i		live lived
6	u-e		use
Advanced consonants			
6	f		laugh
6	g		eggs ghost
6	h		who whose
6	j		giant magic
6	k		school
6	m		climb
6	n		know
6	p		floppy stopped
6	r		narrator
6	t		better little
6	v		I've
6	w		what when where which white why
6	z		because please

* These words may be explored at different points in the programme depending on variations in regional pronunciation.

Phoneme frame

Phoneme frame 1: up to three sounds

Phoneme frame 2: up to four sounds

Phoneme frame 3: up to five sounds

Phoneme frame 3: up to six sounds

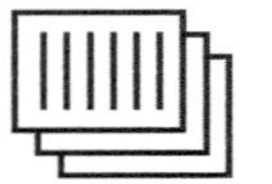

Blank flippies template

Flippies blank – for words with up to four sound spellings

Print out on card and cut out.
Stack them with the biggest (the complete word) on the bottom and in decreasing size so that the smallest is on the top.
Make sure the left-hand edge of the cards are flush. Staple the cards together on the left-hand side.
When the child runs a finger over the cards the sound spellings flip up. Ask the child to say the sounds and match to the flips.

staple

Sounds and their sound spellings 1 poster

a	cat

o	go
o-e	home
oa	boat
ow	grow
oe	toe
ough	though

ea	dream
ee	seen
y	happy
e	be
ie	field
e-e	eve
i	ski

a-e	made
a	angel
ai	train
ay	play
ea	steak
ey	they
eigh	eight

er	her
ur	burn
ir	bird
ear	learn
or	word
our	colour
ar	collar
re	centre
ere	were

e	red
ea	head
a	many
ai	said
ie	friend

ou	loud
ow	down
ough	plough

oi	soil
oy	boy

oo	moon
u	truth
u-e	rule
ew	grew
o	do
ui	suit
ou	soup
ue	blue

u	put
o	month
oo	book
ou	touch
o-e	come
oul	could

i-e	kite
i	mind
y	by
igh	night
ie	pie

or	for
au	haunt
aw	saw
ore	more
ar	war
al	walk
our	your
a	also
oar	roar
ough	bought
augh	taught

air	hair
ere	there
are	care
ear	bear

ar	star
a	father
al	calm
ear	heart

o	got
a	want
au	fault

i	sit
y	myth

u	music
u-e	cube
ew	few
ue	cue

Sounds and their sound spellings 2 poster

s	sat
c	city
sc	scent
ss	less
st	listen
ce	dance
se	house

t	top
tt	better
bt	doubt

p	pet
pp	happy

m	man
mm	summer
mn	hymn
mb	lamb

n	not
kn	knot
nn	sunny
gn	gnat

d	dog
dd	ladder
ed	wagged

g	get
gg	wiggle
gu	guard
gue	plague
gh	ghost

c	can
k	kid
ck	duck
ch	chemist
que	plaque

r	rat
wr	wrong
rr	hurry
rh	rhythm

b	bat
bb	robber
bu	build

f	fun
ph	phone
ff	stuff
gh	cough

h	hat
wh	whose

l	lamp
ll	bell
le	little
el	travel
il	pupil
al	metal
ol	symbol

j	jam
g	giant
ge	large
dge	bridge

v	van
ve	have

w	wig
wh	which

x	fox
xc	except
cc	accept

y	yes

z	zip
s	his
zz	buzz
ze	freeze
se	noise

sh	ship
s	sugar
ch	machine

th	think

ng	ring

ch	chip
tch	match

qu	quit

SECTION 1

sh

sh

fish

shop

Words with a 'sh' sound – word list of 1 syllable words

Initial sh

<u>3 sounds</u>
sham
shed
shin
ship
shod
shop
shot
shun
shut

<u>4 sounds</u>
shaft
shank
shelf
shift
shred
shrub
shrug
shunt

<u>5 sounds</u>
shrank
shrimp
shrink
shrunk

Final sh

<u>2 sounds</u>
ash

<u>3 sounds</u>
bash
bush
cash
dash
dish
dosh
fish
gush
hush
lush
mash
mush
posh
push
sash
wish

<u>4 sounds</u>
blush
brash
brush
clash
crash
crush
flash
flesh
flush
fresh
plush
slash
smash
swish
trash

<u>5 sounds</u>
splash
splish
splosh

Auditory discrimination is the ability to hear differences between sounds. Good auditory discrimination helps us to recognise and identify the sounds in words and so interpret them correctly. Children with poor auditory discrimination may confuse sounds and misinterpret things they have heard. Their spelling and writing may reflect their confusion over which sounds they heard in a word. **Auditory attention and tracking** is the ability to actively listen and follow auditory information from beginning to end. Good auditory attention and tracking helps us to follow a conversation, a story read out loud or a set of instructions, and enables us to focus on key information. Children with poor auditory attention and tracking may find it difficult to follow and respond appropriately to what is being said to them.

This story contains lots of words that contain the sound 'sh', which is the 'target' sound.
Read the story out loud to the child or group of children. Encourage the child to listen carefully and spot any word that contains the target sound. When a target word has been read, the child indicates that they have heard and spotted it by tapping the table, putting up a hand or any other agreed signal, but without shouting out. Stop reading and discuss the word, making any error correction necessary. If a word is missed, re-read the sentence.
Do not show the written story to the child. The target words are highlighted below for you.

Activity 1 Sound target story sh

It was Sam's birthday.

Sam and his dad were going to the pet **shop**.

"What sort of pet do you want, Sam?" **shouted** dad as they got ready to **rush** out of the house.

" I would like a **shiny** snake," said Sam.
"Too scary," said dad.

" I would like a woolly **sheep**," said Sam.
"Too hairy," said dad.

" I would like a **blushing shrimp**," said Sam.
"Too wobbly," said dad.

" I would like a **crashing** whale," said Sam.
"Too knobbly," said dad.

" I would like a **splashy fish**," said Sam.
"Hmmm.... perfect," said dad.

"I'll get my **dish**," thought the **shifty** cat.

Auditory discrimination is the ability to hear differences between sounds. Good auditory discrimination helps us to recognise and identify the sounds in words and so interpret them correctly. Children with poor auditory discrimination may confuse sounds and misinterpret things they have heard. Their spelling and writing may reflect their confusion over what sounds they heard in a word. **Auditory sequential memory** is the ability to remember and recall a series of things that they have heard. Children with poor auditory sequential memory may find it difficult to remember information given earlier in a conversation or set of instructions and may struggle to recall the sequence of sounds in a word.

The silly sentences contain lots of words containing the sound 'sh'.
Read the sentence to the child several times, invite them to join in as you say it and gradually recall it on their own.
Do not show the words to the child.
Ask them to say it as quickly as they can and have some fun with it. Perhaps they can make up their own?
The sentences gradually get longer and more complex.
Break this task into a number of shorter tasks over a number of lessons if necessary.

Activity 2 Tongue twister fun sh

Shay shares shirts.

Shrimps splash fresh fish.

Shireen brushes shy sheep.

She smashes shelves in sheds.

Shops sell sharp shorts and shoes.

Auditory discrimination is the ability to hear differences between sounds. Good auditory discrimination helps us to recognise and identify the sounds in words and so interpret them correctly. Children with poor auditory discrimination may confuse sounds and misinterpret things they have heard. Their spelling and writing may reflect their confusion over which sounds they heard in a word. **Auditory attention and tracking** is the ability to actively listen and follow auditory information from beginning to end. Good auditory attention and tracking helps us to follow a conversation, a story read out loud or a set of instructions, and enables us to focus on key information. Children with poor auditory attention and tracking may find it difficult to follow and respond appropriately to what is being said to them.

Read out the words and ask the child to listen carefully and identify the odd one out, the word that **does not start** with the same sound as the others.
Do not show the words to the child. The odd one out is highlighted for you.
Break this task into a number of shorter tasks over a number of lessons if necessary.

Activity 3 Odd one out — sh

1.	sad	sat	shop	2.	shed	ten	ship
3.	fish	flash	sit	4.	tap	dish	dash
5.	sum	shot	sun	6.	rat	mash	mush
7.	shell	shall	soft	8.	crash	sand	clash
9.	brush	blush	sink	10.	shelf	craft	shred
11.	stop	stab	shrug	12.	trash	smash	swish
13.	shrimp	snap	shrink	14.	splish	splash	flush
15.	shrub	stamp	stand	16.	stink	shift	stump
17.	ash	ant	ask	fan			
18.	tin	shed	top	ten			
19.	shop	sit	sun	set			

Auditory discrimination is the ability to hear differences between sounds. Good auditory discrimination helps us to recognise and identify the sounds in words and so interpret them correctly. Children with poor auditory discrimination may confuse sounds and misinterpret things they have heard. Their spelling and writing may reflect their confusion over which sounds they heard in a word. **Auditory recall memory** is the ability to remember and recall something that they have just heard. Children with poor auditory recall memory may find it difficult to remember sounds and words and respond appropriately.

Read the list of words below clearly, asking the child to listen carefully. At random points tap the table and stop reading, asking the child to remember and say the last word you said. Then ask them to tell you what the first sound in the word is.

Break this task into a number of shorter tasks over a number of lessons if necessary.

Activity 4 What sound am I? sh

1.	shop	sad	fan	sent	shed	shot	fast
2.	vet	ship	sun	still	van	shut	sent
3.	shell	mash	shin	wish	shall	send	push
4.	fish	flash	shift	fresh	shrub	flash	shop
5.	smash	sink	ask	ask	pest	spit	shell
6.	rush	rash	splash	spot	brush	shift	spin
7.	shred	trust	shelf	stink	shrink	trash	
8.	splosh	stump	flush	fresh	shrub	split	
9.	shrunk	crash	smash	crush	swish	splish	
10.	blush	shelf	brush	shift	smash	brush	

Auditory discrimination is the ability to hear differences between sounds. Good auditory discrimination helps us to recognise and identify the sounds in words and so interpret them correctly. Children with poor auditory discrimination may confuse sounds and misinterpret things they have heard. Their spelling and writing may reflect their confusion over what sounds they heard in a word.

Read out the pairs of words. Ask the child to tell you whether or not they start with the same sound. The words get increasingly complex. The pairs highlighted start with the same sounds.

Break this task into a number of shorter tasks over a number of lessons if necessary.

Activity 5 Same or different? sh

1. ash - ask
2. sad - hit
3. shed - shop
4. sip - hop
5. dish - dash
6. shot - shell
7. shut - slip
8. shall - still
9. spin - stop
10. shift - drift
11. mash - mush
12. send - soft
13. shrub - sank
14. pink - push
15. past - hush
16. shrink - flash
17. swish - smash
18. plush - lush
19. wish - ship
20. flush - fresh
21. shrimp - splash
22. stamp - shrunk
23. crash - crush
24. blush - smash
25. clash - bash
26. splosh - splish

Auditory fusion is the ability to hear the subtle gaps between sounds and words. Children with poor auditory fusion may get lost in conversations and when following a list of instructions given verbally.

Say the sounds or read the words in the list one after another at a brisk pace so that there are no obvious gaps between the sounds or the words. Ask the child to listen carefully and then tell you how many sounds or words you have said. Many of the words contain the sound 'sh' and get increasingly complex.

Break this task into a number of shorter tasks over a number of lessons if necessary.

Activity 6 How many did you hear? sh

1. s - **sh** - s
2. **sh** - s - p - p
3. **sh** - **sh** - s - f - **sh**
4. s - s - **sh**
5. f - **sh** - s - v
6. f - f - **sh** - s - v
7. s - s - **sh**
8. **sh** - s
9. sun - shop - sad - shed
10. van - fan - ship
11. sit - sad - shut - wish
12. shot - dish
13. sip - shed - ship
14. shell - mash - shut
15. push - fish - cash - shall
16. soft - sand - shift - swish
17. shelf - self - melt
18. push - rush
19. slip - spit - brush - shift - clash
20. blush - skip - flash
21. swish - trash
22. shift - shrink - splash
23. splosh - shrimp
24. sheep - seem - steam
25. sleep - sheet
26. shoe - soon - spoon
27. show - snow - stone - slow
28. home - hope - shown
29. hurt - shirt - turn
30. shape - same - slate - shave

Auditory attention and tracking is the ability to actively listen and follow auditory information from beginning to end. Good auditory attention and tracking helps us to follow a conversation, a story read out loud or a set of instructions, and enables us to focus on key information. Children with poor auditory attention and tracking may find it difficult to follow and respond appropriately to what is being said to them. **Auditory sequential memory** is the ability to remember and recall a series of things that they have heard. Children with poor auditory sequential memory may find it difficult to remember information given earlier in a conversation or set of instructions and may struggle to recall the sequence of sounds in a word.

In this activity the child has to process the auditory information but also respond by working out the pattern and stating the next sound in the sequence. Read out the list of sounds with a clear space between each. Ask the child to listen and work out what sound would come next. The answers follow in red.

Break this task into a number of shorter tasks over a number of lessons if necessary.

Activity 7 What comes next? sh

1. s **sh** s **sh** s **sh** ...... s
2. **sh** h **sh** h **sh** h ...... sh
3. v **sh** v **sh** v **sh** v
4. a **sh** a **sh** a **sh** ...... a
5. t t **sh** t t **sh** t t **sh** ...... t
6. s s **sh** s s **sh** s s **sh** ...... s
7. **sh** a a **sh** a a **sh** a a ...... sh
8. **sh** p p **sh** p p **sh** p p ...... sh
9. **sh sh** t t **sh sh** t t ...... sh
10. p p **sh sh** p p **sh sh** ...... p
11. f f **sh sh** f f **sh sh** ...... f
12. **sh sh** v v **sh sh** v v ...... sh
13. **sh sh** s **sh sh** s ...... sh
14. f f **sh** f f **sh** f f **sh** ...... f
15. p **sh** p p **sh** p p **sh** p ...... p
16. v **sh sh** v **sh sh** v **sh sh** v
17. f s **sh** f s **sh** f s **sh** ...... f
18. **sh** p f **sh** p f **sh** p f...... sh
19. **sh** s p **sh** s p **sh** s p ...... sh
20. s v **sh** s v **sh** s v **sh** ...... s
21. s **sh sh** v s **sh sh** v ...... s
22. **sh** s s f **sh** s s f ...... sh
23. v **sh sh** f v **sh sh** f v
24. **sh** s s v f **sh** s s v f ...... sh

This activity results in the child discovering the sound spelling which represents the sound 'sh'. Previously the child encountered sound spellings with just one letter but this one is made up of two letters 'working together'.

Support the child to read the words one by one.

For each word support the child to work out the sound spelling corresponding to the sound 'sh' and highlight it.

Ask the child to write the **sh** sound spelling as a heading on the small line in the box below, then write the word **ship** on the line underneath. Encourage the child to say each sound at the same time as writing each sound spelling. For example, the child writes **sh** and says 'sh', writes **i** and says 'i' and writes **p** and says 'p'. Then work through the rest of the words one by one, writing the words in the box below. Point out to the child that this shows that some sound spellings are made up of more than one letter 'working together' to be a 'picture' of the word.

Break this task into a number of shorter tasks over a number of lessons if necessary.

Activity 8 Investigating the sound sh

ship	shop	fish
mash	shut	wish
shin	push	shed
rush	crash	splash

Activity 10 Sound spelling cards sh

Visual memory is the ability to remember and identify a shape or picture that we have previously seen. Children with poor visual memory may struggle to remember pictures, figures, shapes, letters and numbers and may have difficulties with reading, writing and number work.

Ask the child to look at the sound spelling in the yellow box for at least five seconds, covering the white box underneath. Then cover the yellow box so that the sound spelling cannot be seen and reveal the choice of sound spellings in the white box below. Ask the child to select the matching sound spelling from the white box.

Break this task into a number of shorter tasks over a number of lessons if necessary.

Activity 12 Remembering sound spellings sh

sh
s sh

s
sh s

sh
sh h

h
s h

sh
s sh h

s
sh h s

Visual discrimination is the ability to see differences between objects and figures that are similar. Good visual discrimination helps keep us from getting confused when looking at shapes and forms in the environment. Children with poor visual discrimination may find it difficult to recognise letters, may confuse letters such as b and d and may find it difficult to identify mathematical symbols.

Focus on one of the sound spellings featured on this sheet, e.g. **sh** (say the sound 'sh' and point to an example rather than using the letter names to identify the sound spelling). Ask the child to look at all the sound spellings and indicate or put a ring round all the sound spellings which match the target. Repeat for another sound spelling featured on the sheet.

Break this task into a number of shorter tasks over a number of lessons if necessary.

Activity 13 Spot the sound spelling sh

h b sh sh s

b

sh b s

b b

s sh h b

b h sh s

Spatial relations is the ability to perceive the position of objects in relation to ourselves and to each other. This skill helps children to understand relationships between symbols and letters. Children with poor spatial relations may find it difficult to write letters in the correct orientation, write consistently starting at the margin and write letters of the same size.

In the first part, ask the child to copy the sound spellings on the lines below in exactly the same places as they appear above.
In the second part, ask the child to copy the words on the lines below in exactly the same places, saying the matching sound as they write each sound spelling. Note that the sound spellings are for the sounds 'sh', 's', 'n' and 'h', which are visually similar.

Break this task into a number of shorter tasks over a number of lessons if necessary.

Activity 17 Where am I? sh

sh s h sh

s h sh n h

ship dish

shop cash

Visual sequential memory is the ability to remember sequences of figures, symbols and shapes. Children with poor visual sequencing struggle to remember a sequence of letters and follow visual patterns. They may have difficulties writing a sequence of letters to form a word and a sequence of words to form a sentence.

Ask the child to look at the sound spellings in the yellow box for at least five seconds, covering the white box underneath. Then cover the yellow box so that the sound spellings cannot be seen and reveal the sequence of sound spellings in the white box below. Ask the child to remember the missing sound spelling and write it in the space.

Break this task into a number of shorter tasks over a number of lessons if necessary.

Activity 18 Remembering lots of sound spellings sh

s sh
_ sh

h sh
h _

s	h
_	h

s	sh
s	_

s	sh	h
s	sh	_

s	h	sh
s	_	sh

This set of cards is made of up words containing the sound 'sh'. The sound spelling for the target sound in each word is highlighted. Copy onto card and cut out.
Practise dynamic blending for reading, as described in the 'Working through the programme' section, using these cards. Model this process for the child if necessary.

Activity 20 Dynamic blending – word cards sh

shop	shut
shed	shelf
ash	fish
rush	push
cash	wish
posh	fresh
crash	splash

This set of cards is made of up words containing the sound 'sh'. Copy onto card and cut out. Practise dynamic blending for reading, as described in the 'Working through the programme' section, using these cards. Model this process for the child if necessary.

Activity 20 Dynamic blending – word cards sh

shot	ship
shift	shunt
shrink	shrimp
mash	dash
bash	hush
blush	flash
swish	brush

Print out onto card and cut out.
Stack them with the biggest (the complete word) on the bottom and in decreasing size so that the smallest is on the top.
Make sure the left-hand edge of the cards are flush. Staple the cards together on the left-hand side.
When the child runs a finger over the cards the sound spellings flip up. Ask the child to say the sounds and match to the flips.

staple

Activity 24 Flippies for the sound 'sh'

sh	sh	o	sh	o	p				
sh	sh	e	sh	e	l	sh	e	l	f
w	w	i	w	i	sh				
b	b	r	b	r	u	b	r	u	sh
c	c	r	c	r	a	c	r	a	sh

Read the clue on the left for the child.
Use the clue to work out what the answer word is.
Encourage the child to think about the sounds in that word and write a sound spelling for each sound in the boxes on the right, one by one.
The first one is done for you as an example.
Explain to the child that they may not need to use all the boxes and so some are shaded in.
Break this task into a number of shorter tasks over a number of lessons if necessary.

Activity 25 Sound boxes sh

Clue	Sound boxes			
Part of the leg	sh	i	n	
Blow out candles - make a ...				
A place to buy things				
Not open				
Crushed potato				
Sails on the sea				
Walk fast to get somewhere				
Money				
Place for garden tools				
Put books and toys on this				
Go red in the face				

Support the child to read the words on the left.
For each word, support the child to work out how many sounds there are in it and write that number in the grey box.
Then ask the child to count out the number of white boxes needed to write the word, so that there is one box for each sound, and colour in any boxes that are not needed.
Next ask the child to say the sounds in the word, one by one, and at the same time write the matching sound spelling in the boxes one by one.
The first two are done for you as examples.
Break this task into a number of shorter tasks over a number of lessons if necessary.

Activity 26 How many sounds? sh

Word	Number	Writing the sound spellings				
shot	3	sh	o	t		
smash	4	s	m	a	sh	
dish						
cash						
splash						
rush						
shops						
shed						
shrink						

During this activity the child will be asked to slide sounds in and out of words, i.e. practise phoneme manipulation.
A sound might be swapped, added or taken away.
Print the sound spelling cards onto card and cut out.
Activity:

- Spread out all the sound spelling cards so that the child can see them.
- Build a starting word from the prompt list, demonstrating how to dynamically blend the sounds together as you move the sound spelling cards into place.
- Repeat the word, running your finger under the cards so that it corresponds to the sounds within the word.
- Ask the child to change the word to the next word on the prompt list. As you say the new word run your finger under the cards so that it corresponds with the sound you are saying and the matching sound spelling card.

This gives the child the chance to hear and see what is different.

- The child can then swap the appropriate sound spelling cards.
- Repeat this technique with the next word on the list.

Activity 29 Sound swap sh

Sound swap sh

List 1	List 2	List 3
cash	smash	ship
clash	sash	ships
crash	bash	shops
rash	brash	shop
ash	brush	shot
cash	rush	shut
mash	mush	shunt

sh	a	i	o
u	c	l	r
m	s	b	p
t	n		

Support the child to read the words on the left, one by one.
For each word read the clue to the child and then work out what the answer word is.
Explain to the child that they will need to either: add a sound, take away a sound or change a sound to the word on the left to make the answer word, e.g. cot > cost list > lit mat > rat.
Have the child write out the answer word on the right, saying each sound as they write each sound spelling.
An example is done for you.
Break this task into a number of shorter tasks over a number of lessons if necessary.

Activity 30 Sound exchange sh

Starting word	Clue	New word
ship	Place to buy things	shop
shred	Place to leave tools	______
clash	Money	______
rash	American for rubbish	______
rub	Big plant	______
brush	Do things fast	______
wish	Swims in water	______
elf	Put books on this	______
mash	Break up	______
flash	Water down the toilet	______

Place a whiteboard in front of the child.
Choose a word from the list below. Randomise the words you choose so that you are choosing words with a variety of number of sounds.
Draw dots on the whiteboard to match the number of sounds in the word, one dot for each sound. Do not write the word or show the word to the child as this is a purely auditory activity.
Say the word to the child and as you do so run your finger under the dots so that your finger matches the appropriate sound dot and its corresponding sound as you say it.
Then cover the dot that corresponds to the sound you are going to take away – use the list below.
Ask the child to tell you what is left if you take that sound away.
Take away another sound or choose a new word.
Remember to time limit this activity.

Activity 31 Sound sums sh

No. of sounds in starting word	Word	Take away the sound	What is left?
2	ash	sh	a
3	shin	sh	in
4	blush	l	bush
4	crash	k (c)	rash
4	brush	b	rush
4	clash	l	cash
4	swish	s	wish
4	smash	s	mash
4	plush	l	push
4	shelf	sh	elf
4	shred	sh	red
4	shrub	sh	rub
4	shrug	sh	rug
5	splash	p	slash
5	splosh	p	slosh
5	shrink	sh	rink

This set of cards is made up of high frequency words containing the sound 'sh'. Copy onto card and cut out. Practise dynamic blending for reading, as described in the 'Working through the programme' section, using these cards. Model this process for the child if necessary.

Activity 32 Reading high frequency words sh

fish	wish

Starting at 'fish', have the child read each of the words on the shapes as quickly as possible.
Support the child to read the words by giving information about sounds and supporting blending but do not supply the whole word.
Time how long it takes to read all the words to 'splash' and record the time in the box.
Repeat at a later point and see if the child can beat his own time.

Activity 33 Reading race: splash! sh

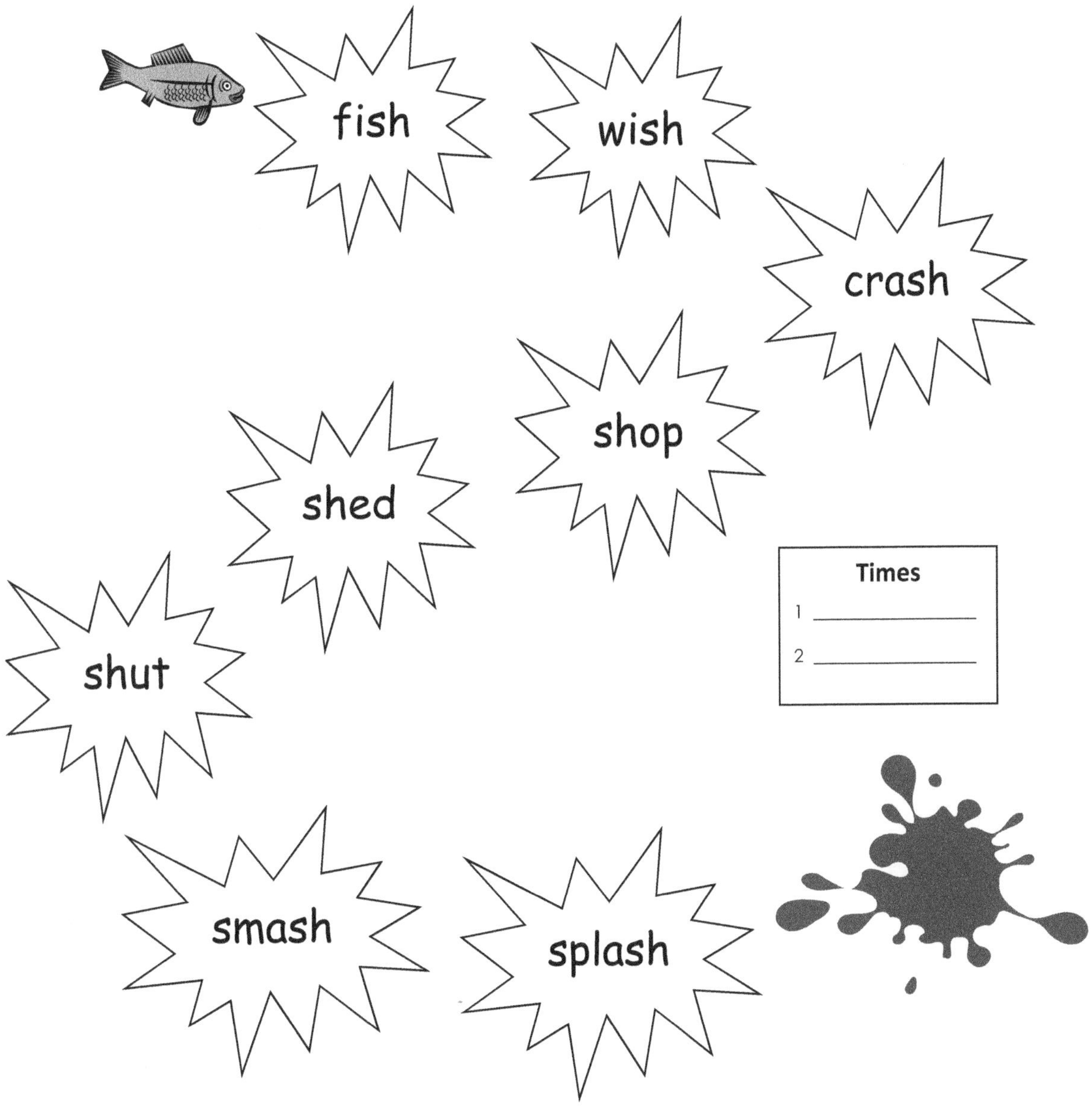

fish

wish

crash

shop

shed

shut

smash

splash

Times
1 ____________
2 ____________

Support the child to read the words one by one.
For each word support the child to think whether there is a 'sh' sound in the word.
Have the child put a ring around or highlight just the words that have a 'sh' sound.
Break this task into a number of shorter tasks over a number of lessons if necessary.

Activity 34 Word tracker sh

sink	shed	shop	stop	ash
mash	sad	shut	wish	most
crash	shin	stand	cash	sits
send	shelf	splash	posh	trash
slip	spots	ships	just	wish

How many 'sh' words did you find? ________

Visual memory is the ability to remember and identify a shape, figure or picture that we have previously seen. Children with poor visual memory may struggle to remember pictures, figures, shapes, letters and numbers and may have difficulties with reading, writing and number work.

Ask the child to look at the word in the yellow box for at least five seconds, covering the white box underneath. Then cover the yellow box so that the word cannot be seen and reveal a choice of words in the white box below. Ask the child to select the word in the white box that matches the one they saw in the yellow box.

Break this task into a number of shorter tasks over a number of lessons if necessary.

Activity 35 Remembering words sh

shop
shot shop

fish
fish dish

shelf
shift shelf

brush
blush brush

crush
crash crush clash

flash
fish flush flash

splash
splish splash splosh

Support the child to read the words one by one.
For each word support the child to think whether the word is a real word that makes sense or is a nonsense word.
Have the child put a ring around or highlight just the real words.
Break this task into a number of shorter tasks over a number of lessons if necessary.

Activity 36 Word detective sh

mish	rush	bash	shelf	mash
push	shop	frosh	ship	shand
crash	flash	shad	hish	smash
shand	drish	cash	brush	losh
hush	trash	smesh	blosh	flush

How many real words did you find? ________

Visual sequential memory is the ability to remember sequences of figures, symbols, pictures and shapes. Children with poor visual sequencing struggle to remember a sequence of letters and follow visual patterns. They may have difficulties writing a sequence of letters to form a word and a sequence of words to form a sentence.

Ask the child to look at the words in the yellow box for at least five seconds, covering the white box underneath. Then cover the yellow box so that the words cannot be seen and reveal the sequence of words in the white box below. Ask the child to remember the missing word from the sequence in the yellow box and write it in the space.

Break this task into a number of shorter tasks over a number of lessons if necessary.

Activity 37 Remembering lots of words sh

shed shut
______ shut

fish push
fish ______

shop dash wish
______ dash wish

shot	bush	cash
shot	______	cash

hush	shrub	smash
hush	shrub	______

mash	shin	brush
mash	______	brush

shift	clash	blush
______	clash	blush

Print out on card and cut out the sound spelling and picture cards for each word.
Read though the instructions in the 'Working through the programme' section at the start of this book prior to working with a child.

Activity 38 Word build sh

w	i	sh		
m	a	sh		
c	r	a	sh	
b	r	u	sh	

sh	e	d		
sh	i	f	t	
sh	e	l	f	

Support the child to read the words on the list one by one.
For each word support the child to think about each of the sounds in the word and their matching sound spellings.
Have the child put a ring around or highlight the sound spelling for each sound.
Break this task into a number of shorter tasks over a number of lessons if necessary.

Activity 39 Word tech sh

ship

smash

wish

shut

brush

splash

shelf

shops

crash

Read the clue on the left for the child.
For each clue support the child to work out what the answer word is.
The sound spellings for the answer word are given to help, but they are mixed up – an anagram.
Have the child use the sound spellings to write the answer word on the line on the right.
Encourage the child to say the associated sound as he writes each sound spelling.
Break this task into a number of shorter tasks over a number of lessons if necessary.

Activity 40 Word scramble sh

Clue	Sound spellings	Word
Place to buy things	p **sh** o	__________
Swims in water	**sh** i f	__________
Money	c **sh** a	__________
Put books on this	f **sh** l e	__________
Part of your leg	i n **sh**	__________
Move as fast as you can	**sh** r u	__________
Not open	t u **sh**	__________
Left after a fire	**sh** a	__________
Itchy spots	**sh** r a	__________
Boat	p **sh** i	__________

Activity 42 Spelling challenge — sh

shop	sh o p	sh o p	___ ___ ___	____________
shut	sh u t	sh u t	___ ___ ___	____________
shelf	sh e l f	sh e l f	___ ___ ___ ___	____________
fish	f i sh	f i sh	___ ___ ___	____________
wish	w i sh	w i sh	___ ___ ___	____________
crash	c r a sh	c r a sh	___ ___ ___ ___	____________
brush	b r u sh	b r u sh	___ ___ ___ ___	____________

Support the child to read the sentences.
In each sentence there is a missing word with two words underneath. Ask the child to choose the word that makes sense and write the word on the line within the sentence. Encourage the child to say the sounds as they write the sound spellings.
Note that the sentences include some high frequency words which contain sounds that the child has not yet encountered in the programme. Support the child to decode these words by supplying information about any unfamiliar sound and its sound spelling and encourage the child to blend for reading. Some sound spellings are highlighted to support this.
Break this task into a number of shorter tasks over a number of lessons if necessary.

Activity 44 Spot the spelling sh

1. I went to the bank to get ____________.
   mash cash

2. Tom put the pots on the ____________.
   shelf self

3. Dad had to ____________ the pram.
   push rush

4. I made a big ____________ in the pond.
   smash splash

5. I like ____________ and chips.
   wish fish

6. Dad sat in the ____________.
   shed shin

Support the child to read the sentences.
Explain that the sentences are OK but that they are very short and could be a bit more interesting!
Then support the child to read the phrases at the bottom of the page and decide which could be used to make each sentence 'better' or 'more interesting'.
Ask the child to write out the sentence, adding the new phrase from the list. Encourage the child to say the sounds at the same time as writing the associated sound spelling when writing each word.
Note that the sentences include high frequency words which contain sounds that the child has not yet encountered in the programme. Support the child to decode these words by supplying information about any unfamiliar sounds and sound spellings and encourage the child to blend for reading. Some sound spellings are highlighted to support this.
Break this task into a number of shorter tasks over a number of lessons if necessary.

Activity 45 Making better sentences sh

1. I went to the shop.

___

___

2. Dad sat in the shed.

___

___

3. The fish swam fast.

___

___

4. I **like** mash.

___

___

5. Mum had to dash.

___

___

but Sam **like**s chips	but it was shut
and mended the **bike**	**becau**se she was in a rush
and **made** a big splash	

Support the child to read each sentence one by one.
Ask the child to re-read the sentence, several times if necessary, and try to remember it.
Then cover the sentence and ask the child to recall the sentence verbally.
Once they can do this confidently, ask the child to write out the sentence from memory.

When writing a word, encourage the child to say the sound as they write each associated sound spelling.
When the word is complete then they are to say the whole word.
When the sentence is complete the child reads out their sentence and then compares it to the original.
Note that the sentences may include high frequency words which contain sounds that the child has not yet encountered in the programme. Support the child to decode these words by supplying information about any unfamiliar sounds and their sound spellings and encouraging the child to blend for reading. Some of these sound spellings are highlighted to help the child when writing the words later.

Alternatively, using text to speech software, the child could type the sentence, with the computer reading back each word and then the completed sentence.

Activity 46 Writing challenge sh

I wish the ship had a crash.

The shed shop was shut.

The fish slid off the dish.

Hush or Sam will rush.

Answers sh

Page 22
Activity 25 Sound boxes

w i sh
sh o p
sh u t
m a sh
sh i p
r u sh
c a sh
sh e d
sh e l f
b l u sh

Page 23
Activity 26 How many sounds?

3 d i sh
3 c a sh
5 s p l a sh
3 r u sh
4 sh o p s
3 sh e d
5 sh r i n k

Page 26
Activity 30 Sound exchange

shred – shed
clash – cash
rash – trash
rub – shrub
brush – rush
wish – fish
elf – shelf
mash – smash
flash – flush

Page 30
Activity 34 Word tracker

shed shop ash
mash shut wish
crash shin cash
shelf splash posh trash
ships wish

15

Page 33
Activity 36 Word detective

rush bash shelf mash
push shop ship
crash flash smash
cash brush
hush trash flush

15

Page 38
Activity 39 Word tech

s m a sh
w i sh
sh u t
b r u sh
s p l a sh
sh e l f
sh o p s
c r a sh

Page 39
Activity 40 Word scramble

shop
fish
cash
shelf
shin
rush
shut
ash
rash
ship

Page 41
Activity 44 Spot the spelling

cash
shelf
push
splash
fish
shed

Page 42
Activity 45 Making better sentences

1. I went to the shop but it was shut.
2. Dad sat in the shed and mended the bike.
3. The fish swam fast and made a big splash.
4. I like mash but Sam likes chips.
5. Mum had to dash because she was in a rush.

SECTION 2

th

th

bath

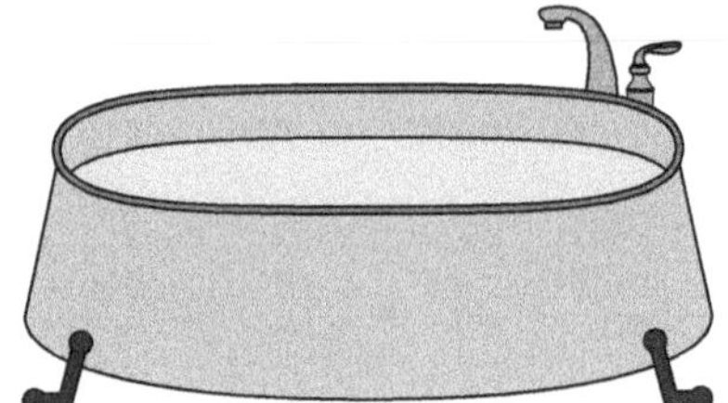

think

with

this

Words with a 'th' sound – word list of 1 syllable words

Initial 'th' (unvoiced)

<u>3 sounds</u>
thin
thud
thug

<u>4 sounds</u>
thank
theft
think
thrash
thresh
throb
thrum
thrush
thump

<u>5 sounds</u>
thrift
thrust

Final 'th' (unvoiced)

<u>3 sounds</u>
moth

<u>3 sounds</u>
bath*
path*

<u>4 sounds</u>
broth
cloth
fifth
froth
maths
sloth
tenth

Voiced and unvoiced sounds

There are subtle differences between how the sound 'th' is produced in different words.
In the voiced sound the vocal folds vibrate and in the unvoiced sound they do not. This explains the way saying the sound 'th' feels different in the words **with** and **moth**.
This is not something that needs to be taught to the child but is something that you will need to be aware of in your teaching should questions arise.

Initial 'th' (voiced)

<u>3 sounds</u>
than
that
them
then
this
thus

Final 'th' (voiced)

<u>3 sounds</u>
with

High frequency words
Containing sounds / sound spellings not yet encountered in the programme

th***eir***	the 'air' sound is represented by the sound spelling **eir**
th***ere***	the 'air' sound is represented by the sound spelling **ere**
th***ese***	the 'e-e' sound is represented by the sound spelling **e-e** and the 'z' sound is represented by the sound spelling **s**
th***ey***	the 'a-e' sound is represented by the sound spelling **ey**
th***ose***	the 'o-e' sound is represented by the sound spelling **o-e** and the 'z' sound is represented by the sound spelling **s**

Auditory discrimination is the ability to hear differences between sounds. Good auditory discrimination helps us to recognise and identify the sounds in words and so interpret them correctly. Children with poor auditory discrimination may confuse sounds and misinterpret things they have heard. Their spelling and writing may reflect their confusion over which sounds they heard in a word. **Auditory attention and tracking** is the ability to actively listen and follow auditory information from beginning to end. Good auditory attention and tracking helps us to follow a conversation, a story read out loud or a set of instructions, and enables us to focus on key information. Children with poor auditory attention and tracking may find it difficult to follow and respond appropriately to what is being said to them.

This story contains lots of words that contain the sound 'th', which is the 'target' sound.
Read the story out loud to the child or group of children. Encourage the child to listen carefully and spot any word that contains the target sound. When a target word has been read, the child indicates that they have heard and spotted it by tapping the table, putting up a hand or any other agreed signal, but without shouting out. Stop reading and discuss the word, making any error correction necessary. If a word is missed, re-read the sentence.
Do not show the written story to the child. The target words are highlighted below for you.

Activity 1 Sound target story th

A moth flew down the garden path.

'This is a beautiful day,' the moth thought to himself.

'The sun is shining high in the sky.'

'I think I would like to play with another moth.'

He looked everywhere for a moth friend: under the picnic cloth, along the path and even in the old bath left in the garden.

Then he heard a loud thump and a thud.

Just behind him a thrush landed.

'I'll be your friend, little moth,' he said.

The moth was thrilled and off they flew together.

Auditory discrimination is the ability to hear differences between sounds. Good auditory discrimination helps us to recognise and identify the sounds in words and so interpret them correctly. Children with poor auditory discrimination may confuse sounds and misinterpret things they have heard. Their spelling and writing may reflect their confusion over what sounds they heard in a word. **Auditory sequential memory** is the ability to remember and recall a series of things that they have heard. Children with poor auditory sequential memory may find it difficult to remember information given earlier in a conversation or set of instructions and may struggle to recall the sequence of sounds in a word.

The silly sentences contain lots of words containing the sound 'th'.
Read the sentence to the child several times, invite them to join in as you say it and gradually recall it on their own.
Do not show the words to the child.
Ask them to say it as quickly as they can and have some fun with it. Perhaps they can make up their own?
The sentences gradually get longer and more complex.
Break this task into a number of shorter tasks over a number of lessons if necessary.

Activity 2 Tongue twister fun — th

Thirty thankful thieves.

Beth threw three things.

Ruth thinks thirsty moths have thick throats.

Auditory discrimination is the ability to hear differences between sounds. Good auditory discrimination helps us to recognise and identify the sounds in words and so interpret them correctly. Children with poor auditory discrimination may confuse sounds and misinterpret things they have heard. Their spelling and writing may reflect their confusion over which sounds they heard in a word. **Auditory attention and tracking** is the ability to actively listen and follow auditory information from beginning to end. Good auditory attention and tracking helps us to follow a conversation, a story read out loud or a set of instructions, and enables us to focus on key information. Children with poor auditory attention and tracking may find it difficult to follow and respond appropriately to what is being said to them.

Read out the words and ask the child to listen carefully and identify the odd one out, the word that **does not start** with the same sound as the others.
Do not show the words to the child. The odd one out is highlighted for you.
Break this task into a number of shorter tasks over a number of lessons if necessary.

Activity 3 Odd one out th

1. shop this ship
2. ten tap that
3. thin thud sit
4. them fish fan
5. moth map then
6. mash than mush
7. thin shed shin
8. thank theft sent
9. push thump posh
10. maths the moths
11. think shelf shift
12. thrush thrash smash
13. fifth this froth
14. flash think flush
15. thin thud tub thug
16. thank fifth thing think
17. this they where them
18. those there these hair

Auditory discrimination is the ability to hear differences between sounds. Good auditory discrimination helps us to recognise and identify the sounds in words and so interpret them correctly. Children with poor auditory discrimination may confuse sounds and misinterpret things they have heard. Their spelling and writing may reflect their confusion over which sounds they heard in a word. **Auditory recall memory** is the ability to remember and recall something that they have just heard. Children with poor auditory recall memory may find it difficult to remember sounds and words and respond appropriately.

Read the list of words below clearly, asking the child to listen carefully. At random points tap the table and stop reading, asking the child to remember and say the last word you said. Then ask them to tell you what the **first** sound in the word is.

Break this task into a number of shorter tasks over a number of lessons if necessary.

Activity 4 What sound am I? th

1.	thin	ship	sad	thud	thug	van	shop
2.	thank	wish	cash	think	fish	shut	this
3.	shell	theft	moth	path	shall	push	that
4.	them	rush	fast	this	bash	shot	then
5.	fresh	cloth	stamp	tenth	shelf	brush	with
6.	shrink	think	splash	blush	thrush	fifth	path
7.	tenth	flush	fresh	thump	shift	thrust	
8.	these	they	where	those	share	there	
9.	third	shirt	world	thirst	skirt	earth	
10.	sheep	three	cream	thief	street	dream	

Auditory discrimination is the ability to hear differences between sounds. Good auditory discrimination helps us to recognise and identify the sounds in words and so interpret them correctly. Children with poor auditory discrimination may confuse sounds and misinterpret things they have heard. Their spelling and writing may reflect their confusion over what sounds they heard in a word.

Read out the pairs of words. Ask the child to tell you whether or not they start with the same sound. The words get increasingly complex. The pairs that start with the same sounds are highlighted.

Break this task into a number of shorter tasks over a number of lessons if necessary.

Activity 5 Same or different? th

1. thin - thud
2. moth - rush
3. this - sit
4. ship - that
5. with - wish
6. than - them
7. shall - thin
8. shin - shop
9. thank - think
10. shift - tenth
11. fifth - froth
12. maths - moths
13. theft - cloth
14. thrash - fresh
15. thrush - crush
16. thump - thresh
17. three - threat
18. third - earth
19. those - sheep
20. these - those
21. way - they
22. stare - thump
23. thief - thorn
24. where - there
25. splash - thrush
26. thought - through

Auditory fusion is the ability to hear the subtle gaps between sounds and words. Children with poor auditory fusion may get lost in conversations and when following a list of instructions given verbally.

Say the sounds or read the words in the list one after another at a brisk pace so that there are no obvious gaps between the sounds or the words. Ask the child to listen carefully and then tell you how many sounds or words you have said. Many of the words contain the sound 'th' and get increasingly complex.

Break this task into a number of shorter tasks over a number of lessons if necessary.

Activity 6 How many did you hear? th

1. t - **th** - s
2. **th** - s - t - t
3. **th** - **th** - s - f - **th**
4. f - s - **th** - v
5. f - **th** - s - v
6. **th** - f - **th** - s - f
7. t - f - **th** - sh
8. **th** - f
9. than - mash - this - shed
10. fan - them - van
11. that - mad - bath - then
12. moth - with
13. thank - shelf - think
14. shell - fifth - shift
15. cloth - fish - thrush - maths
16. tenth - theft - brush - wish
17. shelf - thump - plant
18. thrust - crush
19. these - three - green - sheep
20. tree - thief - steam - these
21. they - tray - stay
22. those - throat - shown
23. there - where - stare
24. thought - bought - shore
25. flirt - shirt - third - work
26. through - shoe - fruit

Auditory attention and tracking is the ability to actively listen and follow auditory information from beginning to end. Good auditory attention and tracking helps us to follow a conversation, a story read out loud or a set of instructions, and enables us to focus on key information. Children with poor auditory attention and tracking may find it difficult to follow and respond appropriately to what is being said to them. **Auditory sequential memory** is the ability to remember and recall a series of things that they have heard. Children with poor auditory sequential memory may find it difficult to remember information given earlier in a conversation or set of instructions and may struggle to recall the sequence of sounds in a word.

In this activity the child has to process the auditory information but also respond by working out the pattern and stating the next sound in the sequence. Read out the list of sounds with a clear space between each. Ask the child to listen and work out what sound would come next. The answers follow in red.

Break this task into a number of shorter tasks over a number of lessons if necessary.

Activity 7 What comes next? th

1. t **th** t **th** t **th** ...... t
2. **th** h **th** h **th** h ...... th
3. f **th** f **th** f **th** ...... f
4. v **th** v **th** v **th** v
5. t t **th** t t **th** t t **th** ...... t
6. s s **th** s s **th** s s **th** ...... s
7. **th** f f **th** f f **th** f f ...... th
8. **th** v v **th** v v **th** v v ...... th
9. **th th** t t **th th** t t ...... sh
10. f f **th th** f f **th th** ...... f
11. **th th** sh **th th** sh ...... th
12. **th th** v v **th th** v v ...... th
13. **th th** s **th th** s ...... th
14. f f **th** f f **th** f f **th** ...... f
15. p **th** p p **th** p p **th** p ...... p
16. v **th th** v **th th** v **th th** v
17. f v **th** f v **th** f v **th** ...... f
18. **th** p f **th** p f **th** p f...... th
19. **th** s p **th** s p **th** s p ...... th
20. s v **th** s v **th** s v **th** ...... s
21. s **th th** v s **th th** v ...... s
22. **th** s s f **th** s s f ...... th
23. v **th th** f v **th th** f v
24. **th** s s v f **th** s s v f ...... th

This activity results in the child discovering the sound spelling which represents the sound 'th'. The child is learning that some sound spellings are made up of more than one letter.

Support the child to read the words one by one.
For each word support the child to work out the sound spelling corresponding to the sound 'th' and highlight it.
There is just one sound spelling to find: **th**, but note that it has two letters.
In the box underneath write the sound spelling **th** as the heading on the small line at the top of the box.
Then work through the word list and write the remainder of the words in the box, noting the **th** sound spelling.
Encourage the child to say each sound as they write each sound spelling in sequence, e.g. say 'th' 'i' 's' as they write **th i s**.

Break this task into a number of shorter tasks over a number of lessons if necessary.

Activity 8 Investigating the sound th

this	then	that
path	moth	thin
with	them	than
thank	cloth	maths

______

______ ______
______ ______
______ ______
______ ______
______ ______
______ ______
______ ______

Activity 10 Sound spelling cards th

th

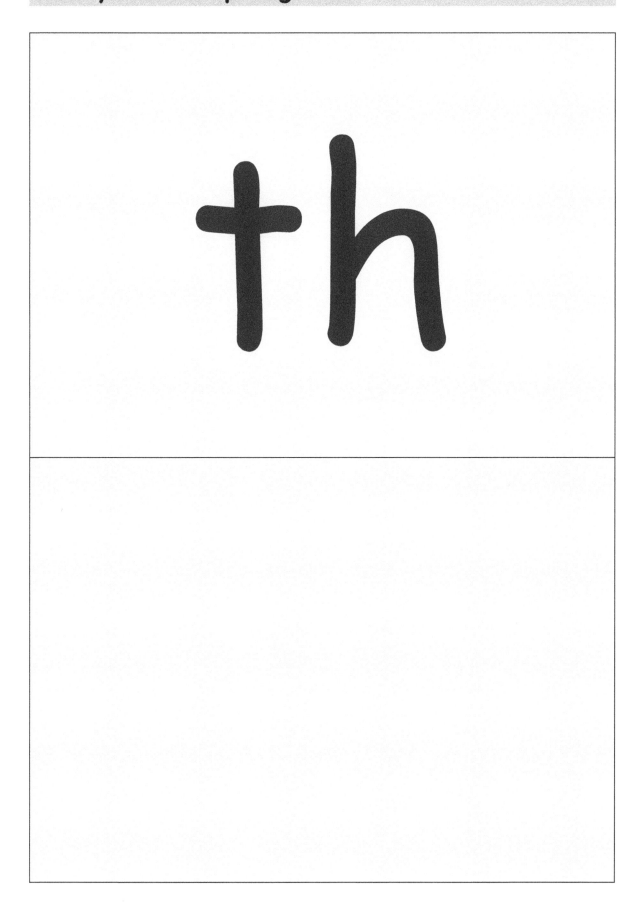

Visual memory is the ability to remember and identify a shape or picture that we have previously seen. Children with poor visual memory may struggle to remember pictures, figures, shapes, letters and numbers and may have difficulties with reading, writing and number work.

Ask the child to look at the sound spelling in the yellow box for at least five seconds, covering the white box underneath. Then cover the yellow box so that the sound spelling cannot be seen and reveal the choice of sound spellings in the white box below. Ask the child to select the matching sound spelling from the white box.

Break this task into a number of shorter tasks over a number of lessons if necessary.

Activity 12 Remembering sound spellings th

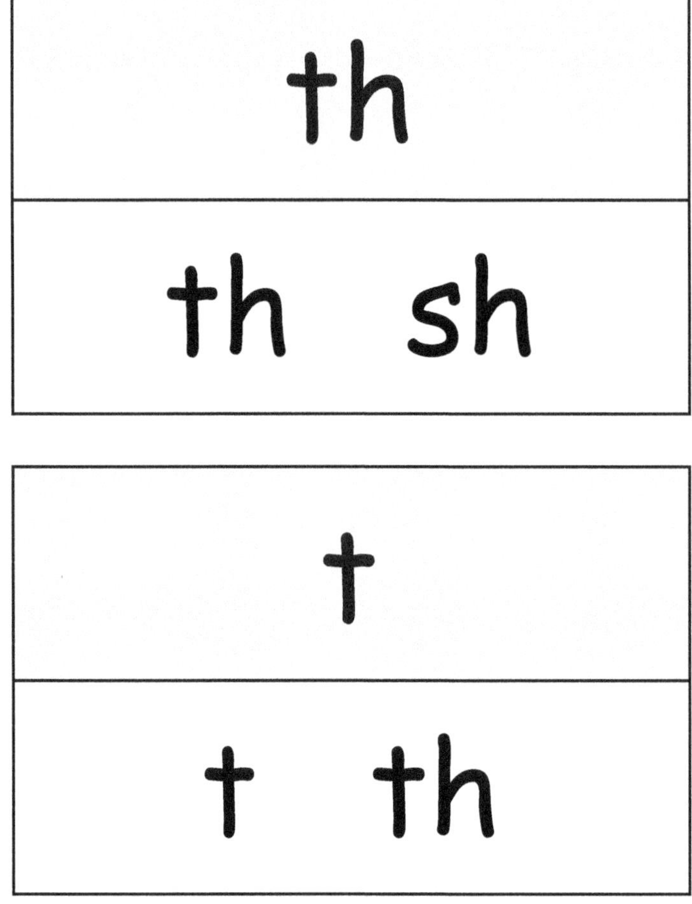

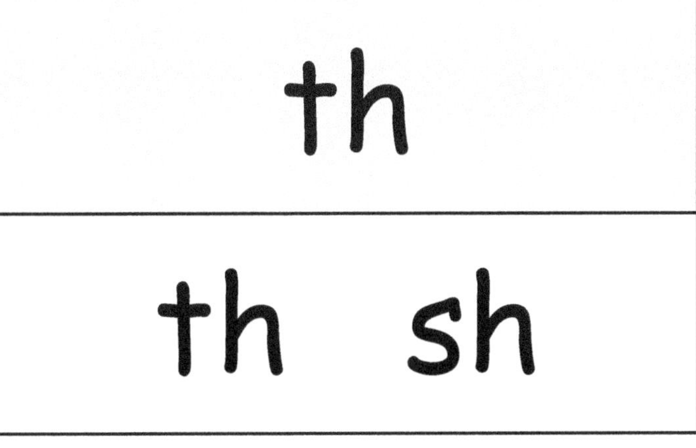

t
th t

th
t th h

t
sh th t

Visual discrimination is the ability to see differences between objects and figures that are similar. Good visual discrimination helps keep us from getting confused when looking at shapes and forms in the environment. Children with poor visual discrimination may find it difficult to recognise letters, may confuse letters such as b and d and may find it difficult to identify mathematical symbols.

Focus on one of the sound spellings featured on this sheet, e.g. **th** (say the sound 'th' and point to an example rather than using the letter names to identify the sound spelling). Ask the child to look at all the sound spellings and indicate or put a ring round all the sound spellings which match the target. Repeat for another sound spelling featured on the sheet.

Break this task into a number of shorter tasks over a number of lessons if necessary.

Activity 13 Spot the sound spelling th

h th th

t t t

th h th

t t h h

th

h h th h

Spatial relations is the ability to perceive the position of objects in relation to ourselves and to each other. This skill helps children to understand relationships between symbols and letters. Children with poor spatial relations may find it difficult to write letters in the correct orientation, write consistently starting at the margin and write letters of the same size.

In the first part, ask the child to copy the sound spellings on the lines below in exactly the same places as they appear above.
In the second part, ask the child to copy the words on the lines below in exactly the same places, saying the matching sound as they write each sound spelling. Note that the sound spellings are for the sounds 'th', 't' and 'h', which are visually similar.

Break this task into a number of shorter tasks over a number of lessons if necessary.

Activity 17 Where am I? th

th t h th

____

t h th th

____

this with

____

that them

____

Visual sequential memory is the ability to remember sequences of figures, symbols and shapes. Children with poor visual sequencing struggle to remember a sequence of letters and follow visual patterns. They may have difficulties writing a sequence of letters to form a word and a sequence of words to form a sentence.

Ask the child to look at the sound spellings in the yellow box for at least five seconds, covering the white box underneath. Then cover the yellow box so that the sound spellings cannot be seen and reveal the sequence of sound spellings in the white box below. Ask the child to remember the missing sound spelling and write it in the space.

Break this task into a number of shorter tasks over a number of lessons if necessary.

Activity 18 Remembering lots of sound spellings th

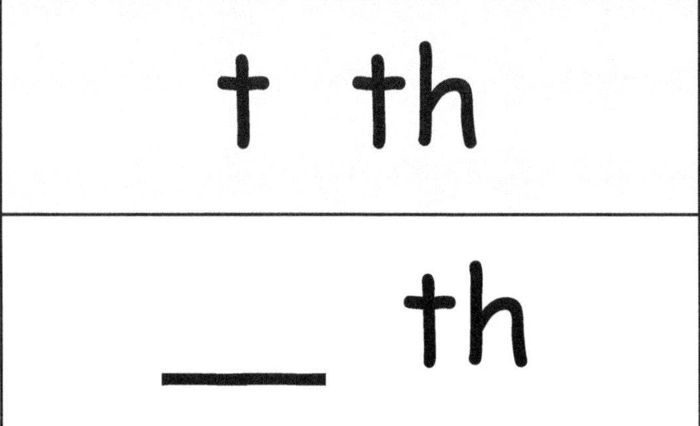

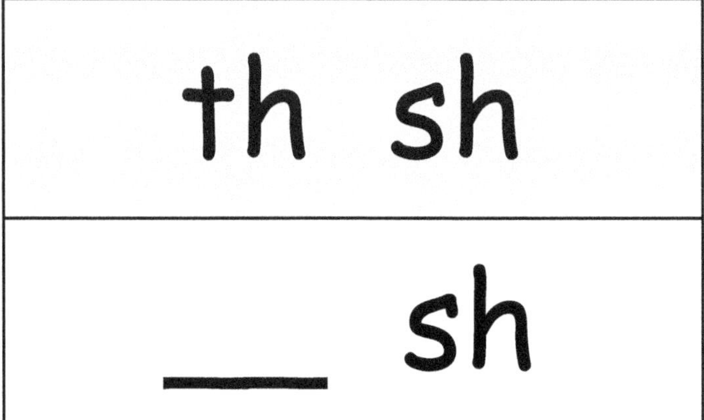

t h
___ h

t th
t ___

t	sh	th
t	sh	___

t	th	sh
t	___	sh

This set of cards is made of up words containing the sound 'th'. The sound spelling for the target sound in each word is highlighted. Copy onto card and cut out.
Practise dynamic blending for reading, as described in the 'Working through the programme' section, using these cards. Model this process for the child if necessary.

Activity 20 Dynamic blending – word cards th

thud	thank
think	thump
moth	cloth
maths	fifth
the	them
with	than
this	that

This set of cards is made of up words containing the sound 'th'. Copy onto card and cut out. Practise dynamic blending for reading, as described in the 'Working through the programme' section, using these cards. Model this process for the child if necessary.

Activity 20 Dynamic blending – word cards th

thin	think
theft	thump
thrush	thrift
moth	bath
cloth	tenth
that	then
this	with

Note that bath only fits into this group of words for some accents where the **a** sound spelling represents an 'a' sound.

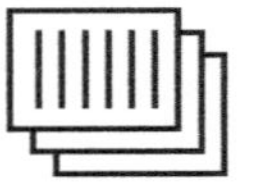

Print out onto card and cut out.
Stack them with the biggest (the complete word) on the bottom and in decreasing size so that the smallest is on the top.
Make sure the left-hand edge of the cards are flush. Staple the cards together on the left-hand side.
When the child runs a finger over the cards the sound spellings flip up. Ask the child to say the sounds and match to the flips.

staple

Activity 24 Flippies for the sound 'th'

th	th i	th i n	
th	th a	th a n	th a n k
m	m a	m a th	m a th s
th	th a	th a t	
w	w i	w i th	

Read the clue on the left for the child.
Use the clue to work out what the answer word is.
Encourage the child to think about the sounds in that word and write a sound spelling for each sound in the boxes on the right, one by one.
The first one is done for you as an example.
Explain to the child that they may not need to use all the boxes and so some are shaded in.
Break this task into a number of shorter tasks over a number of lessons if necessary.

Activity 25 Sound boxes th

Clue	Sound boxes			
Those people	th	e	m	
Together				
Not fat				
Insect – looks like a butterfly				
A speckled bird				
5th as a word				
Stealing is				
Adding and taking away				
Use your brain				
Bubbles on a drink				
Say '............... you' for a present				

Support the child to read the words on the left.
For each word, support the child to work out how many sounds there are in it and write that number in the grey box.
Then ask the child to count out the number of white boxes needed to write the word, so that there is one box for each sound, and colour in any boxes that are not needed.
Next ask the child to say the sounds in the word, one by one, and at the same time write the matching sound spelling in the boxes one by one.
The first two are done for you as examples.
Break this task into a number of shorter tasks over a number of lessons if necessary.

Activity 26 How many sounds? th

Word	Number	Writing the sound spellings				
this	3	th	i	s		
think	4	th	i	n	k	
moth						
thump						
them						
with						
froth						
that						
maths						

During this activity the child will be asked to slide sounds in and out of words, i.e. practise phoneme manipulation.
A sound might be swapped, added or taken away.
Print the sound spelling cards onto card and cut out.
Activity:

- Spread out all the sound spelling cards so that the child can see them.
- Build a starting word from the prompt list, demonstrating how to dynamically blend the sounds together as you move the sound spelling cards into place.
- Repeat the word, running your finger under the cards so that it corresponds to the sounds within the word.
- Ask the child to change the word to the next word on the prompt list. As you say the new word run your finger under the cards so that it corresponds with the sound you are saying and the matching sound spelling card.

This gives the child the chance to hear and see what is different.

- The child can then swap the appropriate sounds spelling cards.
- Repeat this technique with the next word on the list.

Activity 29 Sound swap th

Sound swap th

List 1	List 2	List 3
thin	that	math
think	than	maths
thank	then	moths
thanks	them	moth
tanks		

th	a	e	i
o	n	k	s
t	m		

Support the child to read the words on the left, one by one.
For each word read the clue to the child and then work out what the answer word is.
Explain to the child that they will need to either: add a sound, take away a sound or change a sound to the word on the left to make the answer word, e.g. cot > cost list > lit mat > rat.
Have the child write out the answer word on the right, saying each sound as they write each sound spelling.
An example is done for you.
Break this task into a number of shorter tasks over a number of lessons if necessary.

Activity 30 Sound exchange th

Starting word	Clue	New word
ink	Use your brain	think
moths	Doing sums	______
think	'............... you for the gift'	______
froth	A kind of soup	______
jump	Hit very hard	______
thrash	Song bird	______
then	Those people	______
tenth	10 as a word	______
rust	Rocket power	______

Place a whiteboard in front of the child.
Choose a word from the list below. Randomise the words you choose so that you are choosing words with a variety of number of sounds.
Draw dots on the whiteboard to match the number of sounds in the word, one dot for each sound. Do not write the word or show the word to the child as this is a purely auditory activity.
Say the word to the child and as you do so run your finger under the dots so that your finger matches the appropriate sound dot and its corresponding sound as you say it.
Then cover the dot that corresponds to the sound you are going to take away – use the list below.
Ask the child to tell you what is left if you take that sound away.
Take away another sound or choose a new word.
Remember to time limit this activity.

Activity 31 Sound sums th

No. of sounds in starting word	Word	Take away the sound	What is left?
3	thin	th	in
3	than	th	an
3	that	th	at
4	think	th	ink
4	thrash	th	rash
4	throb	th	rob
4	thrush	th	rush
4	maths	s	math
4	tenth	th	ten
5	thrift	th	rift
5	thrust	th	rust

This set of cards is made up of high frequency words containing the sound 'th'. Copy onto card and cut out. Practise dynamic blending for reading, as described in the 'Working through the programme' section, using these cards. Model this process for the child if necessary.

Activity 32 Reading high frequency words th

this	that
them	then
with	bath
path	

Note that bath only fits into this group of words for some accents where the **a** sound spelling represents an 'a' sound.

Starting at 'think', have the child read each of the words on the shapes as quickly as possible.
Support the child to read the words by giving information about sounds and supporting blending but do not supply the whole word.
Time how long it takes to read all the words to 'throb' and record the time in the box.
Repeat at a later point and see if the child can beat his own time.

Activity 33 Reading race: headache! th

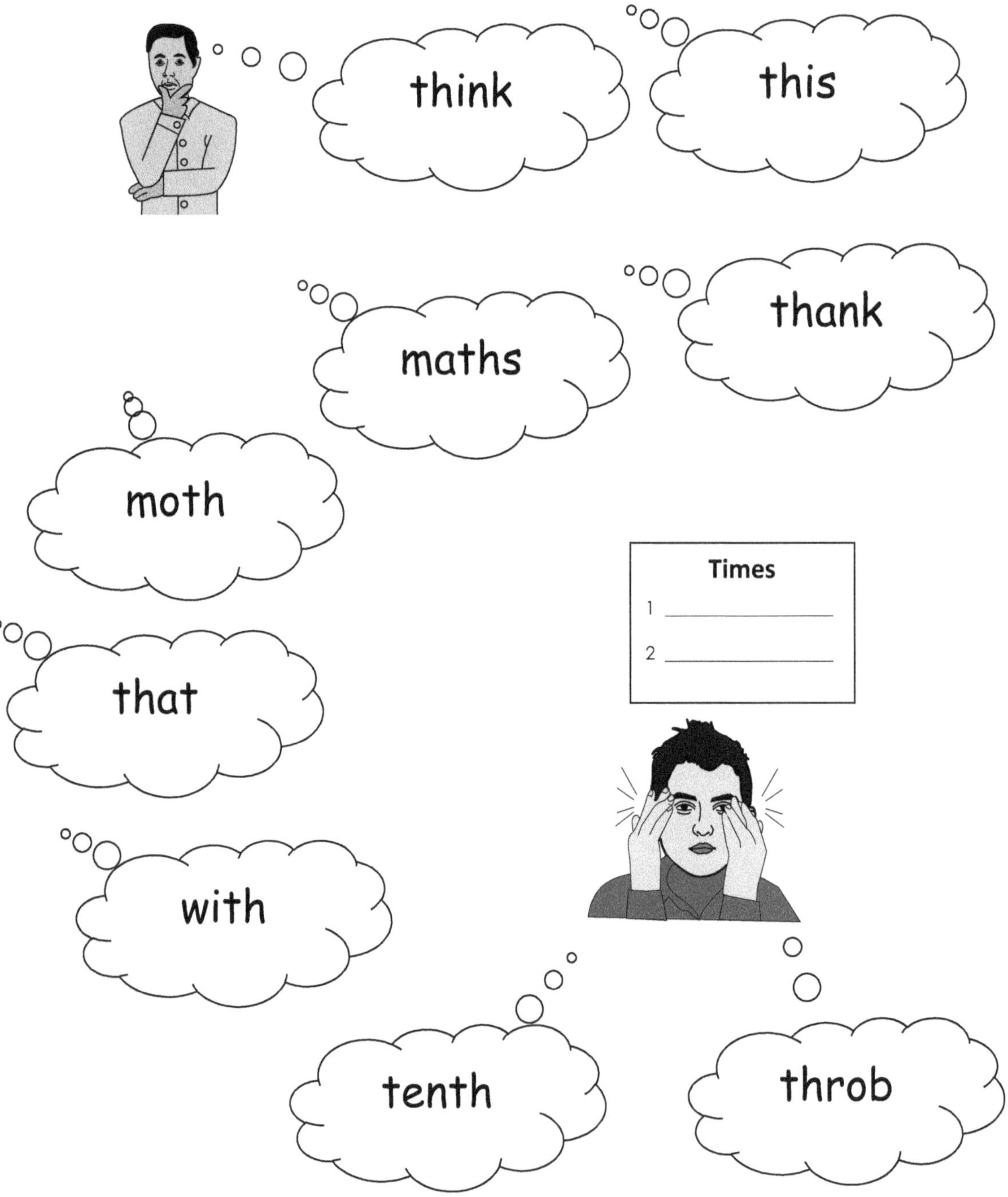

think

this

maths

thank

moth

Times

1 ________________

2 ________________

that

with

tenth

throb

Support the child to read the words one by one.
For each word support the child to think whether there is a 'th' sound in the word.
Have the child put a ring around or highlight just the words that have a 'th' sound.
Break this task into a number of shorter tasks over a number of lessons if necessary.

Activity 34 Word tracker th

tent	then	this	stop	shop
maths	the	shot	that	with
hunt	top	cloth	them	thing
froth	think	left	moth	thump
trust	fifth	thanks	that's	broth

How many 'th' words did you find? ________

Visual memory is the ability to remember and identify a shape, figure or picture that we have previously seen. Children with poor visual memory may struggle to remember pictures, figures, shapes, letters and numbers and may have difficulties with reading, writing and number work.

Ask the child to look at the word in the yellow box for at least five seconds, covering the white box underneath. Then cover the yellow box so that the word cannot be seen and reveal a choice of words in the white box below. Ask the child to select the word in the white box that matches the one they saw in the yellow box.

Break this task into a number of shorter tasks over a number of lessons if necessary.

Activity 35 Remembering words th

thin
thin think

thud
thug thud

moth
moth maths

thank
think thank

tenth
tenth fifth

them
then them than

thrush
thrash thresh thrush

Support the child to read the words one by one.
For each word support the child to think whether the word is a real word that makes sense or is a nonsense word.
Have the child put a ring around or highlight just the real words.
Break this task into a number of shorter tasks over a number of lessons if necessary.

Activity 36 Word detective th

coth	them	thup	maths	weth
this	thed	with	drith	then
gruth	cloths	that's	thod	thanks
moth	thith	fifth	thump	thin
throb	theft	buth	maths	tenth

How many real words did you find? ________

Visual sequential memory is the ability to remember sequences of figures, symbols, pictures and shapes. Children with poor visual sequencing struggle to remember a sequence of letters and follow visual patterns. They may have difficulties writing a sequence of letters to form a word and a sequence of words to form a sentence.

Ask the child to look at the words in the yellow box for at least five seconds, covering the white box underneath. Then cover the yellow box so that the words cannot be seen and reveal the sequence of words in the white box below. Ask the child to remember the missing word from the sequence in the yellow box and write it in the space.

Break this task into a number of shorter tasks over a number of lessons if necessary.

Activity 37 Remembering lots of words th

thin	thud
______	thud

thank	theft
thank	______

maths	tenth
______	tenth

fifth	moth
fifth	_____

cloth	theft	think
cloth	_____	think

thrash	throb	thump
thrash	throb	_____

thrift	thank	thrust
thrift	_____	thrust

Print out on card and cut out the sound spelling and picture cards for each word.
Read though the instructions in the 'Working through the programme' section at the start of this book prior to working with a child.

Activity 38 Word build th

w	i	th		
th	e	m		
th	i	s		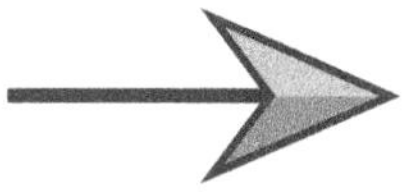
m	o	th		

c	l	o	th	
th	u	m	p	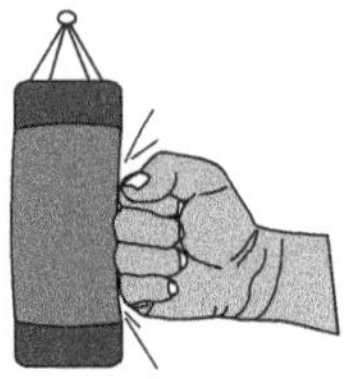
th	a	n	k	

Support the child to read the words on the list one by one.
For each word support the child to think about each of the sounds in the word and their matching sound spellings.
Have the child put a ring around or highlight the sound spelling for each sound.
Break this task into a number of shorter tasks over a number of lessons if necessary.

Activity 39 Word tech th

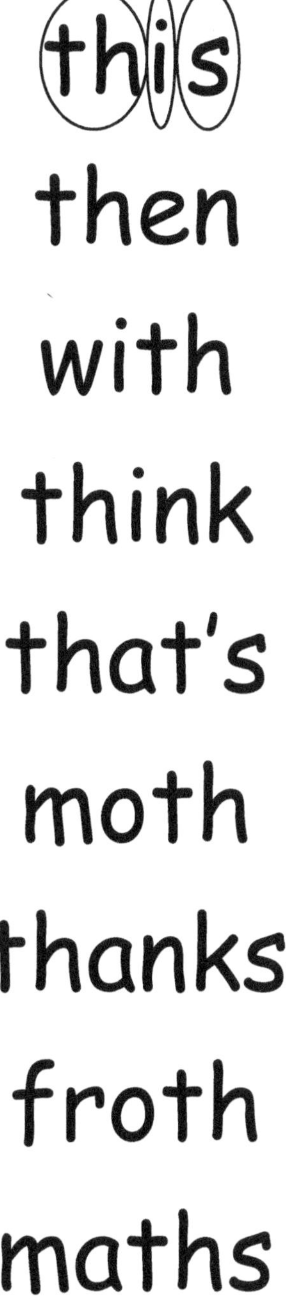

this
then
with
think
that's
moth
thanks
froth
maths

Read the clue on the left for the child.
For each clue support the child to work out what the answer word is.
The sound spellings for the answer word are given to help, but they are mixed up – an anagram.
Have the child use the sound spellings to write the answer word on the line on the right.
Encourage the child to say the associated sound as he writes each sound spelling.
Break this task into a number of shorter tasks over a number of lessons if necessary.

Activity 40 Word scramble th

Clue	Sound spellings	Word
Not this…	**th** t a	________
Slim	i **th** n	________
Fabric or material	c **th** l o	________
Alongside	i w **th**	________
Sums and counting	s a m **th**	________
Grateful	**th** a k n	________
Those people	**th** m e	________
Kind of bird	**th** **sh** r u	________
Rocket power	**th** u s r t	________

*For some accents, only where **a** represents an 'a' sound rather than 'ar' sound:*

Clue	Sound spellings	Word
Place to get clean	b **th** a	________
Leads to front door	**th** p a	________

Activity 42 Spelling challenge th

that	th a t	th a t	___ ___ ___	____________
than	th a n	th a n	___ ___ ___	____________
then	th e n	th e n	___ ___ ___	____________
them	th e m	th e m	___ ___ ___	____________
this	th i s	th i s	___ ___ ___	____________
with	w i th	w i th	___ ___ ___	____________
thank	th a n k	th a n k	___ ___ ___ ___	____________

Support the child to read the sentence and for each spot the spelling mistake. Have the child underline the mistake and then write the accepted spelling on the line underneath. If the child is able then the whole sentence could be written out.

Note that the sentences may include high frequency words which contain sounds that the child has not yet encountered in the programme. Support the child to decode these words by supplying information about the unfamiliar sound and its sound spelling and encourage the child to blend for reading. Some sound spellings are highlighted to support this.

Break this task into a number of shorter tasks over a number of lessons if necessary.

Activity 43 Oops! Correct the spelling th

1. Dad got a math in the net.

___

2. Sam fell down with a thug.

___

3. Mum thins that Rav is with Jan.

___

4. A cat can sit win a dog.

___

5. The thrash sat on the nest.

___

Support the child to read the sentences.
In each sentence there is a missing word with two words underneath. Ask the child to choose the word that makes sense and write the word on the line within the sentence. Encourage the child to say the sounds as they write the sound spellings.
Note that the sentences include some high frequency words which contain sounds that the child has not yet encountered in the programme. Support the child to decode these words by supplying information about any unfamiliar sound and its sound spelling and encourage the child to blend for reading.
Break this task into a number of shorter tasks over a number of lessons if necessary.

Activity 44 Spot the spelling th

1. Sam is a ______________ lad.
   thin then

2. A ______________ is on the twig.
   math moth

3. ______________ ran to the shop.
   Beth With

4. ______________ fish is fresh.
   Them This

5. Dan ______________ the man is sad.
   thinks thins

6. Jan ran fast but was ______________.
   fifth froth

Support the child to read the sentences.
Explain that the sentences are OK but that they are very short and could be a bit more interesting!
Then support the child to read the phrases at the bottom of the page and decide which could be used to make each sentence 'better' or 'more interesting'.
Ask the child to write out the sentence, adding the new phrase from the list. Encourage the child to say the sounds at the same time as writing the associated sound spelling when writing each word.
Note that the sentences include high frequency words which contain sounds that the child has not yet encountered in the programme. Support the child to decode these words by supplying information about any unfamiliar sounds and sound spellings and encourage the child to blend for reading. Some sound spellings are highlighted to support this.
Break this task into a number of shorter tasks over a number of lessons if necessary.

Activity 45 Making better sentences — th

1. Sam likes sums.

____

____

2. Mum fell in the mud.

____

____

3. The thrush sat in the tree.

____

____

4. Dad sat with Jan.

____

____

5. Beth thinks that Sam can run fast.

____

____

and her left leg began to throb	and is good at maths
on the bus to the shops	and put twigs in the nest
but Sam thinks Beth is best	

Support the child to read each sentence one by one.
Ask the child to re-read the sentence, several times if necessary, and try to remember it.
Then cover the sentence and ask the child to recall the sentence verbally.
Once they can do this confidently, ask the child to write out the sentence from memory.

When writing a word, encourage the child to say the sound as they write each associated sound spelling.
When the word is complete then they are to say the whole word.
When the sentence is complete the child reads out their sentence and then compares it to the original.
Note that the sentences may include high frequency words which contain sounds that the child has not yet encountered in the programme. Support the child to decode these words by supplying information about any unfamiliar sounds and their sound spellings and encouraging the child to blend for reading. Some of these sound spellings are highlighted to help the child when writing the words later.

Alternatively, using text to speech software, the child could type the sentence, with the computer reading back each word and then the completed sentence.

Activity 46 Writing challenge th

This is a thin thrush.

That drink's can had froth.

The moth is on the cloth.

Sam is fifth and Jan is tenth.

Answers th

Page 67
Activity 25 Sound boxes

w i th
th i n
m o th
th r u sh
f i f th
th e f t
m a th s
th i n k
f r o th
th a n k

Page 68
Activity 26 How many sounds?

3 m o th
4 th u m p
3 th e m
3 w i th
4 f r o th
3 th a t
4 m a th s

Page 71
Activity 30 Sound exchange

moths – maths
think – thank
froth – broth
jump – thump
thrash – thrush
then – them
tenth – ten
rust – thrust

Page 75
Activity 34 Word tracker

then this
maths the that with
cloth them thing
froth think moth thump
fifth thanks that's broth

17

Page 78
Activity 36 Word detective

them maths
this with then
cloths that's thanks
moth fifth thump thin
throb theft maths tenth

16

Page 83
Activity 39 Word tech

th e n
w i th
th i n k
th a t' s
m o th
th a n k s
f r o th
m a th s

Page 84
Activity 40 Word scramble

that
thin
cloth
with
maths
thank
them
thrush
thrust
bath
path

Page 87
Activity 44 Spot the spelling

thin
moth
Beth
This
thinks
fifth

Page 88
Activity 45 Making better sentences

1. Sam likes sums and is good at maths.
2. Mum fell in the mud and her left leg began to throb.
3. The thrush sat in the tree and put twigs in the nest.
4. Dad sat with Jan on the bus to the shops.
5. Beth thinks that Sam can run fast but Sam thinks Beth is best.

SECTION 3

ng

ng

song

Words with an 'ng' sound – word list of 1 syllable words

3 sounds

bang
bong
bung
ding
dong
dung
fang
gang
hang
hung
king
long
lung
pang
ping
pong
rang
ring
rung
sang
sing
song
sung
thing
ting
wing
zing

4 sounds

bling
bring
clang
cling
clung
fling
flung
slang
sling
slung
sting
stung
swing
throng

5 sounds

spring
sprung
string
strung

Auditory discrimination is the ability to hear differences between sounds. Good auditory discrimination helps us to recognise and identify the sounds in words and so interpret them correctly. Children with poor auditory discrimination may confuse sounds and misinterpret things they have heard. Their spelling and writing may reflect their confusion over which sounds they heard in a word. **Auditory attention and tracking** is the ability to actively listen and follow auditory information from beginning to end. Good auditory attention and tracking helps us to follow a conversation, a story read out loud or a set of instructions, and enables us to focus on key information. Children with poor auditory attention and tracking may find it difficult to follow and respond appropriately to what is being said to them.

Read out the words and ask the child to listen carefully and identify the odd one out, the word that **does not end** with the same sound as the others.
Do not show the words to the child. The odd one out is highlighted for you.
Break this task into a number of shorter tasks over a number of lessons if necessary.

Activity 3 Odd one out ng

1.	run	ran	ring	2.	sit	sing	sat
3.	kip	cup	king	4.	wing	win	when
5.	let	long	lot	6.	fan	fang	fun
7.	hid	had	hang	8.	thing	then	than
9.	brush	blush	bring	10.	slip	slap	sling
11.	swim	swing	swam	12.	clap	clip	cling
13.	fling	flop	flap	14.	stomp	sting	stamp
15.	skin	spring	spin	16.	team	dream	seeing
17.	train	drain	raining	18.	waving	save	brave
19.	fool	pool	cooling	20.	born	morning	lawn

Auditory discrimination is the ability to hear differences between sounds. Good auditory discrimination helps us to recognise and identify the sounds in words and so interpret them correctly. Children with poor auditory discrimination may confuse sounds and misinterpret things they have heard. Their spelling and writing may reflect their confusion over which sounds they heard in a word. **Auditory recall memory** is the ability to remember and recall something that they have just heard. Children with poor auditory recall memory may find it difficult to remember sounds and words and respond appropriately.

Read the list of words below clearly, asking the child to listen carefully. At random points tap the table and stop reading, asking the child to remember and say the last word you said. Then ask them to tell you what the **last** sound in the word is.

Break this task into a number of shorter tasks over a number of lessons if necessary.

Activity 4 What sound am I? ng

1.	past	ship	king	trap	long	drag	snap
2.	flag	ring	grab	spin	fang	song	plug
3.	glad	wing	crab	stop	bang	best	sing
4.	rang	zing	left	camp	thing	drop	list
5.	stand	sting	wish	sink	west	bring	fish
6.	stung	drift	bling	swift	grasp	fling	blast
7.	shrink	flash	swing	think	cling	crash	
8.	fresh	slang	maths	smash	sling	froth	
9.	swish	string	theft	tenth	thrush	bring	
10.	shelf	brush	spring	sprint	fifth	sprung	

Auditory fusion is the ability to hear the subtle gaps between sounds and words. Children with poor auditory fusion may get lost in conversations and when following a list of instructions given verbally.

Say the sounds or read the words in the list one after another at a brisk pace so that there are no obvious gaps between the sounds or the words. Ask the child to listen carefully and then tell you how many sounds or words you have said. Many of the words contain the sound 'ng' and get increasingly complex.

Break this task into a number of shorter tasks over a number of lessons if necessary.

Activity 6 How many did you hear? ng

1. t - p - **ng**
2. **ng** - r - f - v
3. n - g - **ng**
4. g - n - g - **ng** - **ng**
5. **th** - m - n - **ng**
6. **sh** - **th** - **ng** - g - n
7. d - g - **ng**
8. h - k - **ng** - n - l
9. shed - thin - sing
10. this - path - long - wish
11. left - thin - rang
12. fang - wing
13. spot - stop - sting - swim
14. thing - think - fling - king
15. bring - cling
16. swish - sling
17. shelf - sting - fifth - cloth
18. thrush - swing - fling
19. brush - bling - sting - tenth
20. flash - shrimp - string
21. spring - sting - sprint
22. shrink - splash - swing

Auditory attention and tracking is the ability to actively listen and follow auditory information from beginning to end. Good auditory attention and tracking helps us to follow a conversation, a story read out loud or a set of instructions, and enables us to focus on key information. Children with poor auditory attention and tracking may find it difficult to follow and respond appropriately to what is being said to them. **Auditory sequential memory** is the ability to remember and recall a series of things that they have heard. Children with poor auditory sequential memory may find it difficult to remember information given earlier in a conversation or set of instructions and may struggle to recall the sequence of sounds in a word.

In this activity the child has to process the auditory information but also respond by working out the pattern and stating the next sound in the sequence. Read out the list of sounds with a clear space between each. Ask the child to listen and work out what sound would come next. The answers follow in red.

Break this task into a number of shorter tasks over a number of lessons if necessary.

Activity 7 What comes next? ng

1. **ng** g **ng** g **ng** ...... g
2. **ng** n **ng** n **ng** ...... n
3. v **ng** v **ng** v **ng** v
4. m **ng** m **ng** m **ng** ...... m
5. n g **ng** n g **ng** n g ...... ng
6. m m **ng** m m **ng** m m **ng** ...... m
7. **ng** n n **ng** n n **ng** n ...... n
8. **ng** m n **ng** m n **ng** m n ...... ng
9. **ng ng** m n **ng ng** m n ...... ng
10. n g **ng ng** n g **ng ng** ...... n
11. **th th ng ng th th ng** ...... ng
12. **ng ng** v v **ng ng** v v ...... ng
13. **th th ng th th ng th** ...... th
14. m n **ng** m n **ng** m n ...... ng
15. g **ng** m g **ng** m g **ng** ...... m
16. **th ng ng** v **th ng ng** v **th** ...... ng
17. **th sh ng th sh ng th** ...... sh
18. **ng th** f **ng th** f **ng th** f...... ng
19. **ng** n m n **ng** n m n **ng** n ...... m
20. n n **ng** m n n **ng** m ...... n
21. **ng** n **th sh ng** n **th sh** ...... ng
22. **ng** m m g **ng** m m g ...... ng
23. g **ng ng** m g **ng ng** m ...... g
24. **ng** m n g **ng** m n g ...... ng

This activity results in the child discovering the sound spelling which represents the sound 'ng'. The child is learning that some sound spellings are made up of more than one letter.

Support the child to read the words one by one.
For each word support the child to work out the sound spelling corresponding to the sound 'ng' and highlight it.
There is just one sound spelling to find: **ng,** but note that it has two letters.
In the box underneath write the sound spelling **ng** as the heading on the small line at the top of the box.
Then work through the word list and write the remainder of the words in the box, noting the **ng** sound spelling.
Encourage the child to say each sound as they write each sound spelling in sequence, e.g. say 'f' 'a' 'ng' as they write **f a ng**.

Break this task into a number of shorter tasks over a number of lessons if necessary.

Activity 8 Investigating the sound ng

fang	king	sung
long	ring	gang
bang	sting	bring
fling	string	spring

Activity 10 Sound spelling cards ng

Visual memory is the ability to remember and identify a shape or picture that we have previously seen. Children with poor visual memory may struggle to remember pictures, figures, shapes, letters and numbers and may have difficulties with reading, writing and number work.

Ask the child to look at the sound spelling in the yellow box for at least five seconds, covering the white box underneath. Then cover the yellow box so that the sound spelling cannot be seen and reveal the choice of sound spellings in the white box below. Ask the child to select the matching sound spelling from the white box.

Break this task into a number of shorter tasks over a number of lessons if necessary.

Activity 12 Remembering sound spellings ng

ng
n ng

g
ng g

ng
ng n

ng
g ng

ng
g ng n

ng
ng n g

Visual discrimination is the ability to see differences between objects and figures that are similar. Good visual discrimination helps keep us from getting confused when looking at shapes and forms in the environment. Children with poor visual discrimination may find it difficult to recognise letters, may confuse letters such as b and d and may find it difficult to identify mathematical symbols.

Focus on one of the sound spellings featured on this sheet, e.g. **ng** (say the sound 'ng' and point to an example rather than using the letter names to identify the sound spelling). Ask the child to look at all the sound spellings and indicate or put a ring round all the sound spellings which match the target. Repeat for another sound spelling featured on the sheet.

Break this task into a number of shorter tasks over a number of lessons if necessary.

Activity 13 Spot the sound spelling ng

n ng ng n

g g

ng n n

g g n g

g ng

n g ng n

Spatial relations is the ability to perceive the position of objects in relation to ourselves and to each other. This skill helps children to understand relationships between symbols and letters. Children with poor spatial relations may find it difficult to write letters in the correct orientation, write consistently starting at the margin and write letters of the same size.

In the first part, ask the child to copy the sound spellings on the lines below in exactly the same places as they appear above.
In the second part, ask the child to copy the words on the lines below in exactly the same places, saying the matching sound as they write each sound spelling. Note that the sound spellings are for the sounds 'ng', 'n' and 'g', which are visually similar.

Break this task into a number of shorter tasks over a number of lessons if necessary.

Activity 17 Where am I? ng

ng ng

n g ng ng

sing wing

long fang

Visual sequential memory is the ability to remember sequences of figures, symbols and shapes. Children with poor visual sequencing struggle to remember a sequence of letters and follow visual patterns. They may have difficulties writing a sequence of letters to form a word and a sequence of words to form a sentence.

Ask the child to look at the sound spellings in the yellow box for at least five seconds, covering the white box underneath. Then cover the yellow box so that the sound spellings cannot be seen and reveal the sequence of sound spellings in the white box below. Ask the child to remember the missing sound spelling and write it in the space.

Break this task into a number of shorter tasks over a number of lessons if necessary.

Activity 18 Remembering lots of sound spellings ng

g ng
___ ng

ng n
g ___

n g
___ g

n ng
n ___

n ng g
n ng ___

n ng g
n ___ g

This set of cards is made of up words containing the sound 'ng'. The sound spelling for the target sound in each word is highlighted. Copy onto card and cut out.
Practise dynamic blending for reading, as described in the 'Working through the programme' section, using these cards. Model this process for the child if necessary.

Activity 20 Dynamic blending – word cards ng

fang	gang
king	long
rang	sing
wing	thing
bring	fling
sting	swing
spring	string

This set of cards is made of up words containing the sound 'ng'. Copy onto card and cut out.
Practise dynamic blending for reading, as described in the 'Working through the programme' section, using these cards. Model this process for the child if necessary.

Activity 20 Dynamic blending – word cards ng

ding	rung
song	hang
sang	king
lung	thing
sling	flung
cling	bling
string	spring

Print out onto card and cut out.
Stack them with the biggest (the complete word) on the bottom and in decreasing size so that the smallest is on the top.
Make sure the left-hand edge of the cards are flush. Staple the cards together on the left-hand side.
When the child runs a finger over the cards the sound spellings flip up. Ask the child to say the sounds and match to the flips.

staple

Activity 24 Flippies for the sound 'ng'

r	r i	r i ng	
l	l o	l o ng	
th	th i	th i ng	
b	b r	b r i	b r i ng
s	s w	s w i	s w i ng

Read the clue on the left for the child.
Use the clue to work out what the answer word is.
Encourage the child to think about the sounds in that word and write a sound spelling for each sound in the boxes on the right, one by one.
The first one is done for you as an example.
Explain to the child that they may not need to use all the boxes and so some are shaded in.
Break this task into a number of shorter tasks over a number of lessons if necessary.

Activity 25 Sound boxes ng

Clue	Sound boxes				
Not short	l	o	ng		
Sharp tooth					
Male ruler					
Finger jewellery					
Choirs do this					
Hug tightly					
Broken arm support					
Fetch something					
Wasps and bees do this					
Use to tie things					
Season starting the year					

Support the child to read the words on the left.
For each word, support the child to work out how many sounds there are in it and write that number in the grey box.
Then ask the child to count out the number of white boxes needed to write the word, so that there is one box for each sound, and colour in any boxes that are not needed.
Next ask the child to say the sounds in the word, one by one, and at the same time write the matching sound spelling in the boxes one by one.
The first one is done for you as an example.
Break this task into a number of shorter tasks over a number of lessons if necessary.

Activity 26 How many sounds? ng

Word	Number	Writing the sound spellings				
sling	4	s	l	i	ng	
fang						
spring						
king						
bring						
bang						
string						
cling						
stung						

During this activity the child will be asked to slide sounds in and out of words, i.e. practise phoneme manipulation.
A sound might be swapped, added or taken away.
Print the sound spelling cards onto card and cut out.
Activity:

- Spread out all the sound spelling cards so that the child can see them.
- Build a starting word from the prompt list, demonstrating how to dynamically blend the sounds together as you move the sound spelling cards into place.
- Repeat the word, running your finger under the cards so that it corresponds to the sounds within the word.
- Ask the child to change the word to the next word on the prompt list. As you say the new word run your finger under the cards so that it corresponds with the sound you are saying and the matching sound spelling card.

This gives the child the chance to hear and see what is different.

- The child can then swap the appropriate sounds spelling cards.
- Repeat this technique with the next word on the list.

Activity 29 Sound swap ng

Sound swap ng

List 1	List 2	List 3
fang	bring	flung
rang	bling	lung
ring	sling	sung
sing	swing	sang
sting	sing	slang
string	thing	clang
spring		cling

ng	th	a	i
u	f	r	s
t	p	b	l
w	c		

Support the child to read the words on the left, one by one.
For each word read the clue to the child and then work out what the answer word is.
Explain to the child that they will need to either: add a sound, take away a sound or change a sound to the word on the left to make the answer word, e.g. cot > cost list > lit mat > rat.
Have the child write out the answer word on the right, saying each sound as they write each sound spelling.
An example is done for you.
Break this task into a number of shorter tasks over a number of lessons if necessary.

Activity 30 Sound exchange ng

Starting word	Clue	New word
thing	Male ruler	king
hang	Sharp tooth	________
sing	Rocking seat	________
string	Bees and wasps defence	________
ding	Birds have two, to fly	________
bling	Hug tightly	________
sprung	First season of the year	________
sing	Broken arm support	________
flung	Breathing organ	________
ring	Fetch something	________

Place a whiteboard in front of the child.
Choose a word from the list below. Randomise the words you choose so that you are choosing words with a variety of number of sounds.
Draw dots on the whiteboard to match the number of sounds in the word, one dot for each sound. Do not write the word or show the word to the child as this is a purely auditory activity.
Say the word to the child and as you do so run your finger under the dots so that your finger matches the appropriate sound dot and its corresponding sound as you say it.
Then cover the dot that corresponds to the sound you are going to take away – use the list below.
Ask the child to tell you what is left if you take that sound away.
Take away another sound or choose a new word.
Remember to time limit this activity.

Activity 31 Sound sums ng

No. of sounds in starting word	Word	Take away the sound	What is left?
4	bring	b	ring
4	clung	c	lung
4	slang	l	sang
4	sling	l	sing
4	sting	t	sing
4	slung	l	sung
4	stung	t	sung
4	swing	s	wing

This set of cards is made up of high frequency words containing the sound 'ng'. Copy onto card and cut out. Practise dynamic blending for reading, as described in the 'Working through the programme' section, using these cards. Model this process for the child if necessary.

Activity 32 Reading high frequency words ng

king	long
thing	along

Starting at 'ding', have the child read each of the words on the shapes as quickly as possible.
Support the child to read the words by giving information about sounds and supporting blending but do not supply the whole word.
Time how long it takes to read all the words to 'dong' and record the time in the box.
Repeat at a later point and see if the child can beat his own time.

Activity 33 Reading race: ring the bells! ng

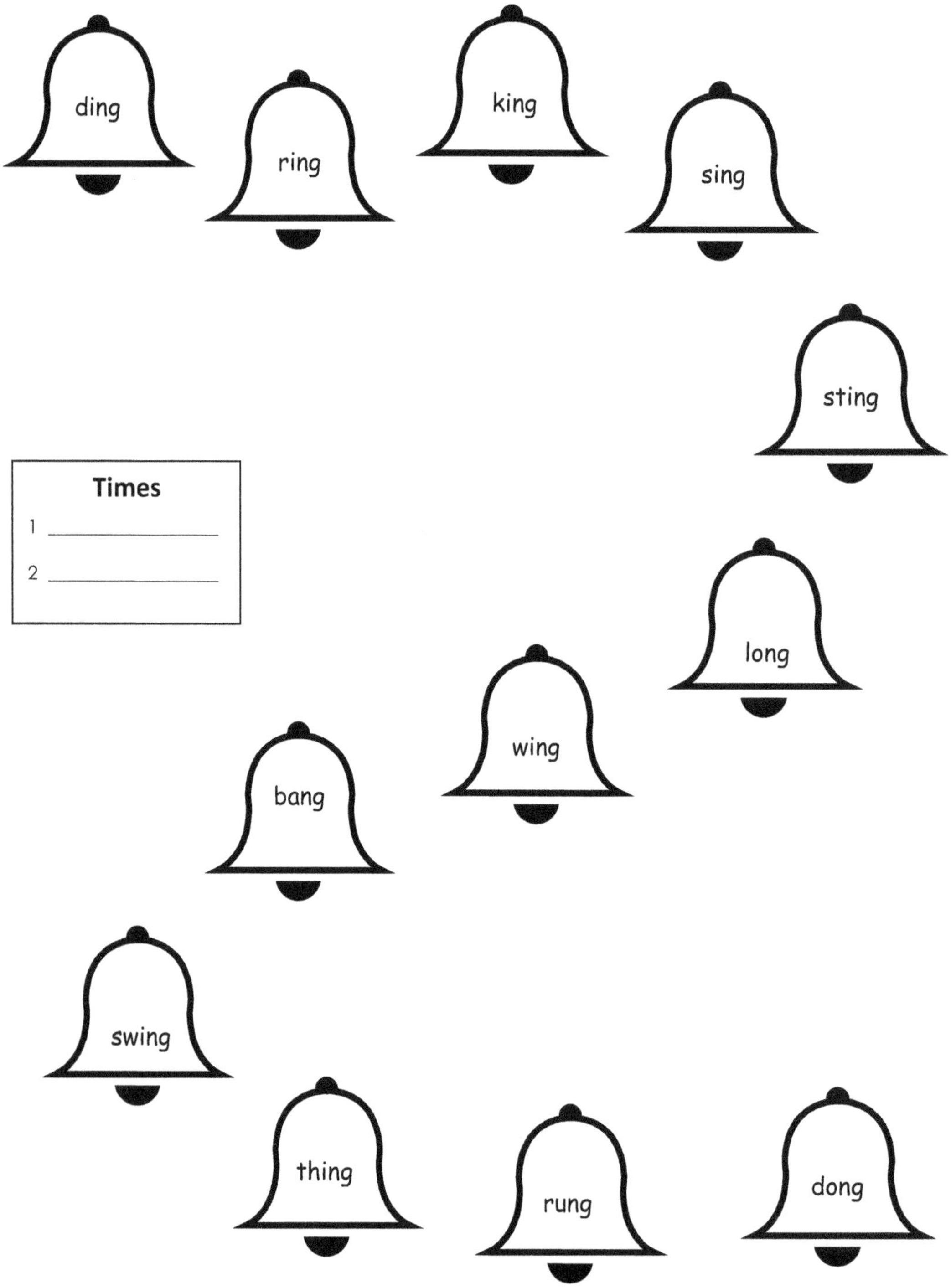

ding

ring

king

sing

sting

long

wing

bang

swing

thing

rung

dong

Times

1 ____________

2 ____________

Support the child to read the words one by one.
For each word support the child to think whether there is a 'ng' sound in the word.
Have the child put a ring around or highlight just the words that have a 'ng' sound.
Break this task into a number of shorter tasks over a number of lessons if necessary.

Activity 34 Word tracker ng

nest	ring	bring	sand	long
sing	sink	slang	plan	fling
sting	shin	thing	think	hung
send	swing	swim	spring	king
wing	string	wind	song	pond

How many 'ng' words did you find? ________

Visual memory is the ability to remember and identify a shape, figure or picture that we have previously seen. Children with poor visual memory may struggle to remember pictures, figures, shapes, letters and numbers and may have difficulties with reading, writing and number work.

Ask the child to look at the word in the yellow box for at least five seconds, covering the white box underneath. Then cover the yellow box so that the word cannot be seen and reveal a choice of words in the white box below. Ask the child to select the word in the white box that matches the one they saw in the yellow box.

Break this task into a number of shorter tasks over a number of lessons if necessary.

Activity 35 Remembering words ng

king
king fang

sing
sang sing

rang
rung rang

long
lung long

bring
bling bring fling

sling
sting slang sling

spring
sprung string strung

Support the child to read the words one by one.
For each word support the child to think whether the word is a real word that makes sense or is a nonsense word.
Have the child put a ring around or highlight just the real words.
Break this task into a number of shorter tasks over a number of lessons if necessary.

Activity 36 Word detective ng

kang	ring	king	cling	nong
sing	swing	tung	spring	spling
blang	fling	fung	long	thing
wing	hing	string	swang	sang
fang	trung	sting	sling	rang

How many real words did you find? ________

Visual sequential memory is the ability to remember sequences of figures, symbols, pictures and shapes. Children with poor visual sequencing struggle to remember a sequence of letters and follow visual patterns. They may have difficulties writing a sequence of letters to form a word and a sequence of words to form a sentence.

Ask the child to look at the words in the yellow box for at least five seconds, covering the white box underneath. Then cover the yellow box so that the words cannot be seen and reveal the sequence of words in the white box below. Ask the child to remember the missing word from the sequence in the yellow box and write it in the space.

Break this task into a number of shorter tasks over a number of lessons if necessary.

Activity 37 Remembering lots of words ng

king sang
______ sang

wing long
wing ______

fang ring sung
______ ring sung

ding hang thing
ding ______ thing

sling swing bring
sling swing ______

cling sting fling
cling ______ fling

thing wing swing
thing wing ______

Print out on card and cut out the sound spelling and picture cards for each word.
Read though the instructions in the 'Working through the programme' section at the start of this book prior to working with a child.

Activity 38 Word build ng

k	i	ng		
s	i	ng		
l	o	ng		
w	i	ng		

b	r	i	ng	
s	w	i	ng	
c	l	i	ng	

Support the child to read the words on the list one by one.
For each word support the child to think about each of the sounds in the word and their matching sound spellings.
Have the child put a ring around or highlight the sound spelling for each sound.
Break this task into a number of shorter tasks over a number of lessons if necessary.

Activity 39 Word tech ng

slang
long
thing
swing
string
king
fang
spring
bring

Read the clue on the left for the child.
For each clue support the child to work out what the answer word is.
The sound spellings for the answer word are given to help, but they are mixed up – an anagram.
Have the child use the sound spellings to write the answer word on the line on the right.
Encourage the child to say the associated sound as he writes each sound spelling.
Break this task into a number of shorter tasks over a number of lessons if necessary.

Activity 40 Word scramble ng

Clue	Sound spellings	Word
Jewellery on the finger	r **ng** i	______
Words set to music	**ng** o s	______
Rocking seat	i s **ng** w	______
Queen and ...	k **ng** i	______
Bouncy coil of wire	i r **ng** p s	______
Fetch something	**ng** r b i	______
Not short	o l **ng**	______
Sharp tooth	**ng** a f	______
Hold on tight	**ng** l c i	______
Choirs do this	s **ng** i	______
Tie things with this	t r s **ng** i	______

Activity 42 Spelling challenge ng

king	k i ng	k i ng	___ ___ ___	________
long	l o ng	l o ng	___ ___ ___	________
sing	s i ng	s i ng	___ ___ ___	________
thing	th i ng	th i ng	___ ___ ___	________
bring	b r i ng	b r i ng	___ ___ ___ ___	________
swing	s w i ng	s w i ng	___ ___ ___ ___	________
spring	s p r i ng	s p r i ng	___ ___ ___ ___ ___	________

Support the child to read the sentences.
In each sentence there is a missing word with two words underneath. Ask the child to choose the word that makes sense and write the word on the line within the sentence. Encourage the child to say the sounds as they write the sound spellings.
Note that the sentences include some high frequency words which contain sounds that the child has not yet encountered in the programme. Support the child to decode these words by supplying information about any unfamiliar sound and its sound spelling and encourage the child to blend for reading. Some sound spellings are highlighted to support this.
Break this task into a number of shorter tasks over a number of lessons if necessary.

Activity 44 Spot the spelling ng

1. Rav can ______________ a song.
   sing sung

2. The dog had just **one** long ______________.
   bang fang

3. Dad must ______________ the drink.
   bling bring

4. The kid sat on the ______________ in the p**ar**k.
   swing swung

5. Sam got ______________ on the leg.
   stung sting

6. The cat play**ed** with the ______________.
   spring string

Support the child to read the sentences.
Explain that the sentences are OK but that they are very short and could be a bit more interesting!
Then support the child to read the phrases at the bottom of the page and decide which could be used to make each sentence 'better' or 'more interesting'.
Ask the child to write out the sentence, adding the new phrase from the list. Encourage the child to say the sounds at the same time as writing the associated sound spelling when writing each word.
Note that the sentences include high frequency words which contain sounds that the child has not yet encountered in the programme. Support the child to decode these words by supplying information about any unfamiliar sounds and sound spellings and encourage the child to blend for reading. Some sound spellings are highlighted to support this.
Break this task into a number of shorter tasks over a number of lessons if necessary.

Activity 45 Making better sentences ng

1. Gran can sing.

____

____

2. Jan sat on the swing.

____

____

3. The king was sad.

____

____

4. A bee can sting.

____

____

5. Rav rang mum.

____

____

and ask**ed** **for** a lift	but it cannot sing
lots of sad songs	and dad push**ed** **her**
bec**au**se he lost a ring	

Support the child to read each sentence one by one.
Ask the child to re-read the sentence, several times if necessary, and try to remember it.
Then cover the sentence and ask the child to recall the sentence verbally.
Once they can do this confidently, ask the child to write out the sentence from memory.

When writing a word, encourage the child to say the sound as they write each associated sound spelling.
When the word is complete then they are to say the whole word.
When the sentence is complete the child reads out their sentence and then compares it to the original.
Note that the sentences may include high frequency words which contain sounds that the child has not yet encountered in the programme. Support the child to decode these words by supplying information about any unfamiliar sounds and their sound spellings and encouraging the child to blend for reading. Some of these sound spellings are highlighted to help the child when writing the words later.

Alternatively, using text to speech software, the child could type the sentence, with the computer reading back each word and then the completed sentence.

Activity 46 Writing challenge ng

The cat had a long fang.

Gran sang a sad song.

Mum lost a ring in the sink.

Sam put the string on the swing.

Answers ng

Page 109
Activity 25 Sound boxes

f a ng
k i ng
r i ng
s i ng
c l i ng
s l i ng
b r i ng
s t i ng
s t r i ng
s p r i ng

Page 110
Activity 26 How many sounds?

3 f a ng
5 s p r i ng
3 k i ng
4 b r i ng
3 b a ng
5 s t r i ng
4 c l i ng
4 s t u ng

Page 113
Activity 30 Sound exchange

hang – fang
sing – swing
string – sting
ding – wing
bling – cling
sprung – spring
sing – sling
flung – lung
ring – bring

Page 117
Activity 34 Word tracker

ring bring long
sing slang fling
sting thing hung
swing spring king
wing string song

15

Page 120
Activity 36 Word detective

ring king cling
sing swing spring
fling long thing
wing string sang
fang sting sling rang

16

Page 125
Activity 39 Word tech

l o ng
th i ng
s w i ng
s t r i ng
k i ng
f a ng
s p r i ng
b r i ng

Page 126
Activity 40 Word scramble

ring
song
swing
king
spring
bring
long
fang
cling
sing
string

Page 128
Activity 44 Spot the spelling

sing
fang
bring
swing
stung
string

Page 129
Activity 45 Making better sentences

1. Gran can sing lots of sad songs.
2. Jan sat on the swing and dad pushed her.
3. The king was sad because he lost a ring.
4. A bee can sting but it cannot sing.
5. Rav rang mum and asked her for a lift.

SECTION 4

ch

ch

chips

tch

pitch

Words with a 'ch' sound – word list of words

Initial ch

3 sounds
chap
chat
chin
chip
chop
chug
chum

4 sounds
champ
chest
chimp
chink
chomp
chump
chunk

Final ch

3 sounds
rich
much
such

4 sounds
bunch
lunch
munch

tch

2 sounds
etch
itch

3 sounds
batch
botch
catch
ditch
dutch
fetch
hatch
hitch
hutch
latch
match
patch
pitch
witch

4 sounds
glitch
snatch
snitch
switch

5 sounds
scratch
scritch

High frequency words
Containing sounds / sound spellings not yet encountered in the programme

which	wh i **ch**	the sound 'w' is represented by the sound spelling **wh**

Auditory discrimination is the ability to hear differences between sounds. Good auditory discrimination helps us to recognise and identify the sounds in words and so interpret them correctly. Children with poor auditory discrimination may confuse sounds and misinterpret things they have heard. Their spelling and writing may reflect their confusion over which sounds they heard in a word. **Auditory attention and tracking** is the ability to actively listen and follow auditory information from beginning to end. Good auditory attention and tracking helps us to follow a conversation, a story read out loud or a set of instructions, and enables us to focus on key information. Children with poor auditory attention and tracking may find it difficult to follow and respond appropriately to what is being said to them.

This story contains lots of words that contain the sound 'ch', which is the 'target' sound.
Read the story out loud to the child or group of children. Encourage the child to listen carefully and spot any word that contains the target sound. Note that there are two ways that 'ch' can be represented: **ch** and **tch,** but the 'ch' sound is the same for both. When a target word has been read, the child indicates that they have heard and spotted it by tapping the table, putting up a hand or any other agreed signal, but without shouting out. Stop reading and discuss the word, making any error correction necessary. If a word is missed, re-read the sentence. Do not show the written story to the child. The target words are highlighted below for you.

Activity 1 Sound target story ch

Dan had an **itch**. It was a bad **itch**. It would not stop.

He had to **scratch** and **scratch**.

"I will go to the **witch**. She will stop it," said Dan.

The **witch** said, "**Fetch** a **chest**. Put in a bag of **chips**

and a big **chop** from the **kitchen**. Bring them to me

and I will give you a spell to stop the **itch**."

Dan did this. But he got a such a **chill**.

"**Achoo**," said Dan.

But he still had the **itch**!

The witch had a good **lunch**!

Do not trust a **twitchy witch** or you will catch a **chill**.

Auditory discrimination is the ability to hear differences between sounds. Good auditory discrimination helps us to recognise and identify the sounds in words and so interpret them correctly. Children with poor auditory discrimination may confuse sounds and misinterpret things they have heard. Their spelling and writing may reflect their confusion over what sounds they heard in a word. **Auditory sequential memory** is the ability to remember and recall a series of things that they have heard. Children with poor auditory sequential memory may find it difficult to remember information given earlier in a conversation or set of instructions and may struggle to recall the sequence of sounds in a word.

The silly sentences contain lots of words containing the sound 'ch'.
Read the sentence to the child several times, invite them to join in as you say it and gradually recall it on their own.
Do not show the words to the child.
Ask them to say it as quickly as they can and have some fun with it. Perhaps they can make up their own?
The sentences gradually get longer and more complex.
Break this task into a number of shorter tasks over a number of lessons if necessary.

Activity 2 Tongue twister fun ch

Chew cheese chunks cheerily.

Cheeky chimps chase chirpy chickens.

Choose chilled chops and chips at the checkout.

Auditory discrimination is the ability to hear differences between sounds. Good auditory discrimination helps us to recognise and identify the sounds in words and so interpret them correctly. Children with poor auditory discrimination may confuse sounds and misinterpret things they have heard. Their spelling and writing may reflect their confusion over which sounds they heard in a word. **Auditory attention and tracking** is the ability to actively listen and follow auditory information from beginning to end. Good auditory attention and tracking helps us to follow a conversation, a story read out loud or a set of instructions, and enables us to focus on key information. Children with poor auditory attention and tracking may find it difficult to follow and respond appropriately to what is being said to them.

Read out the words and ask the child to identify the odd one out. In 1–10 the child focuses on the sound at the **beginning** of the words and in 11–20 the child focuses on the sound at the **end** of the words.
Do not show the words to the child. The odd one out is highlighted for you.
Break this task into a number of shorter tasks over a number of lessons if necessary.

Activity 3 Odd one out ch

1.	win	chin	wet	2.	sun	chat	sat
3.	cat	chap	chum	4.	chop	fan	fed
5.	last	chip	lost	6.	past	chip	pink
7.	hand	help	chest	8.	champ	chunk	shot
9.	think	thank	chimp	10.	that	them	chomp
11.	said	such	sad	12.	ran	run	rich
13.	much	match	mat	14.	fun	fetch	fan
15.	cast	catch	cost	16.	drop	drip	ditch
17.	plum	pram	patch	18.	witch	west	went
19.	snap	snip	snatch	20.	swim	switch	scratch

Auditory discrimination is the ability to hear differences between sounds. Good auditory discrimination helps us to recognise and identify the sounds in words and so interpret them correctly. Children with poor auditory discrimination may confuse sounds and misinterpret things they have heard. Their spelling and writing may reflect their confusion over which sounds they heard in a word. **Auditory recall memory** is the ability to remember and recall something that they have just heard. Children with poor auditory recall memory may find it difficult to remember sounds and words and respond appropriately.

Read the list of words below clearly, asking the child to listen carefully. At random points tap the table and stop reading, asking the child to remember and say the last word you said. Then ask them to tell you what the **first** or the **last** sound in the word is.

Break this task into a number of shorter tasks over a number of lessons if necessary.

Activity 4 What sound am I? ch

1.	rest	cast	chop	send	chat	mask	left
2.	past	jump	rich	mint	itch	much	soft
3.	sink	chat	next	hand	chip	felt	help
4.	trap	gran	catch	camp	such	bent	spin
5.	glad	flag	chin	brag	slip	chum	grab
6.	mash	wish	match	cash	pitch	fish	itch
7.	than	them	chest	that	chimp	this	with
8.	thing	patch	thin	think	fetch	ditch	
9.	such	moth	maths	lunch	fifth	bunch	
10.	witch	bring	snatch	swing	string	scratch	

Auditory discrimination is the ability to hear differences between sounds. Good auditory discrimination helps us to recognise and identify the sounds in words and so interpret them correctly. Children with poor auditory discrimination may confuse sounds and misinterpret things they have heard. Their spelling and writing may reflect their confusion over what sounds they heard in a word.

Read out the pairs of words. For 1–12 ask the child to tell you whether or not they **start** with the same sound and for 13–24 ask whether or not they **end** with the same sounds. The words get increasingly complex.

Break this task into a number of shorter tasks over a number of lessons if necessary.

Activity 5 Same or different? ch

1. shed - chat
2. chip - ship
3. chop - chin
4. chap - that
5. this - champ
6. chest - chimp
7. chair - chunk
8. chomp - thin
9. thank - chair
10. cheap - cheat
11. chain - cheek
12. child - think

13. cash - much
14. rich - such
15. match - pitch
16. push - witch
17. catch - fetch
18. pitch - fish
19. ditch - with
20. hutch - cloth
21. snatch - switch
22. fifth - glitch
23. sting - scratch
24. snitch - dutch

Auditory fusion is the ability to hear the subtle gaps between sounds and words. Children with poor auditory fusion may get lost in conversations and when following a list of instructions given verbally.

Say the sounds or read the words in the list one after another at a brisk pace so that there are no obvious gaps between the sounds or the words. Ask the child to listen carefully and then tell you how many sounds or words you have said. Many of the words contain the sound 'ch' (represented by the sound spellings **ch** and **tch**) and get increasingly complex.

Break this task into a number of shorter tasks over a number of lessons if necessary.

Activity 6 How many did you hear? ch

1. **ch** - **th** - **sh**
2. **th** - **ch** - **sh** - **ng**
3. **ch** - **ch** - c - **th** - **th**
4. c - f - **th** - **ch**
5. f - **ch** - f - **ch**
6. **th** - **ch** - **th** - **sh** - f
7. **ch** - f - **th** - **sh**
8. **ch** - f
9. chip - them - this - chin
10. itch - them - rich
11. that - chap - shop - chat
12. chop - chum
13. fetch - match - think
14. catch - tenth - pitch
15. such - fish - much - moth
16. bunch - brush - lunch
17. witch - cloth - ditch
18. chest - crush
19. patch - think - this - shelf
20. switch - snatch - chimp
21. thank - chunk
22. shift - scratch - shrink

Auditory attention and tracking is the ability to actively listen and follow auditory information from beginning to end. Good auditory attention and tracking helps us to follow a conversation, a story read out loud or a set of instructions, and enables us to focus on key information. Children with poor auditory attention and tracking may find it difficult to follow and respond appropriately to what is being said to them. **Auditory sequential memory** is the ability to remember and recall a series of things that they have heard. Children with poor auditory sequential memory may find it difficult to remember information given earlier in a conversation or set of instructions and may struggle to recall the sequence of sounds in a word.

In this activity the child has to process the auditory information but also respond by working out the pattern and stating the next sound in the sequence. Read out the list of sounds with a clear space between each. Ask the child to listen and work out what sound would come next. The answers follow in red.

Break this task into a number of shorter tasks over a number of lessons if necessary.

Activity 7 What comes next? ch

1. **ch** c **ch** c **ch** c
2. **ch** f **ch** f **ch** ...... f
3. v **ch** v **ch** v **ch** v
4. s **ch** s **ch** s **ch** ...... s
5. n s **ch** n s **ch** n s ...... ch
6. p p **ch** p p **ch** p p **ch** ...... p
7. **ch** x x **ch** x x **ch** x x
8. **ch** m n **ch** m n **ch** m n ...... ch
9. **ch ch** m p **ch ch** m p ...... ch
10. n s **ch ch** n s **ch ch** ...... n
11. **th th ch ch th th ch** ...... ch
12. **ch ch** v v **ch ch** v v ...... ch
13. **sh sh ch sh sh ch sh** ...... sh
14. n **sh ch** n **sh ch** n ...... sh
15. g **ch** t g **ch** t g **ch** ...... t
16. **th ch ch** v **th ch ch** v **th** ...... ch
17. **th sh ch th sh ch th** ...... sh
18. **ch th** f **ch th** f **ch th** f...... ch
19. **ch** c p t **ch** c p t **ch** c ...... p
20. t t **ch** m t t **ch** m ...... t
21. **ch** t **th sh ch** t **th sh** ...... ch
22. **ch** p t c **ch** p t c ...... ch
23. g **ch ch** p g **ch ch** p ...... g
24. **ch** p t g **ch** p t g ...... ch

This activity results in the child discovering that two sound spellings, ch and tch, represent the sound 'ch' in written words.

Support the child to read the word **chin**, work out the sound spelling corresponding to the sound 'ch' and highlight it. The child has discovered the sound spelling **ch** represents the sound 'ch'. Ask the child to write the **ch** sound spelling as a heading on the small line in the first box, then write the word chin on the line underneath. Encourage the child to say each sound at the same time as writing each sound spelling. For example, the child writes **ch** and says 'ch', writes **i** and says 'i' and writes **n** and says 'n'.

Move on to the next word, **match**, and support the child to read it, work out the sound spelling corresponding to the sound 'k' and highlight it. Ask the child to write the **tch** sound spelling as a heading on the small line in the second box, then write the word **match** on the line underneath. Encourage the child to say each sound at the same time as writing each sound spelling. For example, the child writes **m** and says 'm', writes **a** and says 'a' and writes **tch** and says 'ch'.

Then work through the rest of the words one by one, sorting the words into **ch** and **tch** word lists as above. Point out to the child that this shows that there are two ways to write the sound 'ch' when we hear it in a word. Good readers and spellers remember which of these sound spellings go in which word. Point out to the child that this also shows that some sound spellings are made up or more than one letter 'working together' to be a 'picture' of the word. The sound spelling **ch** is made up of two letters and **tch** is made up of three letters. Break this task into a number of shorter tasks over a number of lessons if necessary.

Activity 8 Investigating the sound ch

chin	such	pitch
match	chips	fetch
hutch	much	itch
chest	switch	lunch

Activity 10 Sound spelling cards ch

tch

Visual discrimination is the ability to see differences between objects and figures that are similar. Good visual discrimination helps keep us from getting confused when looking at shapes and forms in the environment. Children with poor visual discrimination may find it difficult to recognise letters, may confuse letters such as b and d and may find it difficult to identify mathematical symbols.

Ask the child to look at the sound spelling in the yellow box then track along the row looking at the other sound spellings.
The child indicates or puts a ring around the sound spelling that is the same as the one in the yellow box. *This includes some sound spellings which represent other sounds but are visually similar.*

Break this task into a number of shorter tasks over a number of lessons if necessary.

Activity 11 Sound spelling tracker ch

ch	th	t	tch	ch
tch	th	ch	tch	t
tch	ch	tch	t	th
ch	t	th	tch	ch
ch	ch	tch	th	t
ch	tch	t	ch	th
tch	ch	th	tch	t
ch	c	ch	th	tch

Visual memory is the ability to remember and identify a shape or picture that we have previously seen. Children with poor visual memory may struggle to remember pictures, figures, shapes, letters and numbers and may have difficulties with reading, writing and number work.

Ask the child to look at the sound spelling in the yellow box for at least five seconds, covering the white box underneath. Then cover the yellow box so that the sound spelling cannot be seen and reveal the choice of sound spellings in the white box below. Ask the child to select the matching sound spelling from the white box.

Break this task into a number of shorter tasks over a number of lessons if necessary.

Activity 12 Remembering sound spellings ch

ch
ch tch

tch
ch tch

ch
tch ch

c
h ch c

ch
ch tch c

tch
ch tch h

Visual discrimination is the ability to see differences between objects and figures that are similar. Good visual discrimination helps keep us from getting confused when looking at shapes and forms in the environment. Children with poor visual discrimination may find it difficult to recognise letters, may confuse letters such as b and d and may find it difficult to identify mathematical symbols.

Focus on one of the sound spellings featured on this sheet, e.g. **tch** (say the sound 'ch' and point to an example rather than using the letter names to identify the sound spelling). Ask the child to look at all the sound spellings and indicate or put a ring round all the sound spellings which match the target. Repeat for another sound spelling featured on the sheet.
Ask the child to look at all the sound spellings and indicate or put a ring round all the letters matching the target.

Break this task into a number of shorter tasks over a number of lessons if necessary.

Activity 13 Spot the sound spelling ch

h tch ch

c c

h

tch tch

ch ch h

c c t h tch

Spatial relations is the ability to perceive the position of objects in relation to ourselves and to each other. This skill helps children to understand relationships between symbols and letters. Children with poor spatial relations may find it difficult to write letters in the correct orientation, write consistently starting at the margin and write letters of the same size.

In the first part, ask the child to copy the sound spellings on the lines below in exactly the same places as they appear above.
In the second part, ask the child to copy the words on the lines below in exactly the same places, saying the matching sound as they write each sound spelling. Note that the sound spellings are for the sounds 'ch', 't', 'c' and 'h', which are visually similar.

Break this task into a number of shorter tasks over a number of lessons if necessary.

Activity 17 Where am I? ch

tch t h ch

h t ch tch c

chips match

much patch

Visual sequential memory is the ability to remember sequences of figures, symbols and shapes. Children with poor visual sequencing struggle to remember a sequence of letters and follow visual patterns. They may have difficulties writing a sequence of letters to form a word and a sequence of words to form a sentence.

Ask the child to look at the sound spellings in the yellow box for at least five seconds, covering the white box underneath. Then cover the yellow box so that the sound spellings cannot be seen and reveal the sequence of sound spellings in the white box below. Ask the child to remember the missing sound spelling and write it in the space.

Break this task into a number of shorter tasks over a number of lessons if necessary.

Activity 18 Remembering lots of sound spellings ch

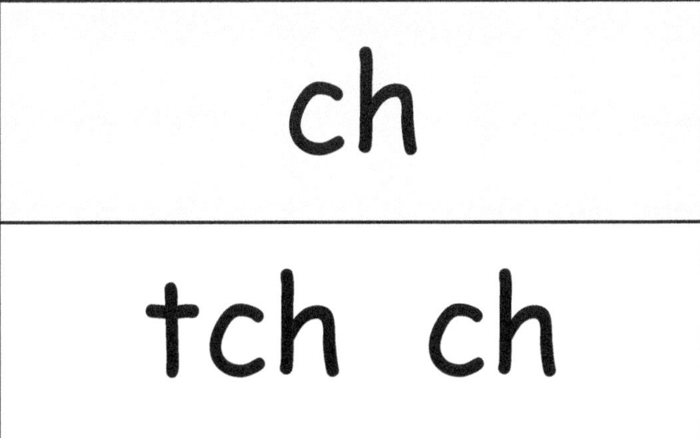

tch
t tch

ch
ch tch

tch
ch tch

ch
c h ch

tch
t ch tch

Having introduced the sound and its corresponding sound spellings, it is important that the child is given the opportunity to practise writing them.
In this activity the child can practise forming the sound spellings in a number of ways:

- copying over the grey letters which act as a guide to accurate letter formation,
- writing individual sound spellings within small boxes (with shading to act as a guide), which develops visual-spatial awareness of the letters and
- writing words with a sound spelling in each box.

Encourage the child to say the sound at the same time as writing the sound spelling.

Activity 19 Writing sound spellings ch

ch ch ch ch

ch ch ch ch ch ch ch

ch							

tch tch tch tch

tch tch tch tch tch tch tch

tch							

ch i p

ch a t

m u ch

r i ch

m a tch

p i tch

ch a m p

This set of cards is made of up words containing the sound 'ch'. The sound spelling for the target sound in each word is highlighted. Copy onto card and cut out.
Practise dynamic blending for reading, as described in the 'Working through the programme' section, using these cards. Model this process for the child if necessary.

Activity 20 Dynamic blending – word cards ch

much	such
lunch	chop
chat	champ
chest	chips
fetch	witch
match	pitch
switch	scratch

This set of cards is made of up words containing the sound 'ch'. Copy onto card and cut out. Practise dynamic blending for reading, as described in the 'Working through the programme' section, using these cards. Model this process for the child if necessary.

Activity 20 Dynamic blending – word cards ch

such	bunch
chap	chin
chops	chimp
chunk	itch
patch	ditch
hutch	latch
glitch	snatch

Print out onto card and cut out.
Stack them with the biggest (the complete word) on the bottom and in decreasing size so that the smallest is on the top.
Make sure the left-hand edge of the cards are flush. Staple the cards together on the left-hand side.
When the child runs a finger over the cards the sound spellings flip up. Ask the child to say the sounds and match to the flips.

staple

Activity 24 Flippies for the sound 'ch'

ch	ch i	ch i p	
b	b u	b u n	b u n ch
i	i tch		
m	m a	m a tch	
s	s w	s w i	s w i tch

Read the clue on the left for the child.
Use the clue to work out what the answer word is.
Encourage the child to think about the sounds in that word and write a sound spelling for each sound in the boxes on the right, one by one.
The first two are done for you as an example.
Explain to the child that they may not need to use all the boxes and so some are shaded in.
Break this task into a number of shorter tasks over a number of lessons if necessary.

Activity 25 Sound boxes ch

Clue	Sound boxes			
Uncomfortable feeling	i	tch		
Under your mouth!	ch	i	n	
A game of football				
Place to play football				
Talk to friends				
Have lots of money				
Rabbit's house				
The winner!				
Meal in the day				
Where pirates keep treasure				
Eat with a burger				

Support the child to read the words on the left.
For each word, support the child to work out how many sounds there are in it and write that number in the grey box.
Then ask the child to count out the number of white boxes needed to write the word, so that there is one box for each sound, and colour in any boxes that are not needed.
Next ask the child to say the sounds in the word, one by one, and at the same time write the matching sound spelling in the boxes one by one.
The first one is done for you as an example.
Break this task into a number of shorter tasks over a number of lessons if necessary.

Activity 26 How many sounds? ch

Word	Number	Writing the sound spellings				
match	3	m	a	tch		
such						
pitch						
lunch						
itch						
champ						
switch						
much						
chips						

During this activity the child will be asked to slide sounds in and out of words, i.e. practise phoneme manipulation.
A sound might be swapped, added or taken away.
Print the sound spelling cards onto card and cut out.
Activity:

- Spread out all the sound spelling cards so that the child can see them.
- Build a starting word from the prompt list, demonstrating how to dynamically blend the sounds together as you move the sound spelling cards into place.
- Repeat the word, running your finger under the cards so that it corresponds to the sounds within the word.
- Ask the child to change the word to the next word on the prompt list. As you say the new word run your finger under the cards so that it corresponds with the sound you are saying and the matching sound spelling card.

This gives the child the chance to hear and see what is different.

- The child can then swap the appropriate sounds spelling cards.
- Repeat this technique with the next word on the list.

Activity 29 Sound swap ch

Sound swap ch

List 1	List 2	List 3
chat	such	match
chap	much	patch
champ	munch	pitch
chimp	bunch	itch
chip	brunch	witch
chips	crunch	
chops		
chop		
chomp		

ch	tch	a	i
o	u	t	p
m	s	n	b
r	p	w	c

Support the child to read the words on the left, one by one.
For each word read the clue to the child and then work out what the answer word is.
Explain to the child that they will need to either: add a sound, take away a sound or change a sound to the word on the left to make the answer word, e.g. cot > cost list > lit mat > rat.
Have the child write out the answer word on the right, saying each sound as they write each sound spelling.
An example is done for you.
Break this task into a number of shorter tasks over a number of lessons if necessary.

Activity 30 Sound exchange ch

Starting word	Clue	New word
chap	The winner	champ
such	A lot, too	
dutch	Rabbit's house	
lunch	A .... of flowers	
ditch	Uncomfortable skin	
witch	Press to turn on light	
chops	Fish and	
chip	Great ape	
patch	Place to play football	
etch	Go get something	

Place a whiteboard in front of the child.
Choose a word from the list below. Randomise the words you choose so that you are choosing words with a variety of number of sounds.
Draw dots on the whiteboard to match the number of sounds in the word, one dot for each sound. Do not write the word or show the word to the child as this is a purely auditory activity.
Say the word to the child and as you do so run your finger under the dots so that your finger matches the appropriate sound dot and its corresponding sound as you say it.
Then cover the dot that corresponds to the sound you are going to take away – use the list below.
Ask the child to tell you what is left if you take that sound away.
Take away another sound or choose a new word.
Remember to time limit this activity.

Activity 31 Sound sums ch

No. of sounds in starting word	Word	Take away the sound	What is left?
3	chat	ch	at
3	chin	ch	in
3	ditch	d	itch
4	champ	ch	amp
4	bunch	ch	bun
4	switch	s	witch

This set of cards is made up of high frequency words containing the sound 'ch'. Copy onto card and cut out. Practise dynamic blending for reading, as described in the 'Working through the programme' section, using these cards. Model this process for the child if necessary.

Activity 32 Reading high frequency words ch

much	children

Starting at 'itch', have the child read each of the words on the shapes as quickly as possible.
Support the child to read the words by giving information about sounds and supporting blending but do not supply the whole word.
Time how long it takes to read all the words to 'scratch' and record the time in the box.
Repeat at a later point and see if the child can beat his own time.

Activity 33 Reading race: scratch that itch! ch

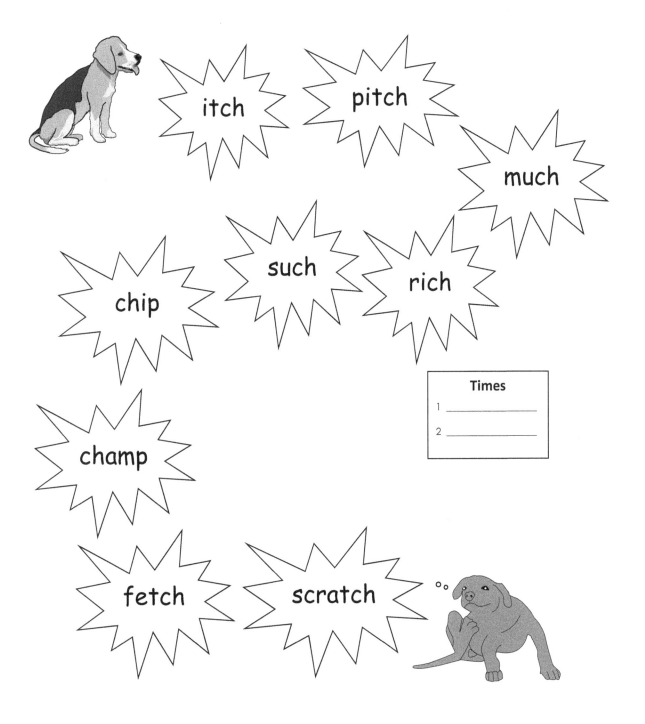

itch

pitch

much

such

rich

chip

champ

fetch

scratch

Times

1 ______________

2 ______________

Support the child to read the words one by one.
For each word support the child to think whether there is a 'ch' sound in the word.
Have the child put a ring around or highlight just the words that have a 'ch' sound.
Remind the child that 'ch' can be represented by two sound spellings: **ch** and **tch**.
Break this task into a number of shorter tasks over a number of lessons if necessary.

Activity 34 Word tracker ch

cat	chat	much	witch	with
chin	patch	shot	cast	itch
match	champ	this	chips	camp
fetch	switch	such	hats	lunch
rich	chop	bunch	maths	scratch

How many 'ch' words did you find? ________

Visual memory is the ability to remember and identify a shape, figure or picture that we have previously seen. Children with poor visual memory may struggle to remember pictures, figures, shapes, letters and numbers and may have difficulties with reading, writing and number work.

Ask the child to look at the word in the yellow box for at least five seconds, covering the white box underneath. Then cover the yellow box so that the word cannot be seen and reveal a choice of words in the white box below. Ask the child to select the word in the white box that matches the one they saw in the yellow box.

Break this task into a number of shorter tasks over a number of lessons if necessary.

Activity 35 Remembering words ch

chat
chap chat

such
such much

chimp
champ chimp

patch
pitch patch

bunch
lunch munch bunch

pitch
patch pitch ditch

scratch
switch scratch scritch

Support the child to read the words one by one.
For each word support the child to think whether the word is a real word that makes sense or is a nonsense word.
Have the child put a ring around or highlight just the real words.
Break this task into a number of shorter tasks over a number of lessons if necessary.

Activity 36 Word detective ch

fotch	pitch	chip	such	luch
match	fitch	rich	dritch	patch
chin	fetch	lunch	gotch	chunk
swetch	hutch	itch	stitch	munch
gritch	flatch	champ	pitch	puch

How many real words did you find? ________

Visual sequential memory is the ability to remember sequences of figures, symbols, pictures and shapes. Children with poor visual sequencing struggle to remember a sequence of letters and follow visual patterns. They may have difficulties writing a sequence of letters to form a word and a sequence of words to form a sentence.

Ask the child to look at the words in the yellow box for at least five seconds, covering the white box underneath. Then cover the yellow box so that the words cannot be seen and reveal the sequence of words in the white box below. Ask the child to remember the missing word from the sequence in the yellow box and write it in the space.

Break this task into a number of shorter tasks over a number of lessons if necessary.

Activity 37 Remembering lots of words ch

chin chat
______ chat

such chip
______ chip

itch fetch
______ fetch

switch	scratch
switch	______

chap	rich	chop
chap	rich	______

patch	catch	pitch
patch	______	pitch

much	match	witch
much	match	______

Print out on card and cut out the sound spelling and picture cards for each word.
Read though the instructions in the 'Working through the programme' section at the start of this book prior to working with a child.

Activity 38 Word build ch

ch	a	t		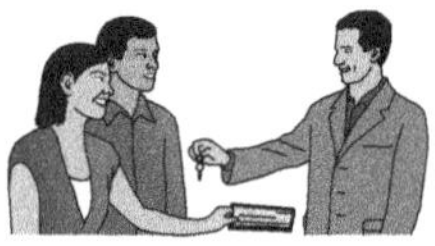
r	i	ch		
ch	a	m	p	
l	u	n	ch	

i	tch			
m	a	tch		
s	w	i	tch	

Support the child to read the words on the list one by one.
For each word support the child to think about each of the sounds in the word and their matching sound spellings.
Have the child put a ring around or highlight the sound spelling for each sound.
Break this task into a number of shorter tasks over a number of lessons if necessary.

Activity 39 Word tech ch

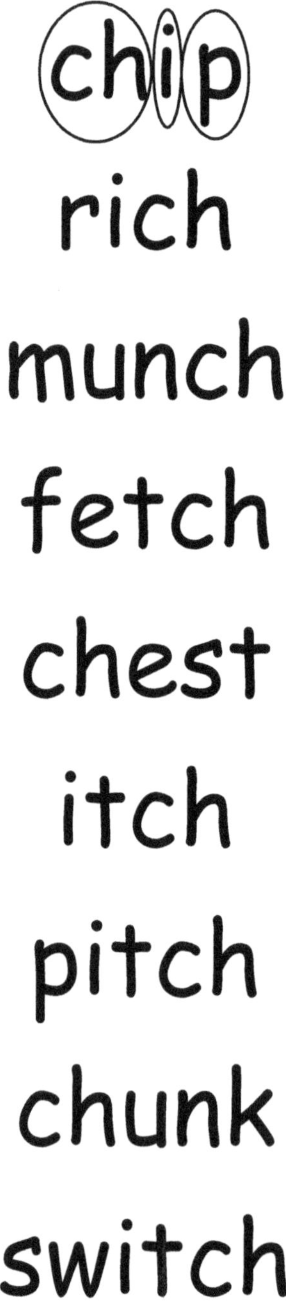

chip
rich
munch
fetch
chest
itch
pitch
chunk
switch

Read the clue on the left for the child.
For each clue support the child to work out what the answer word is.
The sound spellings for the answer word are given to help, but they are mixed up – an anagram.
Have the child use the sound spellings to write the answer word on the line on the right.
Encourage the child to say the associated sound as he writes each sound spelling.
Break this task into a number of shorter tasks over a number of lessons if necessary.

Activity 40 Word scramble ch

Clue	Sound spellings	Word
Magic lady	w **tch** i	______________
Fried potatoes...	**ch** p i s	______________
Have lots of money	i **ch** r	______________
Football game played here	i **tch** p	______________
Holds pirate treasure	e t s **ch**	______________
Turn on and off	**tch** w i s	______________
Rabbit's house	u h **tch**	______________
Meal in the day	**ch** l u n	______________
Makes me scratch	**tch** i	______________
To go get something	**tch** e f	______________
Under your mouth	**ch** n i	______________

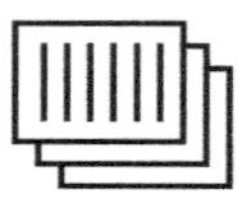

Activity 42 Spelling challenge ch

chat	ch a t	ch a t	___ ___ ___	__________
much	m u ch	m u ch	___ ___ ___	__________
chest	ch e s t	ch e s t	___ ___ ___ ___	__________
lunch	l u n ch	l u n ch	___ ___ ___ ___	__________
catch	c a tch	c a tch	___ ___ ___	__________
pitch	p i tch	p i tch	___ ___ ___	__________
scratch	s c r a tch	s c r a tch	___ ___ ___ ___ ___	__________

Support the child to read the sentence and for each spot the spelling mistake. Remember to refer to the term 'accepted' spelling rather than the 'right' or 'correct' spelling.
Have the child underline the mistake and then write the accepted spelling on the line underneath.
If the child is able then the whole sentence could be written out.
Note that the sentences may include high frequency words which contain sounds that the child has not yet encountered in the programme. Support the child to decode these words by supplying information about the unfamiliar sound and its sound spelling and encourage the child to blend for reading. Some sound spellings are highlighted to support this.
Break this task into a number of shorter tasks over a number of lessons if necessary.

Activity 43 Oops! Correct the spelling ch

1. I sat on the mat and had my luntch.

____

2. The dog ran to fech the stick.

____

3. Sam had sutch fun at the p**ar**k.

____

4. Rav went to the mach.

____

5. The cat had an ich to scratch.

____

6. I can press the swich.

____

Support the child to read each sentence, notice that there is a word missing and think what it might be. The missing word is written underneath in two ways. Remember both spellings are technically correct but only one is the 'accepted' spelling. Refer to the 'Working through the programme' section at the start of this book for an explanation of this term if you need further information.
Ask the child to choose the accepted spelling and write it on the line within the sentence.
Encourage the child to say the sound as they write the associated sound spelling.
Note that the sentences include some high frequency words which contain sounds that the child has not yet encountered in the programme. Support the child to decode these words by supplying information about any unfamiliar sound and its sound spelling and encourage the child to blend for reading. Some sound spellings are highlighted to support this.
Break this task into a number of shorter tasks over a number of lessons if necessary.

Activity 44 Spot the spelling ch

1. The ____________ had a pet cat.
   wich witch

2. The hen will ____________ the egg.
   hatch hach

3. Can Pam ____________ the dog?
   catch cach

4. Dan ran on the ____________ .
   pich pitch

5. The man got hit on the ____________.
   chin tchin

6. Mum said "Do not ____________ the sweets!"
   snatch snach

Support the child to read the sentences.
Explain that the sentences are OK but that they are very short and could be a bit more interesting!
Then support the child to read the phrases at the bottom of the page and decide which could be used to make each sentence 'better' or 'more interesting'.
Ask the child to write out the sentence, adding the new phrase from the list. Encourage the child to say the sounds at the same time as writing the associated sound spelling when writing each word.
Note that the sentences include high frequency words which contain sounds that the child has not yet encountered in the programme. Support the child to decode these words by supplying information about any unfamiliar sounds and sound spellings and encourage the child to blend for reading. Some sound spellings are highlighted to support this.
Break this task into a number of shorter tasks over a number of lessons if necessary.

Activity 45 Making better sentences ch

1. Sam had lunch.

____

____

2. The witch sat on a chest.

____

____

3. The dog ran fast.

____

____

4. Mum got fish and chips.

____

____

5. Tom fell in the ditch.

____

____

full of bugs and slugs	to fetch the twig
and got a scratch on his hand	in the kitchen
but had to rush bef**ore** the shop shut	

Support the child to read each sentence one by one.
Ask the child to re-read the sentence, several times if necessary, and try to remember it.
Then cover the sentence and ask the child to recall the sentence verbally.
Once they can do this confidently, ask the child to write out the sentence from memory.

When writing a word, encourage the child to say the sound as they write each associated sound spelling.
When the word is complete then they are to say the whole word.
When the sentence is complete the child reads out their sentence and then compares it to the original.
Note that the sentences may include high frequency words which contain sounds that the child has not yet encountered in the programme. Support the child to decode these words by supplying information about any unfamiliar sounds and their sound spellings and encouraging the child to blend for reading. Some of these sound spellings are highlighted to help the child when writing the words later.

Alternatively, using text to speech software, the child could type the sentence, with the computer reading back each word and then the completed sentence.

Activity 46 Writing challenge ch

Dad has such a big chin.

The chap had chop and chips.

Sam lit a match on the pitch.

Dan can push the switch.

Answers ch

Page 143 **Activity 8 Investigating the sound 'ch'**	Page 158 **Activity 25 Sound boxes**	Page 159 **Activity 26 How many sounds?**
ch chin such chips much chest lunch **tch** pitch match fetch hutch itch switch	m a tch p i tch ch a t r i ch h u tch ch a m p l u n ch ch e s t ch i p s	3 s u ch 3 p i tch 4 l u n ch 2 i tch 4 ch a m p 4 s w i tch 3 m u ch 4 ch i p s
Page 162 **Activity 30 Sound exchange**	Page 166 **Activity 34 Word tracker**	Page 169 **Activity 36 Word detective**
such – much dutch – hutch lunch – bunch ditch – itch witch – switch chops – chips chip – chimp patch – pitch etch – fetch	chat much witch chin patch itch match champ chips fetch switch such lunch rich chop bunch scratch 17	pitch chip such match rich patch chin fetch lunch chunk hutch itch stitch munch champ pitch 16
Page 174 **Activity 39 Word tech**	Page 175 **Activity 40 Word scramble**	Page 177 **Activity 43 Oops! Correct the spelling**
r i ch m u n ch f e tch ch e s t i tch p i tch ch u n k s w i tch	witch chips rich pitch chest switch hutch lunch itch fetch chin	lunch fetch such match itch switch

Page 178

Activity 44 Spot the spelling

witch
hatch
catch
pitch
chin
snatch

Page 179

Activity 45 Making better sentences

1. Sam had lunch in the kitchen.
2. The witch sat on a chest full of bugs and slugs.
3. The dog ran fast to fetch the twig.
4. Mum got fish and chips but had to rush before the shop shut.
5. Tom fell in the ditch and got a scratch on his hand.

SECTION 5

k

c

cat

k

king

ck

stick

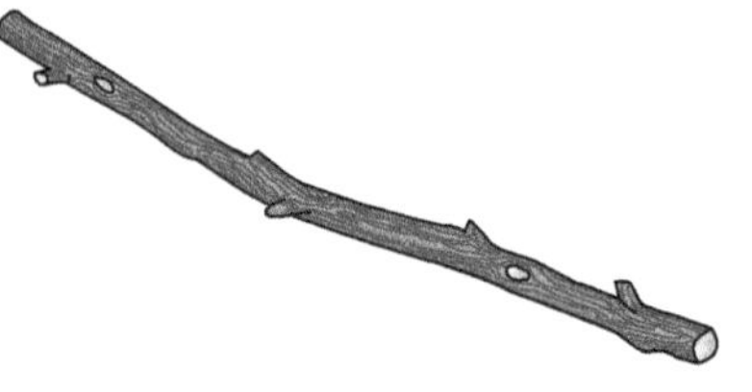

Words with a 'k' sound – word list of 1 syllable words

c

3 sounds

act
cab
can
cap
cat
cod
cog
con
cop
cot
cub
cud
cup
cut
sac

4 sounds

camp
cast
cli**ng**
colt
cost
cult
fact
pact

k

3 sounds

ask
elk
ilk
ink
kid
kin
ki**ng**
kip
kit

4 sounds

bank
cask
desk
mask
milk
silk
sink
tank
trek
wink

5 sounds

blank
blink
drank

ck

3 sounds

back
chick
deck
dock
duck
jack
kick
lack
lick
lock
luck
mock
muck
neck
pack
peck
pick
rack
rock
sack
shack
shock
sick
sock
tack
thick

4 sounds

black
block
brick
cluck
crack
flock
pluck
prick
slack
slick
smack
snack
stack
stick
stock
stuck
track
trick

5 sounds

struck

c	k	ck
5 sounds	5 sounds	3 sounds
clamp	drink	tick
clank	flask	tock
clasp	shrink	tuck
clump	stink	wick
clunk	thank	
cramp	think	
crisp		

Auditory discrimination is the ability to hear differences between sounds. Good auditory discrimination helps us to recognise and identify the sounds in words and so interpret them correctly. Children with poor auditory discrimination may confuse sounds and misinterpret things they have heard. Their spelling and writing may reflect their confusion over which sounds they heard in a word. **Auditory attention and tracking** is the ability to actively listen and follow auditory information from beginning to end. Good auditory attention and tracking helps us to follow a conversation, a story read out loud or a set of instructions, and enables us to focus on key information. Children with poor auditory attention and tracking may find it difficult to follow and respond appropriately to what is being said to them.

This story contains lots of words that contain the sound 'k', which is the 'target' sound.
Read the story out loud to the child or group of children. Encourage the child to listen carefully and spot any word that contains the target sound. Note that there are three ways that 'k' can be represented: **c, k** and **ck,** but the 'k' sound is the same for both. When a target word has been read, the child indicates that they have heard and spotted it by tapping the table, putting up a hand or any other agreed signal, but without shouting out. Stop reading and discuss the word, making any error correction necessary. If a word is missed, re-read the sentence.
Do not show the written story to the child. The target words are highlighted below for you.

Activity 1 Sound target story k

Cal was sick. He did not feel well.

He got up and called for his mum.

Mum gave him a drink and he went back to bed.

Cal's mum gave him a cuddle and tucked him into bed.

He had a kip.

When he woke up he felt better.

Mum made him a snack and a cup of tea.

I think I can get up now.

I hope I can go to the park on my bike tomorrow.

Auditory discrimination is the ability to hear differences between sounds. Good auditory discrimination helps us to recognise and identify the sounds in words and so interpret them correctly. Children with poor auditory discrimination may confuse sounds and misinterpret things they have heard. Their spelling and writing may reflect their confusion over what sounds they heard in a word. **Auditory sequential memory** is the ability to remember and recall a series of things that they have heard. Children with poor auditory sequential memory may find it difficult to remember information given earlier in a conversation or set of instructions and may struggle to recall the sequence of sounds in a word.

The silly sentences contain lots of words containing the sound 'k'.
Read the sentence to the child several times, invite them to join in as you say it and gradually recall it on their own.
Do not show the words to the child.
Ask them to say it as quickly as they can and have some fun with it. Perhaps they can make up their own?
The sentences gradually get longer and more complex.
Break this task into a number of shorter tasks over a number of lessons if necessary.

Activity 2 Tongue twister fun k

Kai cuts cakes.

Kids can kick cans.

Kings kiss cuddly cooks.

Crazy clowns carry cool caps.

Cold cats claw cloth cushions carefully.

Auditory discrimination is the ability to hear differences between sounds. Good auditory discrimination helps us to recognise and identify the sounds in words and so interpret them correctly. Children with poor auditory discrimination may confuse sounds and misinterpret things they have heard. Their spelling and writing may reflect their confusion over which sounds they heard in a word. **Auditory attention and tracking** is the ability to actively listen and follow auditory information from beginning to end. Good auditory attention and tracking helps us to follow a conversation, a story read out loud or a set of instructions, and enables us to focus on key information. Children with poor auditory attention and tracking may find it difficult to follow and respond appropriately to what is being said to them.

Read out the words and ask the child to identify the odd one out. In 1–10 the child focuses on the sound at the **beginning** of the words, and in 11–20 the child focuses on the sound at the **end** of the words.
Do not show the words to the child. The odd one out is highlighted for you.
Break this task into a number of shorter tasks over a number of lessons if necessary.

Activity 3 Odd one out k

1.	dog	cub	dad	2.	man	kid	map
3.	cop	chin	cut	4.	kit	hot	hit
5.	sink	silk	cast	6.	camp	pick	pack
7.	cost	deck	duck	8.	stick	shock	stick
9.	track	trick	clump	10.	cramp	chick	clunk
11.	sand	sock	sick	12.	desk	dust	duck
13.	pack	pick	pant	14.	crack	stand	stamp
15.	brick	black	blast	16.	snack	track	clap
17.	shock	shift	shrink	18.	thrush	think	thick
19.	track	trick	tramp	20.	crisp	struck	cramp

Auditory discrimination is the ability to hear differences between sounds. Good auditory discrimination helps us to recognise and identify the sounds in words and so interpret them correctly. Children with poor auditory discrimination may confuse sounds and misinterpret things they have heard. Their spelling and writing may reflect their confusion over which sounds they heard in a word. **Auditory recall memory** is the ability to remember and recall something that they have just heard. Children with poor auditory recall memory may find it difficult to remember sounds and words and respond appropriately.

Read the list of words below clearly, asking the child to listen carefully. At random points tap the table and stop reading, asking the child to remember and say the last word you said. Then ask them to tell you what the **first** or the **last** sound in the word is.

Break this task into a number of shorter tasks over a number of lessons if necessary.

Activity 4 What sound am I? k

1.	act	cub	cot	can	ink	kid	ask
2.	cut	kit	king	cab	camp	bank	desk
3.	fact	sick	milk	cost	kick	cling	sink
4.	lock	mask	tank	rock	sack	neck	shot
5.	thick	shock	chop	wink	ship	them	sock
6.	snack	clamp	stick	blank	crisp	drink	
7.	flock	crack	flask	trick	stuck	black	
8.	thank	slack	blink	stink	flock	struck	

Auditory discrimination is the ability to hear differences between sounds. Good auditory discrimination helps us to recognise and identify the sounds in words and so interpret them correctly. Children with poor auditory discrimination may confuse sounds and misinterpret things they have heard. Their spelling and writing may reflect their confusion over what sounds they heard in a word.

Read out the pairs of words. For 1–12 ask the child to tell you whether or not they **start** with the same sound and for 13–24 ask whether or not they **end** with the same sounds. The words get increasingly complex.

Break this task into a number of shorter tasks over a number of lessons if necessary.

Activity 5 Same or different? k

1. cut - sun
2. cot - cub
3. ask - act
4. kid - can
5. wink - king
6. cast - camp
7. pack - pick
8. kick - kip
9. duck - chick
10. sick - sock
11. back - neck
12. track - trick

13. cab - cat
14. ink - ask
15. cop - cup
16. luck - lock
17. king - sink
18. hand - milk
19. think - thing
20. stock - block
21. crack - switch
22. stick - flock
23. blink - snack
24. struck - black

Auditory fusion is the ability to hear the subtle gaps between sounds and words. Children with poor auditory fusion may get lost in conversations and when following a list of instructions given verbally.

Read the words in the list one after another at a brisk pace so that are not obvious gaps between the sounds or the words. Ask the child to listen carefully and then tell you how many sounds or words you have said. Many of the words contain the sound 'k' (represented by the sound spellings **c, k** and **ck**) and get increasingly complex.

Break this task into a number of shorter tasks over a number of lessons if necessary.

Activity 6 How many did you hear? k

1. k - **th** - k
2. k - **ch** - k - ng
3. k - **ch** - **sh** - **th** - k
4. c - s - **th** - k
5. f - k - s - **ch**
6. k - **ch** - t - **sh** - f
7. k - f - k - **sh**
8. k - f
9. cab - cut - lock - kick
10. ink - dock - cat
11. cup - kid - neck - kit
12. pack - king
13. milk - cot - mask
14. camp - sack - pick
15. rock - sick - desk - sink
16. duck - cling - muck
17. rack - tank - chick
18. blink - shock
19. drink - flock - stick - crisp
20. stink - track - think
21. slack - trick
22. struck - block - cram

Auditory attention and tracking is the ability to actively listen and follow auditory information from beginning to end. Good auditory attention and tracking helps us to follow a conversation, a story read out loud or a set of instructions, and enables us to focus on key information. Children with poor auditory attention and tracking may find it difficult to follow and respond appropriately to what is being said to them. **Auditory sequential memory** is the ability to remember and recall a series of things that they have heard. Children with poor auditory sequential memory may find it difficult to remember information given earlier in a conversation or set of instructions and may struggle to recall the sequence of sounds in a word.

In this activity the child has to process the auditory information but also respond by working out the pattern and stating the next sound in the sequence. Read out the list of sounds with a clear space between each. Ask the child to listen and work out what sound would come next. The answers follow in red.

Break this task into a number of shorter tasks over a number of lessons if necessary.

Activity 7 What comes next? k

1. k c k c k c
2. k f k f k ...... f
3. k **ch** k **ch** k **ch** ...... k
4. s k s k s k ...... s
5. p s k p s k p s ...... k
6. p p k p p k p p k ...... p
7. k x x k x x k x x
8. **sh** k **sh** **sh** k **sh** **sh** ...... k
9. k k p t k k p t ...... k
10. t t k f t t k f ...... t
11. k **sh** **th** k **sh** **th** ...... k
12. **ch** **ch** k k **ch** **ch** k k ...... ch
13. k k **sh** **th** k k **sh** **th** ...... k
14. d k t d k t d k t ...... d
15. d **ch** k d **ch** k d **ch** ...... k
16. **th** **ch** **ch** k **th** **ch** **ch** k **th** ...... ch
17. k d t p k d t p ...... k
18. k k k p k k k p ...... k
19. **ch** k p t **ch** k p t **ch** k ...... p
20. t t k p t t k p ...... t
21. **ch** k **th** **sh** **ch** k **th** **sh** ... ch
22. **ch** k t p **ch** k t p ...... ch
23. k **ch** **ch** p k **ch** **ch** p ...... k
24. **ch** k t g **ch** k t g ...... ch

This activity results in the child discovering that three sound spellings, c, k and ck, represent the sound 'k' in written words. The child is familiar with c and k from Book 1.

Support the child to read the word **cab**, work out the sound spelling corresponding to the sound 'k' and highlight it. The child has discovered the sound spelling **c** represents the sound 'k'. Ask the child to write the **c** sound spelling as a heading on the small line in the first box, then write the word **cab** on the line underneath. Encourage the child to say each sound at the same time as writing each sound spelling. For example, the child writes **c** and says 'k', writes **a** and says 'a' and writes **b** and says 'b'.

Move on to the next word, **sink**, and support the child to read it, work out the sound spelling corresponding to the sound 'k' and highlight it. Ask the child to write the **k** sound spelling as a heading on the small line in the second box, then write the word **sink** on the line underneath. Encourage the child to say each sound at the same time as writing each sound spelling. For example, the child writes **s** and says 's', writes **i** and says 'n', writes **n** and says 'n' and writes **k** and says 'k'.

Move on to the next word, **sack**, and support the child to read it, work out the sound spelling corresponding to the sound 'k' and highlight it. Ask the child to write the **ck** sound spelling as a heading on the small line in the third box, then write the word **sack** on the line underneath. Encourage the child to say each sound at the same time as writing each sound spelling. For example, the child writes **s** and says 's', writes **a** and says 'a', and writes **ck** and says 'k'.

Then work through the rest of the words one by one, sorting the words into **c, k** and **ck** word lists as above. Point out to the child that this shows that there are three ways to write the sound 'k' when we hear it in a word. Good readers and spellers remember which of these sound spellings go in which word.

Break this task into a number of shorter tasks over a number of lessons if necessary.

Activity 8 Investigating the sound k

cab	back	king
sink	cat	stick
sack	bank	kid
brick	black	camp
cloth	drink	snack

Activity 10 Sound spelling cards k

c	k
ck	

Visual discrimination is the ability to see differences between objects and figures that are similar. Good visual discrimination helps keep us from getting confused when looking at shapes and forms in the environment. Children with poor visual discrimination may find it difficult to recognise letters, may confuse letters such as b and d and may find it difficult to identify mathematical symbols.

Ask the child to look at the sound spelling in the yellow box then track along the row looking at the other sound spellings.
The child indicates or puts a ring around the sound spelling that is the same as the one in the yellow box.
This includes some sound spellings which represent other sounds but are visually similar.

Break this task into a number of shorter tasks over a number of lessons if necessary.

Activity 11 Sound spelling tracker k

ck	ch	ck	tch	k
k	ck	k	ch	h
ck	k	tch	ch	ck
c	a	e	c	o
ck	c	k	ck	ch
k	k	f	t	h
ck	ck	c	k	ch
c	o	e	c	a

Visual memory is the ability to remember and identify a shape or picture that we have previously seen. Children with poor visual memory may struggle to remember pictures, figures, shapes, letters and numbers and may have difficulties with reading, writing and number work.

Ask the child to look at the sound spelling in the yellow box for at least 5 seconds, covering the white box underneath. Then cover the yellow box so that the sound spelling cannot be seen and reveal the choice of sound spellings in the white box below. Ask the child to select the matching sound spelling from the white box.

Break this task into a number of shorter tasks over a number of lessons if necessary.

Activity 12 Remembering sound spellings k

ck
ch ck

ck
ck ch

k
k t

c
o c

ck
ch th ck

ck
ch ck th

Visual discrimination is the ability to see differences between objects and figures that are similar. Good visual discrimination helps keep us from getting confused when looking at shapes and forms in the environment. Children with poor visual discrimination may find it difficult to recognise letters, may confuse letters such as b and d and may find it difficult to identify mathematical symbols.

Focus on one of the sound spellings featured on this sheet, e.g. **ck** (say the sound 'k' and point to an example rather than using the letter names to identify the sound spelling). Ask the child to look at all the sound spellings and indicate or put a ring round all the sound spellings which match the target. Repeat for another sound spelling featured on the sheet.

Break this task into a number of shorter tasks over a number of lessons if necessary.

Activity 13 Spot the sound spelling k

k ck ck

c k k

ck ck

ch ck k

ck c k k ch

Form constancy is the ability to generalise forms and figures and identify them even if they are slightly different from that usually seen. This skill helps us distinguish differences in size, shape and orientation or position. Children with poor form constancy may frequently reverse letters and numbers.

Ask the child to look at the sound spelling on the left and match to a sound spelling on the right (written differently), drawing a line to connect each.

Activity 14 Which is the same? k

ck	k
k	ch
c	c
ch	ck

Visual closure is the ability to identify an object, shape or symbol from a visually incomplete or disorganised presentation and to see where the different parts of a whole fit together, i.e. to recognise something when seeing only part of it. This skill helps us understand things quickly because our visual system doesn't have to process every detail to recognise what we're seeing.

Ask the child to look at the sound spelling in the white box then track left to right along the row.
Ask the child to indicate or put a ring around the sound spelling that is the same as that in the white box.

Break this task into a number of shorter tasks over a number of lessons if necessary.

Activity 15 Bits missing k

ck	ch	ck	th
k	f	k	t
ck	th	ch	ck
c	c	s	u
k	t	f	k
ck	ch	ck	th
ck	th	ch	ck
c	s	u	c

Spatial relations is the ability to perceive the position of objects in relation to ourselves and to each other. This skill helps children to understand relationships between symbols and letters. Children with poor spatial relations may find it difficult to write letters in the correct orientation, write consistently starting at the margin and write letters of the same size.

In the first part, ask the child to copy the sound spellings on the lines below in exactly the same places as they appear above.
In the second part, ask the child to copy the words on the lines below in exactly the same places, saying the matching sound as they write each sound spelling.

Break this task into a number of shorter tasks over a number of lessons if necessary.

Activity 17 Where am I? k

ck c k ck

k ck c

kid back

crust snack

Visual sequential memory is the ability to remember sequences of figures, symbols and shapes. Children with poor visual sequencing struggle to remember a sequence of letters and follow visual patterns. They may have difficulties writing a sequence of letters to form a word and a sequence of words to form a sentence.

Ask the child to look at the sound spellings in the yellow box for at least five seconds, covering the white box underneath. Then cover the yellow box so that the sound spellings cannot be seen and reveal the sequence of sound spellings in the white box below. Ask the child to remember the missing sound spelling and write it in the space.

Break this task into a number of shorter tasks over a number of lessons if necessary.

Activity 18 Remembering lots of sound spellings k

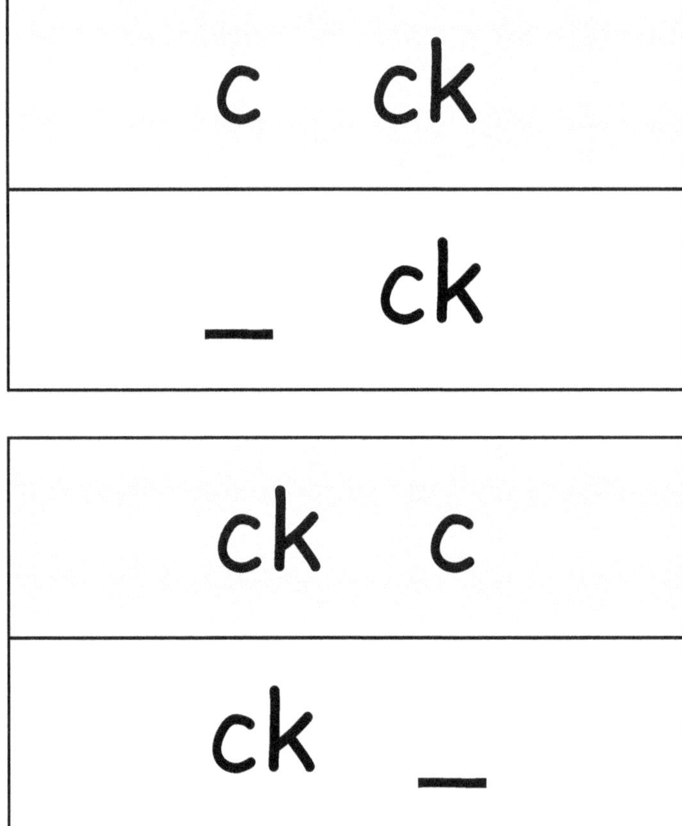

k ck
_ ck

c ck
ck _

c ck k
c ck _

k c ck
k _ ck

Having introduced the sound and its corresponding sound spellings, it is important that the child is given the opportunity to practise writing them.
In this activity the child can practise forming the sound spellings in a number of ways:

- copying over the grey letters which act as a guide to accurate letter formation,
- writing individual sound spellings within small boxes (with shading to act as a guide), which develops visual-spatial awareness of the letters and
- writing words with a sound spelling in each box.

Encourage the child to say the sound at the same time as writing the sound spelling.

Activity 19 Writing sound spellings k

c	c	c	c	c	c	c

c c c c c c c

c						

k k k k k k k

k k k k k k k

k						

ck ck ck ck ck

ck ck ck ck ck ck ck

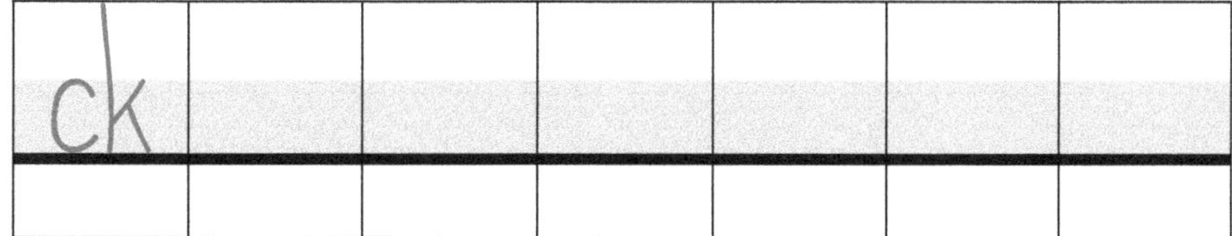

c a n

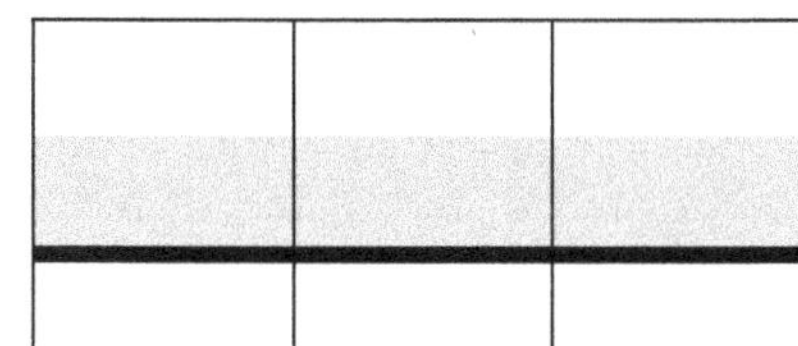

k i d

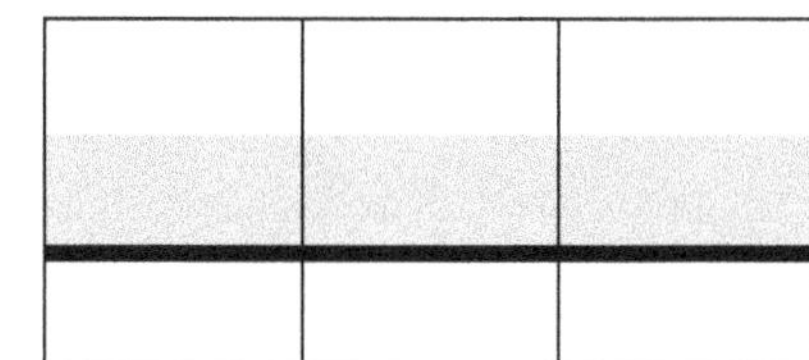

s t i **ck**

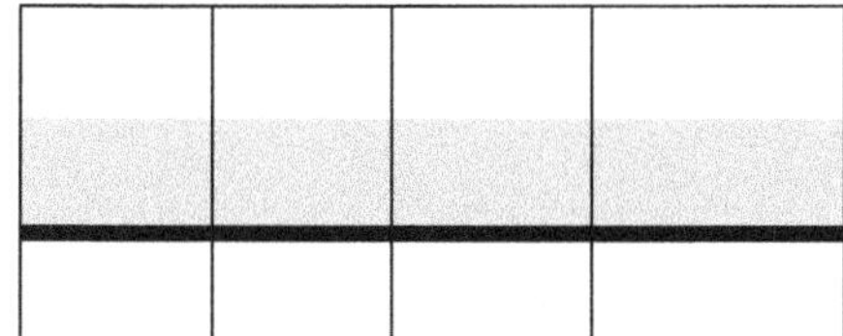

k i **ck**

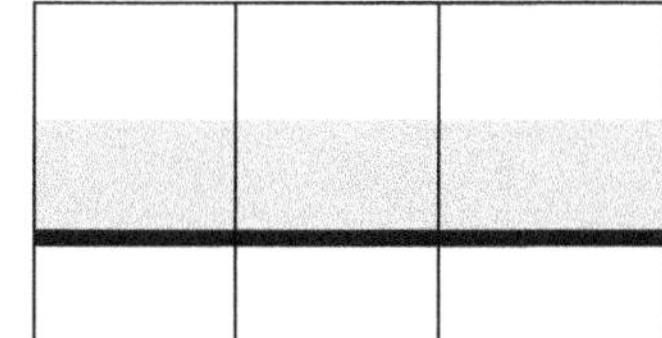

This set of cards is made of up words containing the sound 'k'. The sound spelling for the target sound in each word is highlighted. Copy onto card and cut out.
Practise dynamic blending for reading, as described in the 'Working through the programme' section, using these cards. Model this process for the child if necessary.

Activity 20 Dynamic blending – word cards k

act	cut
cost	clip
kid	ink
tank	sink
drink	sick
lock	pack
black	stick

This set of cards is made of up words containing the sound 'k'. Copy onto card and cut out.
Practise dynamic blending for reading, as described in the 'Working through the programme' section, using these cards. Model this process for the child if necessary.

Activity 20 Dynamic blending – word cards k

cup	cab
camp	cling
kip	king
sink	milk
thank	pick
sack	snack
brick	truck

Print out onto card and cut out.
Stack them with the biggest (the complete word) on the bottom and in decreasing size so that the smallest is on the top.
Make sure the left-hand edge of the cards are flush. Staple the cards together on the left-hand side.
When the child runs a finger over the cards the sound spellings flip up. Ask the child to say the sounds and match to the flips.

staple

Activity 24 Flippies for the sound 'k'

c	c a	c a m	c a m p
f	f a	f a c	f a c t
k	k i	k i t	
l	l u	l u ck	
t	t r	t r i	t r i ck

Read the clue on the left for the child.
Use the clue to work out what the answer word is.
Encourage the child to think about the sounds in that word and write a sound spelling for each sound in the boxes on the right, one by one.
The first one is done for you as an example.
Explain to the child that they may not need to use all the boxes and so some are shaded in.
Break this task into a number of shorter tasks over a number of lessons if necessary.

Activity 25 Sound boxes k

Clue	Sound boxes			
Another word for taxi	c	a	b	
PE clothes				
Question				
Perform on stage				
Not the front				
Holds your drink				
A child				
Build houses with these				
Drink that comes from cows				
Have a little to eat				
Throw for a dog to fetch				

Support the child to read the words on the left.
For each word, support the child to work out how many sounds there are in it and write that number in the grey box.
Then ask the child to count out the number of white boxes needed to write the word, so that there is one box for each sound, and colour in any boxes that are not needed.
Next ask the child to say the sounds in the word, one by one, and at the same time write the matching sound spelling in the boxes one by one.
The first one is done for you as an example.
Break this task into a number of shorter tasks over a number of lessons if necessary.

Activity 26 How many sounds? k

Word	Number	Writing the sound spellings				
rock	3	r	o	ck		
brick						
kid						
drink						
clap						
struck						
tank						
clock						
cats						

During this activity the child will be asked to slide sounds in and out of words, i.e. practise phoneme manipulation.
A sound might be swapped, added or taken away.
Print the sound spelling cards onto card and cut out.
Activity:

- Spread out all the sound spelling cards so that the child can see them.
- Build a starting word from the prompt list, demonstrating how to dynamically blend the sounds together as you move the sound spelling cards into place.
- Repeat the word, running your finger under the cards so that it corresponds to the sounds within the word.
- Ask the child to change the word to the next word on the prompt list. As you say the new word run your finger under the cards so that it corresponds with the sound you are saying and the matching sound spelling card.

This gives the child the chance to hear and see what is different.

- The child can then swap the appropriate sounds spelling cards.
- Repeat this technique with the next word on the list.

Activity 29 Sound swap k

Sound swap k

List 1	List 2	List 3
pick	snack	kin
sick	cap	kip
stick	cat	kit
stuck	cast	kits
tuck	cost	kicks
tack	cot	kick
track	cut	
sack	cuts	
snack		

c	k	ck	a
i	o	u	p
s	t	r	n
d			

Support the child to read the words on the left, one by one.
For each word read the clue to the child and then work out what the answer word is.
Explain to the child that they will need to either: add a sound, take away a sound or change a sound to the word on the left to make the answer word, e.g. cot > cost list > lit mat > rat.
Have the child write out the answer word on the right, saying each sound as they write each sound spelling.
An example is done for you.
Break this task into a number of shorter tasks over a number of lessons if necessary.

Activity 30 Sound exchange k

Starting word	Clue	New word
ink	Quickly close one eye	wink
trick	Build houses with these	
clap	Wear this on your head	
sink	Bad smell	
cost	Baby's bed	
stick	Glued down firmly	
kid	PE clothes	
kick	Not well	
clock	Put a key in this	
fact	Perform on stage	

Place a whiteboard in front of the child.
Choose a word from the list below. Randomise the words you choose so that you are choosing words with a variety of number of sounds.
Draw dots on the whiteboard to match the number of sounds in the word, one dot for each sound. Do not write the word or show the word to the child as this is a purely auditory activity.
Say the word to the child and as you do so run your finger under the dots so that your finger matches the appropriate sound dot and its corresponding sound as you say it.
Then cover the dot that corresponds to the sound you are going to take away – use the list below. There are lots more words you could use for this activity – refer to the teacher word list at the start of this chapter.
Ask the child to tell you what is left if you take that sound away.
Take away another sound or choose a new word.
Remember to time limit this activity.

Activity 31 Sound sums k

No. of sounds in starting word	Word	Take away the sound	What is left?
3	can	k (c)	an
3	cat	k (c)	at
3	cup	k (c)	up
3	ink	k	in
3	kit	k	it
4	camp	m	cap
4	cost	s	cot
4	bank	k	ban
4	tank	k	tan
4	black	l	back
4	black	b	lack
4	block	b	lock
4	cluck	k (c)	luck
4	snack	n	sack

No. of sounds in starting word	Word	Take away the sound	What is left?
4	stick	s	tick
4	stick	t	sick
4	stock	t	sock
5	clamp	k (c)	lamp
5	clamp	l	camp
5	clamp	m	clap
5	clamp	p	clam
5	clump	k (c)	lump
5	cramp	k (c)	ramp
5	struck	s	truck
5	blank	l	bank
5	blink	b	link

This set of cards is made up of high frequency words containing the sound 'k'. Copy onto card and cut out. Practise dynamic blending for reading, as described in the 'Working through the programme' section, using these cards. Model this process for the child if necessary.

Activity 32 Reading high frequency words k

duck	back

Starting at 'ink', have the child read each of the words on the shapes as quickly as possible.Support the child to read the words by giving information about sounds and supporting blending do not supply the whole word. Time how long it takes to read all the words to 'desk' and record the time in the box.
Repeat at a later point and see if the child can beat his own time.

Activity 33 Reading race: write away! k

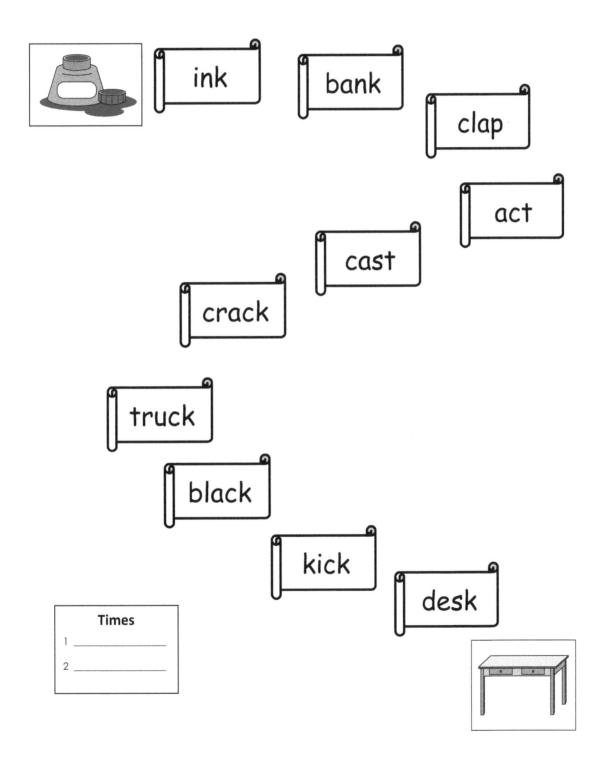

ink

bank

clap

act

cast

crack

truck

black

kick

desk

Times

1 ____________

2 ____________

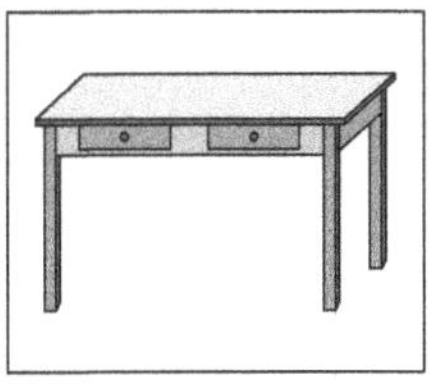

Support the child to read the words one by one.
For each word support the child to think whether there is a 'k' sound in the word.
Have the child put a ring around or highlight just the words that have a 'k' sound.
Remind the child that 'k' can be represented by three sound spellings: **c, k** and **ck**.
Break this task into a number of shorter tasks over a number of lessons if necessary.

Activity 34 Word tracker k

chat	cub	muck	act	much
clock	king	sink	chin	clap
pitch	champ	cost	chips	sick
pack	kid	bank	cats	drink
rock	rich	clip	chip	kit

How many 'k' words did you find? ________

Visual memory is the ability to remember and identify a shape, figure or picture that we have previously seen. Children with poor visual memory may struggle to remember pictures, figures, shapes, letters and numbers and may have difficulties with reading, writing and number work.

Ask the child to look at the word in the yellow box for at least five seconds, covering the white box underneath. Then cover the yellow box so that the word cannot be seen and reveal a choice of words in the white box below. Ask the child to select the word in the white box that matches the one they saw in the yellow box.

Break this task into a number of shorter tasks over a number of lessons if necessary.

Activity 35 Remembering words k

cap
cop cap

kid
kid kit

sack
sock sack

cost
cost cast

mask
mink mask milk

snack
stack smack snack

stick
stick stack stack

Support the child to read the words one by one.
For each word support the child to think whether the word is a real word that makes sense or is a nonsense word.
Have the child put a ring around or highlight just the real words.
Break this task into a number of shorter tasks over a number of lessons if necessary.

Activity 36 Word detective k

dink	milk	casp	kid	rock
chunk	camp	cap	steck	drink
pack	clup	ink	juck	chunk
stink	duck	caz	stack	clock
rock	weck	desk	flock	pank

How many real words did you find? _______

Visual sequential memory is the ability to remember sequences of figures, symbols, pictures and shapes. Children with poor visual sequencing struggle to remember a sequence of letters and follow visual patterns. They may have difficulties writing a sequence of letters to form a word and a sequence of words to form a sentence.

Ask the child to look at the words in the yellow box for at least five seconds, covering the white box underneath. Then cover the yellow box so that the words cannot be seen and reveal the sequence of words in the white box below. Ask the child to remember the missing word from the sequence in the yellow box and write it in the space.

Break this task into a number of shorter tasks over a number of lessons if necessary.

Activity 37 Remembering lots of words k

cub kid
______ kid

back pick
back ______

cat ask rock
______ ask rock

act sink lock
ding ______ thing

desk camp sack
desk camp ______

bank sock fact
bank ______ fact

clump blink track
clump blink ______

Print out on card and cut out the sound spelling and picture cards for each word.
Read though the instructions in the 'Working through the programme' section at the start of this book prior to working with a child.

Activity 38 Word build k

r	o	ck		
c	l	o	ck	
t	r	u	ck	
c	u	b		

c	a	m	p	
k	i	t		
s	i	n	k	

Support the child to read the words on the list one by one.
For each word support the child to think about each of the sounds in the word and their matching sound spellings.
Have the child put a ring around or highlight the sound spelling for each sound.
Break this task into a number of shorter tasks over a number of lessons if necessary.

Activity 39 Word tech k

back
clap
brick
sink
act
truck
drink
clock
kid

Read the clue on the left for the child.
For each clue support the child to work out what the answer word is.
The sound spellings for the answer word are given to help, but they are mixed up – an anagram.
Have the child use the sound spellings to write the answer word on the line on the right.
Encourage the child to say the associated sound as he writes each sound spelling.
Break this task into a number of shorter tasks over a number of lessons if necessary.

Activity 40 Word scramble k

Clue	Sound spellings	Word
Says, "Quack, quack"!	d **ck** u	duck
Not well	**ck** i s	________
Says, "Miaow!"	a t c	________
Put up a tent	a m p c	________
Army car	n t k a	________
Hat	p c a	________
Tells the time	l o c **ck**	________
________ the ball	**ck** k i	________
Big stone	**ck** r o	________
Thirsty? Have a	d i k n r	________
Close with a key	**ck** o l	________
Big van	r **ck** u t	________

Activity 42 Spelling challenge k

can	c a n	c a n	___ ___ ___	________
cat	c a t	c a n	___ ___ ___	________
kid	k i d	k i d	___ ___ ___	________
desk	d e s k	d e s k	___ ___ ___ ___	________
back	b a ck	b a ck	___ ___ ___	________
duck	d u ck	d u ck	___ ___ ___	________
black	b l a ck	b l a ck	___ ___ ___ ___	________

Support the child to read the sentence and for each spot the spelling mistake. Remember to refer to the term 'accepted' spelling rather than the 'right' or 'correct' spelling.
Have the child underline the mistake and then write the accepted spelling on the line underneath.
If the child is able then the whole sentence could be written out.
Note that the sentences may include high frequency words which contain sounds that the child has not yet encountered in the programme. Support the child to decode these words by supplying information about the unfamiliar sound and its sound spelling and encourage the child to blend for reading.
Break this task into a number of shorter tasks over a number of lessons if necessary.

Activity 43 Oops! Correct the spelling k

12. The duk sat on the pond.

____

13. Jan put a cup on the desc.

____

14. I had a snak on the mat.

____

15. In spring Tom went to kamp.

____

16. Ben put the briks in a stack.

____

17. I drink milc.

____

Support the child to read each sentence, notice that there is a word missing and think what it might be. The missing word is written underneath in two ways. Remember both spellings are technically correct but only one is the 'accepted' spelling. Refer to the 'Working through the programme' section at the start of this book for an explanation of this term if you need further information.

Ask the child to choose the accepted spelling and write it on the line within the sentence.

Encourage the child to say the sound as they write the associated sound spelling.

Note that the sentences include some high frequency words which contain sounds that the child has not yet encountered in the programme. Support the child to decode these words by supplying information about any unfamiliar sound and its sound spelling and encourage the child to blend for reading. Some sound spellings are highlighted to support this.

Break this task into a number of shorter tasks over a number of lessons if necessary.

Activity 44 Spot the spelling k

1. A clock ____________ .

   tics ticks

2. The hens ____________ in the grass.

   pek peck

3. I can see a ____________ on the pond.

   duck duc

4. Gran had a ____________ cat.

   blac black

5. I cut my leg on a ____________.

   rock rok

6. The dog picked up the ____________.

   stick stic

7. I like to drink ____________.

   milck milk

Support the child to read the sentences.
Explain that the sentences are OK but that they are very short and could be a bit more interesting!
Then support the child to read the phrases at the bottom of the page and decide which could be used to make each sentence 'better' or 'more interesting'.
Ask the child to write out the sentence, adding the new phrase from the list. Encourage the child to say the sounds at the same time as writing the associated sound spelling when writing each word.
Note that the sentences include high frequency words which contain sounds that the child has not yet encountered in the programme. Support the child to decode these words by supplying information about any unfamiliar sounds and sound spellings and encourage the child to blend for reading. Some sound spellings are highlighted to support this.
Break this task into a number of shorter tasks over a number of lessons if necessary

Activity 45 Making better sentences k

1. Sam kick**ed** the b**all**.

____

____

2. The hen was with a chick.

____

____

3. Rav put his cap on the desk.

____

____

4. The clock went 'tick, tock'.

____

____

5. Jan drank the milk.

____

____

and had a snack into the back of the net and th**ey** peck**ed** the grass	and Dan sat on it then struck ten o'clock

Support the child to read each sentence one by one.
Ask the child to re-read the sentence, several times if necessary, and try to remember it.
Then cover the sentence and ask the child to recall the sentence verbally.
Once they can do this confidently, ask the child to write out the sentence from memory.

When writing a word, encourage the child to say the sound as they write each associated sound spelling.
When the word is complete then they are to say the whole word.
When the sentence is complete the child reads out their sentence and then compares it to the original.
Note that the sentences may include high frequency words which contain sounds that the child has not yet encountered in the programme. Support the child to decode these words by supplying information about any unfamiliar sounds and their sound spellings and encouraging the child to blend for reading. Some of these sound spellings are highlighted to help the child when writing the words later.

Alternatively, using text to speech software, the child could type the sentence, with the computer reading back each word and then the completed sentence.

Activity 46 Writing challenge k

Kids, stop at the stack of sticks.

Jack can kick the bricks.

I cut the soft sack.

Beth had crisps for snack.

Answers

k

Page 194
Activity 8 Investigating the sound 'k'

c
cab cat camp cloth

k
king sink bank kid drink

ck
back stick sack brick black snack

Page 211
Activity 25 Sound boxes

k i t
a s k
a c t
b a ck
c u p
k i d
b r i ck
m i l k
s n a ck
s t i ck

Page 212
Activity 26 How many sounds?

4 b r i ck
3 k i d
5 d r i n k
4 c l a p
5 s t r u ck
4 t a n k
4 c l o ck
4 c a t s

Page 215
Activity 30 Sound exchange

trick – brick
clap – cap
sink – stink
cost – cot
stick – stuck
kid – kit
clock – lock
fact – act

Page 220
Activity 34 Word tracker

cub muck act
clock king sink clap
cost sick
pack kid bank cats drink
rock clip kit

17

Page 223
Activity 36 Word detective

milk kid rock
chunk camp cap drink
pack ink chunk
stink duck stack clock
rock desk flock

17

Page 228
Activity 39 Word tech

c l a p
b r i ck
s i n k
a c t
t r u ck
d r i n k
c l o ck
k i d

Page 229
Activity 40 Word scramble

sick
cat
camp
tank
cap
clock
kick
rock
drink
lock
truck

Page 231
Activity 43 Oops! Correct the spelling

duck
desk
snack
camp
bricks
milk

Page 232
Activity 44 Spot the spelling

ticks
peck
duck
black
rock
stick
milk

Page 233
Activity 45 Making better sentences

1. Sam kicked the ball into the back of the net.
2. The hen was with a chick and they pecked the grass.
3. Rav put his cap on the desk and Dan sat on it.
4. The clock went 'tick tock' then struck ten o'clock.
5. Jan drank the milk and had a snack.

SECTION 6

qu

qu

quit

Words with the sounds 'kw' represented by qu

squid
quack
quench
quest
quick
quid
quilt
quin
quip
quit
quiz

High frequency words
Containing sounds / sound spellings not yet encountered in the programme

quite	**qu** i t e	the 'i-e' sound is represented by the sound spelling **i-e**
queen	**qu** ee n	the 'ee' sound is represented by the sound spelling **ee**
quiet	**qu** i e t	2 syllable word with an 'i-e' sound represented by the sound spelling **i**

Auditory discrimination is the ability to hear differences between sounds. Good auditory discrimination helps us to recognise and identify the sounds in words and so interpret them correctly. Children with poor auditory discrimination may confuse sounds and misinterpret things they have heard. Their spelling and writing may reflect their confusion over which sounds they heard in a word. **Auditory attention and tracking** is the ability to actively listen and follow auditory information from beginning to end. Good auditory attention and tracking helps us to follow a conversation, a story read out loud or a set of instructions, and enables us to focus on key information. Children with poor auditory attention and tracking may find it difficult to follow and respond appropriately to what is being said to them.

This story contains lots of words that contain the sound 'kw' represented by the sound spelling **qu**.
Read the story out loud to the child or group of children. Encourage the child to listen carefully and spot any word that contains the target sound. When a target word has been read, the child indicates that they have heard and spotted it by tapping the table, putting up a hand or any other agreed signal, but without shouting out. Stop reading and discuss the word, making any error correction necessary. If a word is missed, re-read the sentence.
Do not show the written story to the child. The target words are highlighted below for you.

Activity 1 Sound target story qu

Ayesha was queen of the forest. Her father, the old king, set her a quest to find the golden quilt. No one had seen it for hundreds of years.

She set off one quiet morning, eager to reach the edge of the forest as quickly as possible.

At midday she stopped by a stream to drink and quench her thirst. On she traveled for the rest of the day until she was quite exhausted.

Just when she was ready to quit, she heard magical music in the air. She followed it for what seemed like hours. Then stretched out on the branches of a tree she saw the golden light of the quilt. "Only a true queen can find this quilt," said a magical voice.

"Hale Queen Ayesha!"

This activity results in the child learning about the sound spelling qu. The letter q is usually followed by the letter u and they represent two sounds 'k' and 'w'. Since q and u are always seen together they are usually treated as one sound spelling qu which represents 'kw'. There is no need to explain this in detail to the child, simply present qu as a picture of 'kw'.

Support the child to read the words one by one.
For each word support the child to work out the sound spelling corresponding to the sound 'kw' and highlight it.
There is just one sound spelling to find: **qu**.
In the box underneath write the sound spelling **qu** as the heading on the small line at the top of the box.
Then work through the word list and write the remainder of the words in the box, noting the **qu** sound spelling.
Encourage the child to say each sound as they write each sound spelling in sequence, e.g. say 'kw' 'i' 'd' as they write **qu i d**.

Break this task into a number of shorter tasks over a number of lessons if necessary.

Activity 8 Investigating the sound qu

quid	squid	quick
quack	quiz	quit
quest	quin	quilt

Activity 10 Sound spelling cards qu

Visual discrimination is the ability to see differences between objects and figures that are similar. Good visual discrimination helps keep us from getting confused when looking at shapes and forms in the environment. Children with poor visual discrimination may find it difficult to recognise letters, may confuse letters such as b and d and may find it difficult to identify mathematical symbols.

Ask the child to look at the sound spelling in the yellow box then track along the row looking at the other sound spellings.
The child indicates or puts a ring around the sound spelling that is the same as the one in the yellow box.
This includes some sound spellings which represent other sounds but are visually similar.

Break this task into a number of shorter tasks over a number of lessons if necessary.

Activity 11 Sound spelling tracker sh th ng qu

qu	ng	qu	u	g
sh	ch	tch	sh	th
th	th	sh	tch	ch
ng	qu	g	n	ng
qu	u	g	qu	ng
ng	qu	ng	u	g
th	sh	th	tch	ch
sh	s	ch	th	sh

Visual memory is the ability to remember and identify a shape or picture that we have previously seen. Children with poor visual memory may struggle to remember pictures, figures, shapes, letters and numbers and may have difficulties with reading, writing and number work.

Ask the child to look at the sound spelling in the yellow box for at least five seconds, covering the white box underneath. Then cover the yellow box so that the sound spelling cannot be seen and reveal the choice of sound spellings in the white box below. Ask the child to select the matching sound spelling from the white box.

Break this task into a number of shorter tasks over a number of lessons if necessary.

Activity 12 Remembering sound spellings qu

qu
qu ng

ng
n ng

tch
ch tch th

qu
u n qu

ch
ch ck th

qu
u qu n

sh
ch sh th

Form constancy is the ability to generalise forms and figures and identify them even if they are slightly different from that usually seen. This skill helps us distinguish differences in size, shape and orientation or position. Children with poor form constancy may frequently reverse letters and numbers.

Ask the child to look at the letter on the left and match to a letter on the right (written differently), drawing a line to connect each.

Activity 14 Which is the same? sh th ng ch qu

ng	th
qu	sh
th	ng
tch	ch
sh	qu
ch	tch

Visual closure is the ability to identify an object, shape or symbol from a visually incomplete or disorganised presentation and to see where the different parts of a whole fit together, i.e. to recognise something when seeing only part of it. This skill helps us understand things quickly because our visual system doesn't have to process every detail to recognise what we're seeing.

Ask the child to look at the sound spelling in the white box then track left to right along the row.
Ask the child to indicate or put a ring around the sound spelling that is the same as that in the white box.
This covers some of the sounds spellings recently discovered.

Break this task into a number of shorter tasks over a number of lessons if necessary.

Activity 15 Bits missing qu

qu	ng	qu	u
ng	qu	u	ng
ch	ch	sh	th
qu	u	qu	ng
tch	th	ch	tch
th	tch	th	ch
qu	qu	ng	g
sh	ch	sh	th

Figure gound is the ability to find patterns or shapes when hidden within a busy background without getting confused by surrounding images. This skill keeps children from getting lost in the details, for example when looking at pictures in books or reading. Children with poor figure ground become easily confused with too much print on the page, affecting their concentration and attention.

Ask the child to look at the sound spellings, which are overlapping. Ask the child to first find and count all the **sh** sound spellings (refer to the sound not the letter names), then the **qu** etc. The child records how many of each sound spelling are found.

Break this task into a number of shorter tasks over a number of lessons if necessary.

Activity 16 Busy sound spellings sh th ng ch ck qu

How many?

qu	ng	ch
sh	th	ck

Spatial relations is the ability to perceive the position of objects in relation to ourselves and to each other. This skill helps children to understand relationships between symbols and letters. Children with poor spatial relations may find it difficult to write letters in the correct orientation, write consistently starting at the margin and write letters of the same size.

In the first part, ask the child to copy the sound spellings on the lines below in exactly the same places as they appear above.
In the second part, ask the child to copy the words on the lines below in exactly the same places, saying the matching sound as they write each sound spelling. Note that the sound spellings are for the sounds 'qu', 'u' and 'n', which are visually similar.

Break this task into a number of shorter tasks over a number of lessons if necessary.

Activity 17 Where am I? qu

qu u n qu

u qu u u u u

quit quiz

quack quest

Visual sequential memory is the ability to remember sequences of figures, symbols and shapes. Children with poor visual sequencing struggle to remember a sequence of letters and follow visual patterns. They may have difficulties writing a sequence of letters to form a word and a sequence of words to form a sentence.

Ask the child to look at the sound spellings in the yellow box for at least five seconds, covering the white box underneath. Then cover the yellow box so that the sound spellings cannot be seen and reveal the sequence of sound spellings in the white box below. Ask the child to remember the missing sound spelling and write it in the space.

Break this task into a number of shorter tasks over a number of lessons if necessary.

Activity 18 Remembering lots of sound spellings — sh th ng ch qu

qu tch
___ tch

ng sh
ng ___

ch ng th
ch ng ___

ch qu ng
ch ___ ng

th ng qu
th ___ qu

qu ch ng
___ ch ng

sh th qu
sh ___ qu

Having introduced the sounds and their corresponding sound spellings, it is important that the child is given the opportunity to practise writing them.
In this activity the child can practise forming the sound spellings in a number of ways:

- copying over the grey letters which act as a guide to accurate letter formation,
- writing individual sound spellings within small boxes (with shading to act as a guide), which develops visual-spatial awareness of the letters and
- writing words with a sound spelling in each box.

Encourage the child to say the sound at the same time as writing the sound spelling.

Activity 19 Writing sound spellings sh th ng qu

sh sh sh sh sh

sh sh sh sh sh sh sh

th th th th th

th th th th th th th

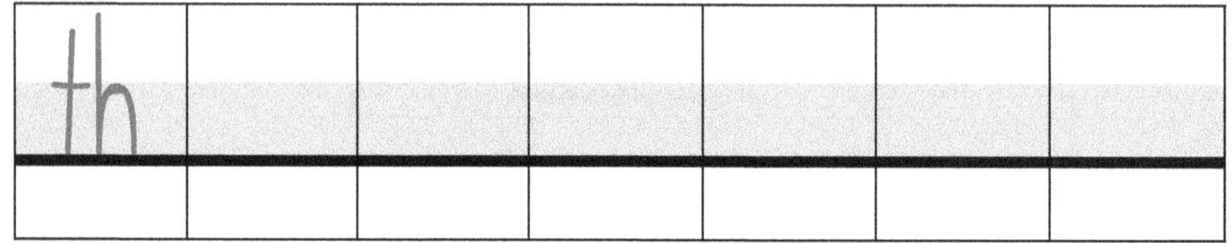

ng ng ng ng ng

ng ng ng ng ng ng ng

ng						

qu qu qu qu qu

qu qu qu qu qu qu qu

qu						

w	i	sh

sh	i	p

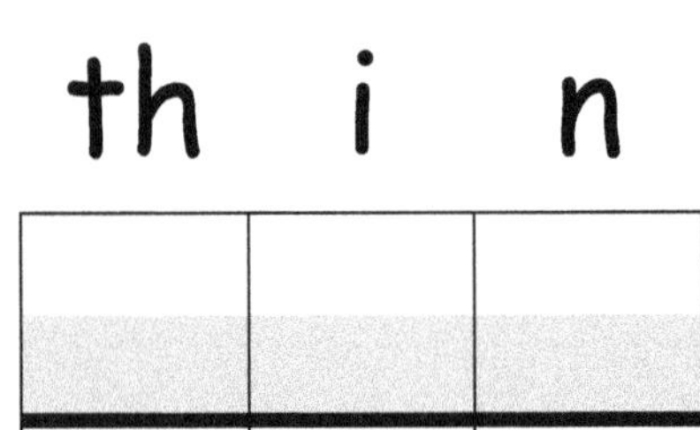

w i th

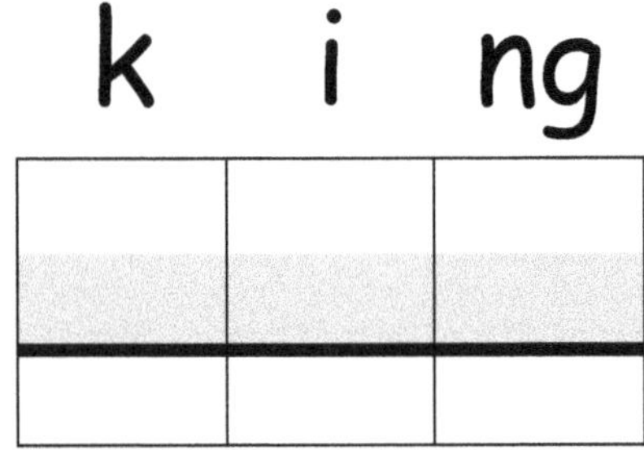

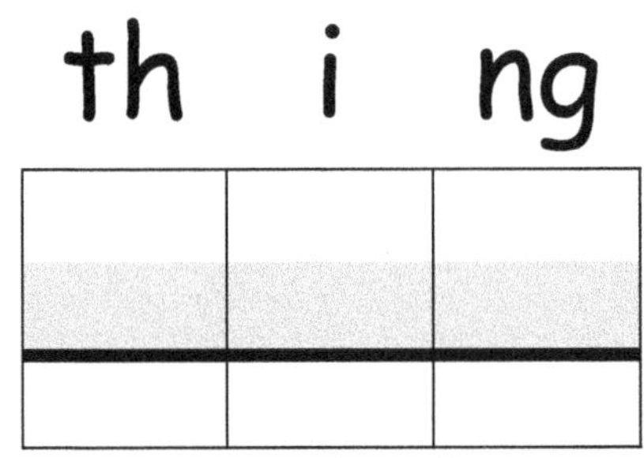

qu i t

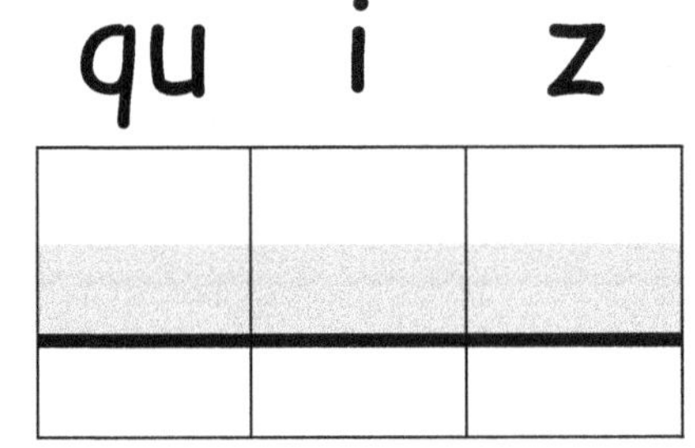

qu i l t

This set of cards is made of up words containing the sound 'kw' represented by the sound spelling **qu**. The sound spelling for the target sound in each word is highlighted. Copy onto card and cut out. Practise dynamic blending for reading, as described in the 'Working through the programme' section, using these cards. Model this process for the child if necessary.

Activity 20 Dynamic blending – word cards qu

quiz	quit
quid	quin
quick	quest
quack	quilt
quench	

This set of cards is made of up words containing the sound 'kw' represented by the sound spelling **qu.** Copy onto card and cut out.
Practise dynamic blending for reading, as described in the 'Working through the programme' section, using these cards. Model this process for the child if necessary.

Activity 20 Dynamic blending – word cards qu

quiz	quit
quid	quin
quick	quest
quilt	quack
quench	

Print out onto card and cut out.
Stack them with the biggest (the complete word) on the bottom and in decreasing size so that the smallest is on the top.
Make sure the left-hand edge of the cards are flush. Staple the cards together on the left-hand side.
When the child runs a finger over the cards the sound spellings flip up. Ask the child to say the sounds and match to the flips.

staple

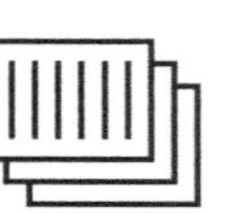

Activity 24 Flippies for the sounds 'kw' represented by the sound spelling qu

s	s qu	s qu i	s qu i d
qu	qu a	qu a ck	
qu	qu i	qu i ck	
qu	qu i	qu i z	
qu	qu e	qu e s	qu e s t

During this activity the child will be asked to slide sounds in and out of words, i.e. practise phoneme manipulation.
A sound might be swapped, added or taken away.
Print the sound spelling cards onto card and cut out.
Activity:

- Spread out all the sound spelling cards so that the child can see them.
- Build a starting word from the prompt list, demonstrating how to dynamically blend the sounds together as you move the sound spelling cards into place.
- Repeat the word, running your finger under the cards so that it corresponds to the sounds within the word.
- Ask the child to change the word to the next word on the prompt list. As you say the new word run your finger under the cards so that it corresponds with the sound you are saying and the matching sound spelling card.

This gives the child the chance to hear and see what is different.

- The child can then swap the appropriate sounds spelling cards.
- Repeat this technique with the next word on the list.

Activity 29 Sound swap qu

Sound swap qu

List 1

quilt

quit

quiz

quick

quid

squid

qu	ck	i	l
t	z	d	s

Support the child to read the words on the left, one by one.
For each word read the clue to the child and then work out what the answer word is.
Explain to the child that they will need to either: add a sound, take away a sound or change a sound to the word on the left to make the answer word, e.g. cot > cost list > lit mat > rat.
Have the child write out the answer word on the right, saying each sound as they write each sound spelling.
An example is done for you.
Break this task into a number of shorter tasks over a number of lessons if necessary.

Activity 30 Sound exchange qu

Starting word	Clue	New word
quip	Puzzle competition	quiz
squid	A pound	
quit	Bed cover	
quick	Duck noise	
quin	Give up	
quests	Adventure	

Place a whiteboard in front of the child.
Choose a word from the list below. Randomise the words you choose so that you are choosing words with a variety of number of sounds.
Draw dots on the whiteboard to match the number of sounds in the word, one dot for each sound. Do not write the word or show the word to the child as this is a purely auditory activity.
Say the word to the child and as you do so run your finger under the dots so that your finger matches the appropriate sound dot and its corresponding sound as you say it.
Then cover the dot that corresponds to the sound you are going to take away – use the list below.
Ask the child to tell you what is left if you take that sound away.
Take away another sound or choose a new word.
Remember to time limit this activity.

Activity 31 Sound sums qu

No. of sounds in starting word	Word	Take away the sound	What is left?
3	quit	qu	it
3	quin	qu	in
3	quiz	qu	'iz' is
4	quilt	l	quit
4	quilt	t	'quil' quill
4	squid	s	quid

Starting at 'quiz', have the child read each of the words on the shapes as quickly as possible.
Support the child to read the words by giving information about sounds and supporting blending but do not supply the whole word.
Time how long it takes to read all the words to 'quit' and record the time in the box.
Repeat at a later point and see if the child can beat his own time.

Activity 33 Reading race: quiz quest qu

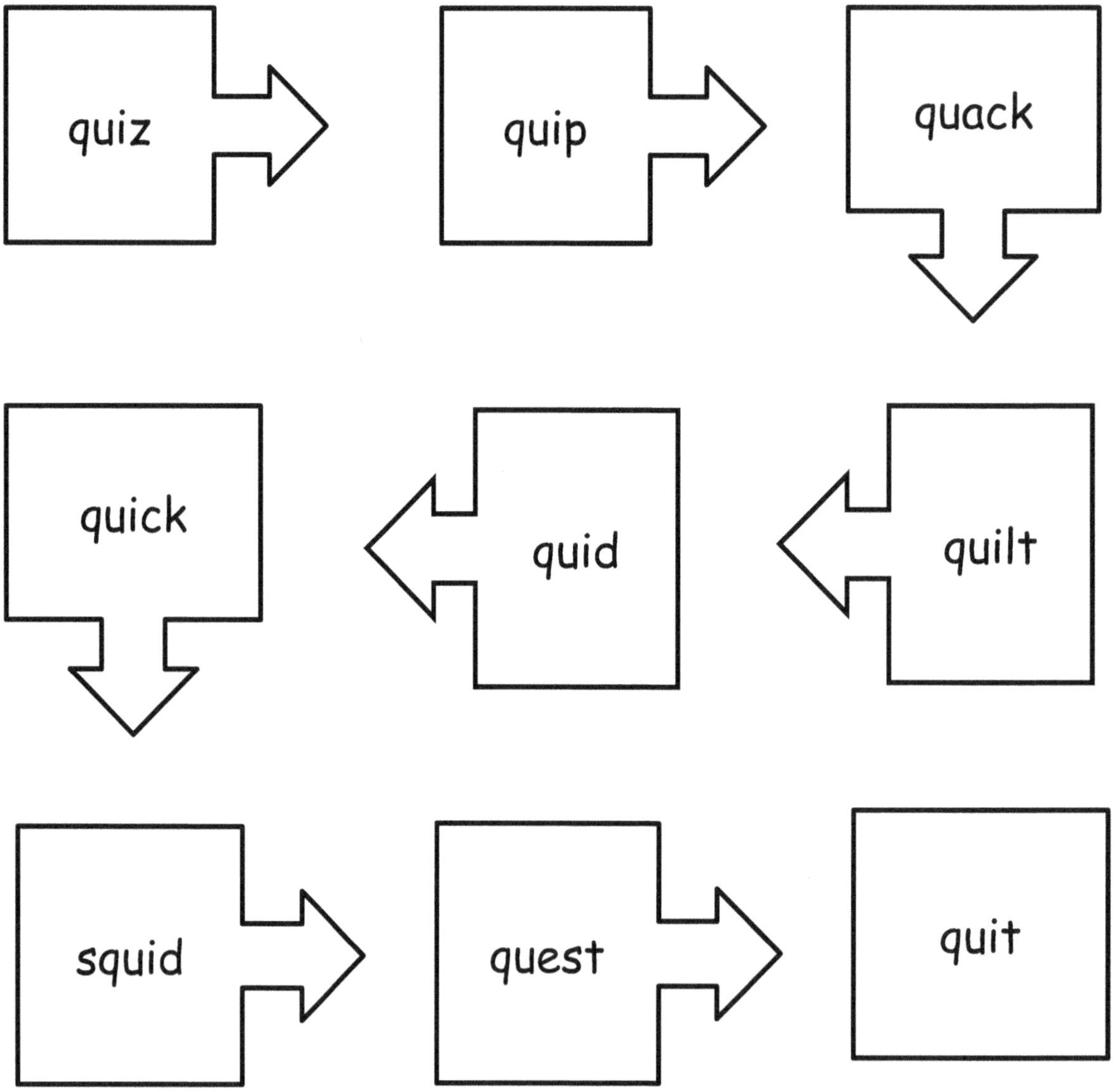

quiz → quip → quack ↓

quick ↓ ← quid ← quilt

squid → quest → quit

Times

1 ______________

2 ______________

Support the child to read the words one by one.
For each word support the child to think whether there is a 'qu' sound in the word.
Have the child put a ring around or highlight just the words that have a 'qu' sound.
Break this task into a number of shorter tasks over a number of lessons if necessary.

Activity 34 Word tracker qu

duck	quack	quid	scat	quiz
quit	sunk	skin	quest	mask
quick	crash	squid	king	scratch
send	clash	quilt	stick	quip
slip	quin	desk	quench	pitch

How many 'qu' words did you find? ________

Visual memory is the ability to remember and identify a shape, figure or picture that we have previously seen. Children with poor visual memory may struggle to remember pictures, figures, shapes, letters and numbers and may have difficulties with reading, writing and number work.

Ask the child to look at the word in the yellow box for at least five seconds, covering the white box underneath. Then cover the yellow box so that the word cannot be seen and reveal a choice of words in the white box below. Ask the child to select the word in the white box that matches the one they saw in the yellow box.

Break this task into a number of shorter tasks over a number of lessons if necessary.

Activity 35 Remembering words qu

quit
quit quid

quiz
quip quiz

quid
quip quid

quilt
quilt quit

squid
quid quit squid

quack
quick quack quilt

quench
quest quick quench

Support the child to read the words one by one.
For each word support the child to think whether the word is a real word that makes sense or is a nonsense word.
Have the child put a ring around or highlight just the real words.
Break this task into a number of shorter tasks over a number of lessons if necessary.

Activity 36 Word detective qu

quib	quit	quag	quench	quop
quet	quack	quesk	quock	quest
quilt	quilk	quiz	quom	quid
quop	quen	quask	quick	quot

How many real words did you find? ________

Visual sequential memory is the ability to remember sequences of figures, symbols, pictures and shapes. Children with poor visual sequencing struggle to remember a sequence of letters and follow visual patterns. They may have difficulties writing a sequence of letters to form a word and a sequence of words to form a sentence.

Ask the child to look at the words in the yellow box for at least five seconds, covering the white box underneath. Then cover the yellow box so that the words cannot be seen and reveal the sequence of words in the white box below. Ask the child to remember the missing word from the sequence in the yellow box and write it in the space.

Break this task into a number of shorter tasks over a number of lessons if necessary.

Activity 37 Remembering lots of words qu

quid quit quip
quid ______ quip

quiz quin quit
______ quin quit

quick	quack	quest
quick	quack	______

quilt	quench	squid
quilt	______	squid

Print out on card and cut out the sound spelling and picture cards for each word.
Read though the instructions in the 'Working through the programme' section at the start of this book prior to working with a child.

Activity 38 Word build qu

qu	i	d		
qu	i	t		
qu	i	z		
qu	i	ck		

s	qu	i	d	
qu	i	l	t	
qu	e	s	t	

Support the child to read the words on the list one by one.
For each word support the child to think about each of the sounds in the word and their matching sound spellings.
Have the child put a ring around or highlight the sound spelling for each sound.
Break this task into a number of shorter tasks over a number of lessons if necessary.

Activity 39 Word tech qu

quid
squid
quit
quick
quilt
quack
quest
quiz
quid

Read the clue on the left for the child.
For each clue support the child to work out what the answer word is.
The sound spellings for the answer word are given to help, but they are mixed up – an anagram.
Have the child use the sound spellings to write the answer word on the line on the right.
Encourage the child to say the associated sound as he writes each sound spelling.
Break this task into a number of shorter tasks over a number of lessons if necessary.

Activity 40 Word scramble qu

Clue	Sound spellings	Word
What a duck says...	qu ck a	quack
Bed cover	qu i t l	______
A pound	d i qu	______
Give up	i qu t	______
Questions game	z i qu	______
An adventure	t e qu s	______
Fast	ck qu i	______
Sea animal	d i qu s	______

Activity 42 Spelling challenge qu

quit	qu i t	qu i t	___ ___ ___	___________
quid	qu i d	qu i d	___ ___ ___	___________
quiz	qu i z	qu i z	___ ___ ___	___________
quick	qu i **ck**	qu i ck	___ ___ ___	___________
quack	qu a **ck**	qu a ck	___ ___ ___	___________
quest	qu e s t	qu e s t	___ ___ ___ ___	___________
quench	qu e n **ch**	qu e n ch	___ ___ ___ ___	___________

Support the child to read each sentence, notice that there is a word missing and think what it might be. The missing word is written underneath in two ways. Remember both spellings are technically correct but only one is the 'accepted' spelling. Refer to the 'Working through the programme' section at the start of this book for an explanation of this term if you need further information.

Ask the child to choose the accepted spelling and write it on the line within the sentence. Encourage the child to say the sound as they write the associated sound spelling.

Note that the sentences include some high frequency words which contain sounds that the child has not yet encountered in the programme. Support the child to decode these words by supplying information about any unfamiliar sound and its sound spelling and encourage the child to blend for reading. Some sound spellings are highlighted to support this.

Break this task into a number of shorter tasks over a number of lessons if necessary.

Activity 44 Spot the spelling qu

1. Tom went on a ____________ to find the ring.
   quest quilt

2. The ____________ was soft and warm.
   quick quilt

3. The ducks said ____________ when we fed them.
   quick quack

4. Jan had a drink to ____________ her thirst.
   quench quest

5. Sam ____________ the football team.
   quit quilt

6. We came first in the ____________.
   quid quiz

Support the child to read the sentences.
Explain that the sentences are OK but that they are very short and could be a bit more interesting!
Then support the child to read the phrases at the bottom of the page and decide which could be used to make each sentence 'better' or 'more interesting'.
Ask the child to write out the sentence, adding the new phrase from the list. Encourage the child to say the sounds at the same time as writing the associated sound spelling when writing each word.
Note that the sentences include high frequency words which contain sounds that the child has not yet encountered in the programme. Support the child to decode these words by supplying information about any unfamiliar sounds and sound spellings and encourage the child to blend for reading. Some sound spellings are highlighted to support this.
Break this task into a number of shorter tasks over a number of lessons if necessary.

Activity 45 Making better sentences qu

1. The duck s**ai**d "quack".

____

____

2. Sam quit.

____

____

3. "I am quick," s**ai**d Tom.

____

____

4. The lads set o**ff** on a quest.

____

____

5. Jan went to the quiz.

____

____

and jump**ed** into the pond	to find the magic land
but Jan ask**ed** him back	as he ran for the bus
and won a quid	

Support the child to read each sentence one by one.
Ask the child to re-read the sentence, several times if necessary, and try to remember it.
Then cover the sentence and ask the child to recall the sentence verbally.
Once they can do this confidently, ask the child to write out the sentence from memory.

When writing a word, encourage the child to say the sound as they write each associated sound spelling.
When the word is complete then they are to say the whole word.
When the sentence is complete the child reads out their sentence and then compares it to the original.
Note that the sentences may include high frequency words which contain sounds that the child has not yet encountered in the programme. Support the child to decode these words by supplying information about any unfamiliar sounds and their sound spellings and encouraging the child to blend for reading. Some of these sound spellings are highlighted to help the child when writing the words later.

Alternatively, using text to speech software, the child could type the sentence, with the computer reading back each word and then the completed sentence.

Activity 46 Writing challenge qu

Sam had to quit.

Rav can run fast and is quick.

The bag cost ten quid.

The quest was long and Tom got lost.

Answers qu

Page 263 **Activity 34 Word tracker**	Page 266 **Activity 36 Word detective**	Page 271 **Activity 39 Word tech**
quack quid quiz quit quest quick squid quilt quip quin quench 11	quit quench quack quest quilt quiz quid quick 8	s qu i d qu i t qu i ck qu i l t qu a ck qu e s t qu i z qu i d
Page 272 **Activity 40 Word scramble**	Page 274 **Activity 44 Spot the spelling**	Page 275 **Activity 45 Making better sentences**
quilt quid quit quiz quest quick squid	quest quilt quack quench quit quiz	1. The duck said "quack" and jumped into the pond. 2. Sam quit, but Jan asked him back. 3. "I am quick," said Tom as he ran for the bus. 4. The lads set off on a quest to find the magic land. 5. Jan went to the quiz and won a quid.

SECTION 7

f

f fun

ff sniff

ph graph

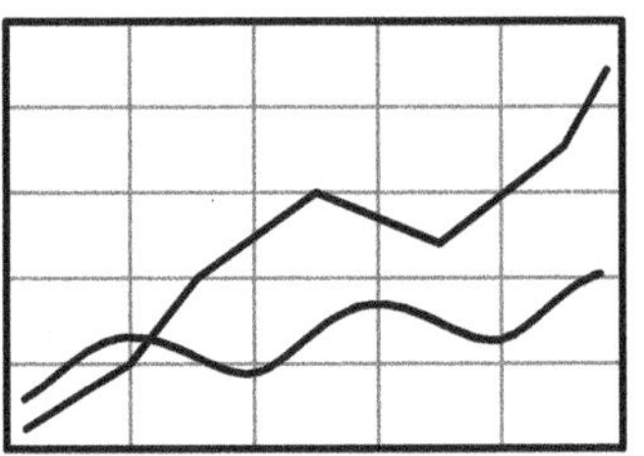

Words with an 'f' sound – word list of 1 syllable words

f

3 sounds

aft
fab
fad
fan
fang
fat
fed
fen
fez
fib
fig
fin
fit
fox
fun
oft

4 sounds

fact
fast
felt
fist
flab
flan
flap
flash
flat
fled
flip
flit
flog
flop
font
frog
from
fund
left
lift
raft
rift
self
shelf

5 sounds

craft
draft
drift
flank
frost

ff

2 sounds

off

3 sounds

biff
cuff
huff
puff
riff
ruff
tiff
toff

4 sounds

bluff
cliff
fluff
scoff
scuff
sniff
staff
stiff
stuff

5 sounds

scruff

ph

4 sounds

graph
phlox

gh

3 sounds

rough
tough

High frequency words

Containing sounds / sound spellings not yet encountered in the programme

phone	**ph** o n e	the 'o-e' sound is represented by the sound spelling **o-e** *the ph sound spelling mostly occurs in multisyllable words*
rough tough	r **ou gh** t **ou gh**	these words contain the 'f' sound but also note the 'u' sound is represented by the sound spelling **ou**

Auditory discrimination is the ability to hear differences between sounds. Good auditory discrimination helps us to recognise and identify the sounds in words and so interpret them correctly. Children with poor auditory discrimination may confuse sounds and misinterpret things they have heard. Their spelling and writing may reflect their confusion over which sounds they heard in a word. **Auditory attention and tracking** is the ability to actively listen and follow auditory information from beginning to end. Good auditory attention and tracking helps us to follow a conversation, a story read out loud or a set of instructions, and enables us to focus on key information. Children with poor auditory attention and tracking may find it difficult to follow and respond appropriately to what is being said to them.

This story contains lots of words that contain the sound 'f', which is the 'target' sound.
Read the story out loud to the child or group of children. Encourage the child to listen carefully and spot any word that contains the target sound. When a target word has been read, the child indicates that they have heard and spotted it by tapping the table, putting up a hand or any other agreed signal, but without shouting out. Stop reading and discuss the word, making any error correction necessary. If a word is missed, re-read the sentence. Do not show the written story to the child. The target words are highlighted below for you.

Activity 1 Sound target story f

Foxes are related to dogs. They have a pointed face, large ears and a full, fluffy tail. Their fur is usually a reddy brown colour with white under the belly and on the feet.

Foxes are frequently seen living close to us in towns and cities. Having large fangs and sharp claws, they can look very fierce but mostly they keep out of our way.

In towns and cities, foxes mostly sniff out scraps of food left by people and often will flip over bins to find tasty morsels. They like to feast on leftover fish and chips and burgers.

In the country, foxes have to hunt for their food to survive. They take chickens as well as wild food such as mice and birds. This makes them very unpopular with farmers.

Auditory discrimination is the ability to hear differences between sounds. Good auditory discrimination helps us to recognise and identify the sounds in words and so interpret them correctly. Children with poor auditory discrimination may confuse sounds and misinterpret things they have heard. Their spelling and writing may reflect their confusion over what sounds they heard in a word. **Auditory sequential memory** is the ability to remember and recall a series of things that they have heard. Children with poor auditory sequential memory may find it difficult to remember information given earlier in a conversation or set of instructions and may struggle to recall the sequence of sounds in a word.

The silly sentences contain lots of words containing the sound 'f'.
Read the sentence to the child several times, invite them to join in as you say it and gradually recall it on their own.
Do not show the words to the child.
Ask them to say it as quickly as they can and have some fun with it. Perhaps they can make up their own?
The sentences gradually get longer and more complex.
Break this task into a number of shorter tasks over a number of lessons if necessary.

Activity 2 Tongue twister fun f

Fifty flopping frogs.

Flo fixes funny flutes.

Fast foxes have furry feet.

Fussy fleas fly from fluffy friends.

Auditory discrimination is the ability to hear differences between sounds. Good auditory discrimination helps us to recognise and identify the sounds in words and so interpret them correctly. Children with poor auditory discrimination may confuse sounds and misinterpret things they have heard. Their spelling and writing may reflect their confusion over which sounds they heard in a word. **Auditory attention and tracking** is the ability to actively listen and follow auditory information from beginning to end. Good auditory attention and tracking helps us to follow a conversation, a story read out loud or a set of instructions, and enables us to focus on key information. Children with poor auditory attention and tracking may find it difficult to follow and respond appropriately to what is being said to them.

Read out the words and ask the child to identify the odd one out. In 1–10 the child focuses on the sound at the **beginning** of the words and in 11–20 the child focuses on the sound at the **end** of the words.
Do not show the words to the child. The odd one out is highlighted for you.
Break this task into a number of shorter tasks over a number of lessons if necessary.

Activity 3 Odd one out f

1.	wet	fit	win	2.	can	fan	cat
3.	fed	dad	fun	4.	fox	ran	run
5.	lamp	list	felt	6.	grab	from	felt
7.	fast	desk	damp	8.	stop	frog	spot
9.	crash	crush	flash	10.	drift	frost	drink
11.	off	if	up	12.	will	biff	tell
13.	man	sun	tiff	14.	cuff	cash	rush
15.	brush	crash	stuff	16.	stand	cliff	send
17.	trust	fluff	plant	18.	graph	moth	path
19.	stick	track	scruff	20.	bring	sniff	thing

Auditory discrimination is the ability to hear differences between sounds. Good auditory discrimination helps us to recognise and identify the sounds in words and so interpret them correctly. Children with poor auditory discrimination may confuse sounds and misinterpret things they have heard. Their spelling and writing may reflect their confusion over which sounds they heard in a word. **Auditory recall memory** is the ability to remember and recall something that they have just heard. Children with poor auditory recall memory may find it difficult to remember sounds and words and respond appropriately.

Read the list of words below clearly, asking the child to listen carefully. At random points tap the table and stop reading, asking the child to remember and say the last word you said. Then ask them to tell you what the **first** or the **last** sound in the word is.

Break this task into a number of shorter tasks over a number of lessons if necessary.

Activity 4 What sound am I? f

1.	if	up	am	on	in	off	it
2.	fan	sun	fed	let	fin	win	fat
3.	red	biff	ten	fox	got	cuff	jet
4.	fast	jump	left	hand	felt	last	raft
5.	grab	frog	stop	flag	clap	from	drop
6.	flat	lift	flip	best	flop	desk	sniff
7.	stuff	brush	graph	flash	cough	brick	fluff
8.	crab	staff	draft	tough	shelf	craft	grip
9.	scruff	scrap	drift	crisp	frost	strip	cliff

Auditory discrimination is the ability to hear differences between sounds. Good auditory discrimination helps us to recognise and identify the sounds in words and so interpret them correctly. Children with poor auditory discrimination may confuse sounds and misinterpret things they have heard. Their spelling and writing may reflect their confusion over what sounds they heard in a word.

Read out the pairs of words. For 1–12 ask the child to tell you whether or not they start with the same sound and for 13–21 ask whether or not they end with the same sounds. The words get increasingly complex.

Break this task into a number of shorter tasks over a number of lessons if necessary.

Activity 5 Same or different? f

1. fed - fib
2. set - fan
3. let - fit
4. fox - fat
5. fun - hot
6. fin - jam
7. felt - fast
8. flag - stop
9. drop - frog
10. flip - flat
11. brush - flash
12. trust - frost
13. off - if
14. had - biff
15. cuff - cup
16. cliff - stuff
17. sniff - snap
18. trap - fluff
19. staff - graph
20. stick - stuff
21. scruff - bluff

Auditory fusion is the ability to hear the subtle gaps between sounds and words. Children with poor auditory fusion may get lost in conversations and when following a list of instructions given verbally.

Say the sounds or read the words in the list one after another at a brisk pace so that there are no obvious gaps between the sounds or the words. Ask the child to listen carefully and then tell you how many sounds or words you have said. Many of the words contain the sound 'f' (represented by the sound spellings **f, ff, ph** and **gh**) and get increasingly complex.

Break this task into a number of shorter tasks over a number of lessons if necessary.

Activity 6 How many did you hear? f

1. s - f - t - r
2. **sh** - **ch** - f
3. **sh** - **ch** - f - **th** - s
4. h - s - f - p
5. f - **sh** - s - h
6. w - f - t - r - **sh**
7. h - f - l
8. p - h - f - r
9. fan - set - fib - off
10. if - ink - had
11. fin - fun - jam - kid
12. fit - fox - sit
13. biff - rough - tiff
14. left - fast - hand
15. felt - lift - shelf - raft
16. from - flip
17. flat - drip - frog
18. stuff - flop - sniff
19. cliff - shift - fluff - graph
20. staff - drift
21. frost - scruff - bluff
22. craft - gruff - draft

Auditory attention and tracking is the ability to actively listen and follow auditory information from beginning to end. Good auditory attention and tracking helps us to follow a conversation, a story read out loud or a set of instructions, and enables us to focus on key information. Children with poor auditory attention and tracking may find it difficult to follow and respond appropriately to what is being said to them. **Auditory sequential memory** is the ability to remember and recall a series of things that they have heard. Children with poor auditory sequential memory may find it difficult to remember information given earlier in a conversation or set of instructions and may struggle to recall the sequence of sounds in a word.

In this activity the child has to process the auditory information but also respond by working out the pattern and stating the next sound in the sequence. Read out the list of sounds with a clear space between each. Ask the child to listen and work out what sound would come next. The answers follow in red.

Break this task into a number of shorter tasks over a number of lessons if necessary.

Activity 7 What comes next? f

1. f s f s f s ...... f
2. m f m f m ...... f
3. f **sh** f **sh** f **sh** ...... f
4. h f h f h f ...... h
5. f h **sh** f h **sh** ...... f
6. s f f s f f s f f ...... s
7. f s **sh** f s **sh** f s **sh** ...... f
8. **ch sh** f **ch sh** f **ch sh** f ...... ch
9. p p f t p p f t ...... p
10. s f f **sh** s f f **sh** ...... s
11. f **sh th** f **sh th** ...... f
12. **sh ch** f s **sh ch** f s ...... sh
13. f f **sh th** f f **sh th** ...... f
14. f h p t f h p t ...... f
15. **sh** f h s **sh** f h s ...... sh
16. **th sh ch** f **th sh ch** f **th** ... sh
17. f s m s f s m s ...... f
18. s f f f s f f f ...... s
19. h s s f h s s f ...... h
20. h f f s h f f s ...... h
21. **sh** f s h **sh** f s h ... sh
22. s f f **th** s f f **th** ...... s
23. v f s **sh** v f s **sh** v
24. h v **sh** f h v **sh** f ...... h

This activity results in the child discovering all the sound spellings for the sound and sorting the words into corresponding lists.
Support the child to read the words one by one.
For each word support the child to work out the sound spelling corresponding to the sound 'f' and highlight it.
There are four sound spellings to find: **f, ff, ph** and **gh**.
Be aware that the sound spellings **gh** and **ph** occur less frequently than the others and tend to occur in multisyllable words. In order to raise the child's awareness of these sound spellings the words used are either unusual, e.g. phlox (a flower) or contain a sound spelling that the child has not yet met, e.g. **ou** representing the sound 'u' in the words tough and rough. Deal with this by saying the 'u' sound when the child is tracking through the word, is blending the sounds and gets to the sound spelling **ou**. Tell them that they will find out more about this sound spelling later.
In the boxes underneath write the sound spelling, **f, ff, ph** or **gh,** as the heading on the small line at the top of the box, as the child discovers it.
Then work through the word list and sort the words into lists according to the sound spelling.
Encourage the child to say each sound as they write each sound spelling in sequence,
e.g. say 'o' 'f' as they write **o ff**.
Break this task into a number of shorter tasks over a number of lessons if necessary.

Activity 8 Investigating the sound f

off	sniff	tough
from	phlox	frog
graph	left	stuff
rough	flat	flash
cliff	frost	cuff

Activity 10 Sound spelling cards f

f	ff
ph	gh

Visual discrimination is the ability to see differences between objects and figures that are similar. Good visual discrimination helps keep us from getting confused when looking at shapes and forms in the environment. Children with poor visual discrimination may find it difficult to recognise letters, may confuse letters such as b and d and may find it difficult to identify mathematical symbols.

Ask the child to look at the sound spelling in the yellow box then track along the row looking at the other sound spellings.
The child indicates or puts a ring around the sound spelling that is the same as the one in the yellow box.
This includes some sound spellings which represent other sounds but are visually similar.

Break this task into a number of shorter tasks over a number of lessons if necessary.

Activity 11 Sound spelling tracker f

ff	tt	ff	f	t
f	k	l	t	f
ph	sh	ch	ph	th
ff	tt	t	f	ff
gh	g	h	ph	gh
f	ff	t	f	k
ff	tt	ff	f	t
ph	gh	h	p	ph

Visual memory is the ability to remember and identify a shape or picture that we have previously seen. Children with poor visual memory may struggle to remember pictures, figures, shapes, letters and numbers and may have difficulties with reading, writing and number work.

Ask the child to look at the sound spelling in the yellow box for at least five seconds, covering the white box underneath. Then cover the yellow box so that the sound spelling cannot be seen and reveal the choice of sound spellings in the white box below. Ask the child to select the matching sound spelling from the white box.

Break this task into a number of shorter tasks over a number of lessons if necessary.

Activity 12 Remembering sound spellings f

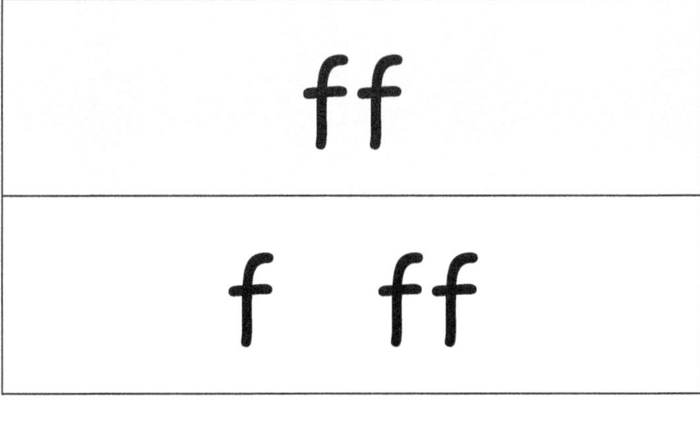

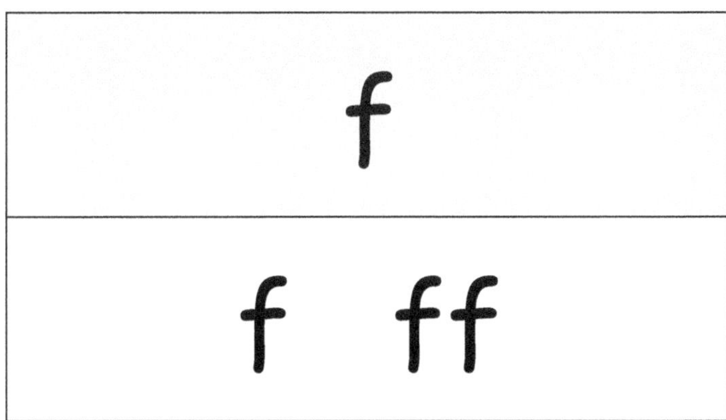

ph
ff ph f

gh
ph gh ff

ff
f ff ph

f
ff f ph

ff
f ph ff

Visual discrimination is the ability to see differences between objects and figures that are similar. Good visual discrimination helps keep us from getting confused when looking at shapes and forms in the environment. Children with poor visual discrimination may find it difficult to recognise letters, may confuse letters such as b and d and may find it difficult to identify mathematical symbols.

Focus on one of the sound spellings featured on this sheet, e.g. **ff** (say the sound 'f' and point to an example rather than using the letter names to identify the sound spelling). Ask the child to look at all the sound spellings and indicate or put a ring round all the sound spellings which match the target. Repeat for another sound spelling featured on the sheet.

Break this task into a number of shorter tasks over a number of lessons if necessary.

Activity 13 Spot the sound spelling f

f ph ff ff gh

f f f

gh ph f

ff ff f f ff

ff ph ff f

Form constancy is the ability to generalise forms and figures and identify them even if they are slightly different from that usually seen. This skill helps us distinguish differences in size, shape, and orientation or position. Children with poor form constancy may frequently reverse letters and numbers.

Ask the child to look at the sound spelling on the left and match to a sound spelling on the right (written differently), drawing a line to connect each.

Activity 14 Which is the same? f

ff	ph
f	gh
ph	ff
gh	f
ff	gh
f	ph
ph	ff
gh	f

Visual closure is the ability to identify an object, shape or symbol from a visually incomplete or disorganised presentation and to see where the different parts of a whole fit together, i.e. to recognise something when seeing only part of it. This skill helps us understand things quickly because our visual system doesn't have to process every detail to recognise what we're seeing.

Ask the child to look at the sound spelling in the white box then track left to right along the row.
Ask the child to indicate or put a ring around the sound spelling that is the same as that in the white box.

Break this task into a number of shorter tasks over a number of lessons if necessary.

Activity 15 Bits missing f

ff	f	ff	ph
f	t	f	k
ff	ph	ff	f
ph	ff	gh	ph
f	t	f	ff
gh	ph	gh	ff
ff	ff	f	t
ph	gh	ph	ff

Spatial relations is the ability to perceive the position of objects in relation to ourselves and to each other. This skill helps children to understand relationships between symbols and letters. Children with poor spatial relations may find it difficult to write letters in the correct orientation, write consistently starting at the margin and write letters of the same size.

In the first part, ask the child to copy the sound spellings on the lines below in exactly the same places as they appear above.
In the second part, ask the child to copy the words on the lines below in exactly the same places, saying the matching sound as they write each sound spelling.

Break this task into a number of shorter tasks over a number of lessons if necessary.

Activity 17 Where am I? f

ff ff f f

ph ff f gh

from off

fluff graph

Visual sequential memory is the ability to remember sequences of figures, symbols and shapes. Children with poor visual sequencing struggle to remember a sequence of letters and follow visual patterns. They may have difficulties writing a sequence of letters to form a word and a sequence of words to form a sentence.

Ask the child to look at the sound spellings in the yellow box for at least five seconds, covering the white box underneath. Then cover the yellow box so that the sound spellings cannot be seen and reveal the sequence of sound spellings in the white box below. Ask the child to remember the missing sound spelling and write it in the space.

Break this task into a number of shorter tasks over a number of lessons if necessary.

Activity 18 Remembering lots of sound spellings f

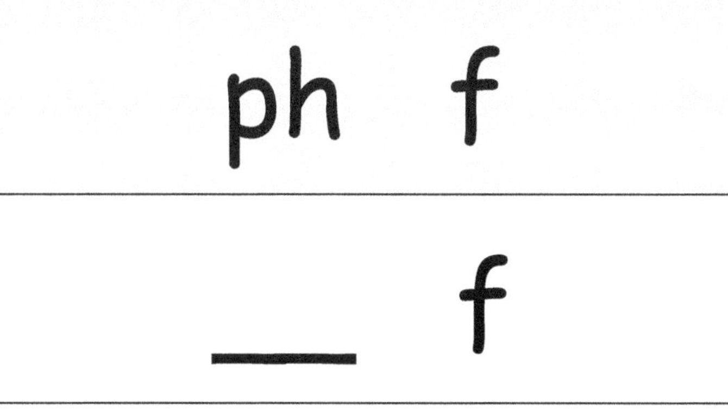

ff f
ff ___

ff f ph
ff f ___

gh ph f
gh ___ f

ph f ff
ph ___ ff

ff f gh
___ f gh

f ph gh
f ___ gh

Having introduced the sound and its corresponding sound spellings, it is important that the child is given the opportunity to practise writing them.
In this activity the child can practise forming the sound spellings in a number of ways:

- copying over the grey letters which act as a guide to accurate letter formation,
- writing individual sound spellings within small boxes (with shading to act as a guide), which develops visual-spatial awareness of the letters and
- writing words with a sound spelling in each box.

Encourage the child to say the sound at the same time as writing the sound spelling.

Activity 19 Writing sound spellings f

f f f f f f f

f f f f f f f

f							

ff ff ff ff ff

ff ff ff ff ff

ff							

ph ph ph ph ph

ph ph ph ph ph ph ph

ph

o ff

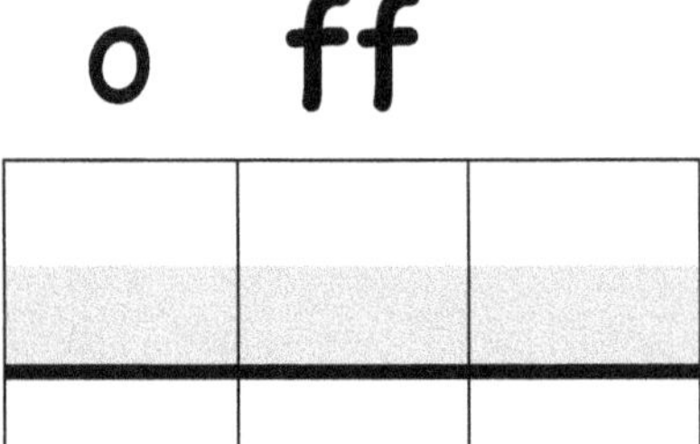

b i ff

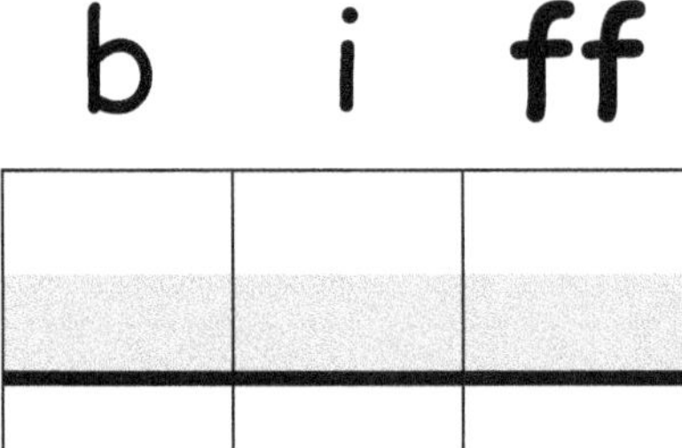

f r o m

l e f t

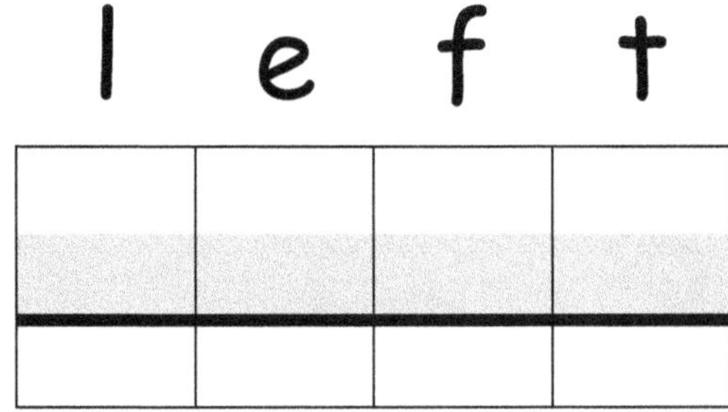

s n i ff

g r a **ph**

This set of cards is made of up words containing the sound 'f'. The sound spelling for the target sound in each word is highlighted. Copy onto card and cut out.
Practise dynamic blending for reading, as described in the 'Working through the programme' section, using these cards. Model this process for the child if necessary.

Activity 20 Dynamic blending – word cards f

fan	fed
flat	flap
left	drift
frost	off
staff	sniff
cliff	graph
Phil	cough

This set of cards is made of up words containing the sound 'f'. Copy onto card and cut out.
Practise dynamic blending for reading, as described in the 'Working through the programme' section, using these cards. Model this process for the child if necessary.

Activity 20 Dynamic blending – word cards f

fox	fun
fig	fist
lift	frog
craft	shelf
cuff	bluff
stiff	fluff
phlox	tough

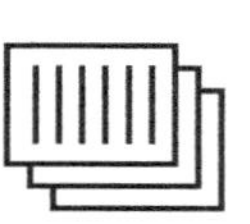

Print out onto card and cut out.
Stack them with the biggest (the complete word) on the bottom and in decreasing size so that the smallest is on the top.
Make sure the left-hand edge of the cards are flush. Staple the cards together on the left-hand side.
When the child runs a finger over the cards the sound spellings flip up. Ask the child to say the sounds and match to the flips.

staple

Activity 24 Flippies for the sound 'f'

f	f a	f a s	f a s t	
l	l e	l e f	l e f t	
o	o ff			
s	s n	s n i	s n i ff	
g	g r	g r a	g r a ph	

Read the clue on the left for the child.
Use the clue to work out what the answer word is.
Encourage the child to think about the sounds in that word and write a sound spelling for each sound in the boxes on the right, one by one.
The first two are done for you as an example.
Explain to the child that they may not need to use all the boxes and so some are shaded in.
Break this task into a number of shorter tasks over a number of lessons if necessary.

Activity 25 Sound boxes f

Clue	Sound boxes			
Very quick	f	a	s	t
Not on	o	ff		
Blows cold air				
A white lie				
Had food				
Fish's flipper				
Workers				
Chart				
Not right				
Take in a smell				
Looks like a toad				

Support the child to read the words on the left.
For each word, support the child to work out how many sounds there are in it and write that number in the grey box.
Then ask the child to count out the number of white boxes needed to write the word, so that there is one box for each sound, and colour in any boxes that are not needed.
Next ask the child to say the sounds in the word, one by one, and at the same time write the matching sound spelling in the boxes one by one.
The first one is done for you as an example.
Break this task into a number of shorter tasks over a number of lessons if necessary.

Activity 26 How many sounds? f

Word	Number	Writing the sound spellings				
cuff	3	c	u	ff		
off						
left						
fan						
fluff						
frost						
sniff						
graph						
flat						

During this activity the child will be asked to slide sounds in and out of words, i.e. practise phoneme manipulation.
A sound might be swapped, added or taken away.
Print the sound spelling cards onto card and cut out.
Activity:

- Spread out all the sound spelling cards so that the child can see them.
- Build a starting word from the prompt list, demonstrating how to dynamically blend the sounds together as you move the sound spelling cards into place.
- Repeat the word, running your finger under the cards so that it corresponds to the sounds within the word.
- Ask the child to change the word to the next word on the prompt list. As you say the new word run your finger under the cards so that it corresponds with the sound you are saying and the matching sound spelling card.

This gives the child the chance to hear and see what is different.

- The child can then swap the appropriate sounds spelling cards.
- Repeat this technique with the next word on the list.

Activity 29 Sound swap f

Sound swap f

List 1	List 2	List 3
fun	off	lift
fan	toff	left
flan	tiff	let
flat	stiff	lent
fat	staff	lend
fit	stuff	led
fist		fled
list		fed
lift		

f	ff	a	e
i	o	u	n
l	t	s	d

Support the child to read the words on the left, one by one.
For each word read the clue to the child and then work out what the answer word is.
Explain to the child that they will need to either: add a sound, take away a sound or change a sound to the word on the left to make the answer word, e.g. cot > cost list > lit mat > rat.
Have the child write out the answer word on the right, saying each sound as they write each sound spelling.
An example is done for you.
Break this task into a number of shorter tasks over a number of lessons if necessary.

Activity 30 Sound exchange f

Starting word	Clue	New word
toff	Not on	off
fin	Healthy	________
from	Looks like a toad	________
left	Elevator in the UK	________
act	A piece of information	________
stuff	Workers	________
flips	Part of the mouth	________
rift	Float away	________
fan	Flipper	________
craft	Flat style boat	________

Place a whiteboard in front of the child.
Choose a word from the list below. Randomise the words you choose so that you are choosing words with a variety of number of sounds.
Draw dots on the whiteboard to match the number of sounds in the word, one dot for each sound. Do not write the word or show the word to the child as this is a purely auditory activity.
Say the word to the child and as you do so run your finger under the dots so that your finger matches the appropriate sound dot and its corresponding sound as you say it.
Then cover the dot that corresponds to the sound you are going to take away – use the list below. There are lots more words you could use for this activity – refer to the teacher word list at the start of this chapter.
Ask the child to tell you what is left if you take that sound away.
Take away another sound or choose a new word.
Remember to time limit this activity.

Activity 31 Sound sums f

No. of sounds in starting word	Word	Take away the sound	What is left?
3	fan	f	an
3	fat	f	at
3	fin	f	in
4	fact	f	act
4	fist	s	fit
4	flan	l	fan
4	flap	f	lap
4	flash	f	lash
4	fled	f	led
4	flip	f	lip
4	flit	f	lit
4	flog	f	log
4	flog	l	fog
4	frog	r	fog
4	fund	d	fun

No. of sounds in starting word	Word	Take away the sound	What is left?
4	left	f	let
4	lift	f	lit
4	raft	f	rat
4	self	s	elf
4	shelf	sh	elf
4	stiff	s	tiff
5	craft	k (c)	raft
5	draft	d	raft
5	draft	r	daft
5	drift	d	rift
5	scruff	r	scuff

This set of cards is made up of high frequency words containing the sound 'f'. Copy onto card and cut out. Practise dynamic blending for reading, as described in the 'Working through the programme' section, using these cards. Model this process for the child if necessary.

Activity 32 Reading high frequency words f

off	

Starting at 'frog', have the child read each of the words on the shapes as quickly as possible.
Support the child to read the words by giving information about sounds and supporting blending but do not supply the whole word.
Time how long it takes to read all the words to 'raft' and record the time in the box.
Repeat at a later point and see if the child can beat his own time.

Activity 33 Reading race: get the frog to the raft f

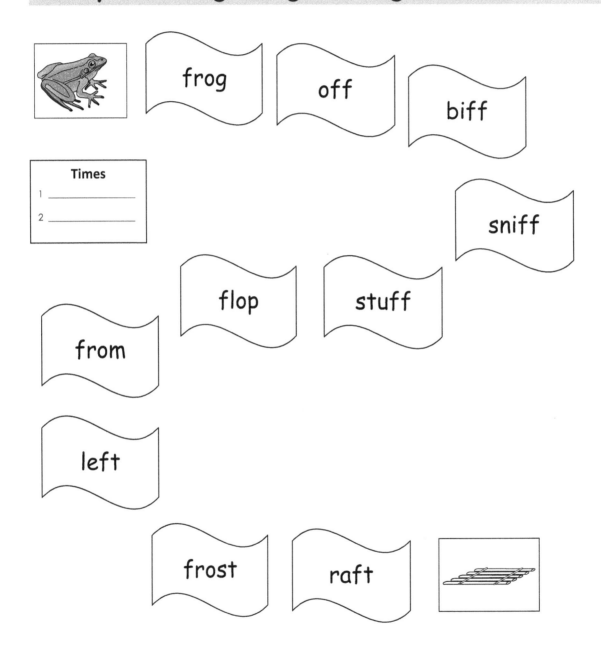

frog

off

biff

Times

1 ______________

2 ______________

sniff

flop

stuff

from

left

frost

raft

Support the child to read the words one by one.
For each word support the child to think whether there is an 'f' sound in the word.
Have the child put a ring around or highlight just the words that have an 'f' sound.
Remind the child that 'f' can be represented by four sound spellings: **f, ff, gh** and **ph**.
Note that the words tough and rough contain the sound spelling ***ou*** *representing an 'u' sound.*
Break this task into a number of shorter tasks over a number of lessons if necessary.

Activity 34 Word tracker f

last	frog	left	truck	stuff
clock	from	graph	sniff	flap
fun	lift	off	chips	stick
draft	fluff	tough	cats	Phil
rough	fan	flash	desk	raft

How many 'f' words did you find? _______

Visual memory is the ability to remember and identify a shape, figure or picture that we have previously seen. Children with poor visual memory may struggle to remember pictures, figures, shapes, letters and numbers and may have difficulties with reading, writing and number work.

Ask the child to look at the word in the yellow box for at least five seconds, covering the white box underneath. Then cover the yellow box so that the word cannot be seen and reveal a choice of words in the white box below. Ask the child to select the word in the white box that matches the one they saw in the yellow box.

Break this task into a number of shorter tasks over a number of lessons if necessary.

Activity 35 Remembering words f

fun
fin fun

frog
from frog

lift
lift left

biff
tiff biff

cliff
cliff staff

graph
grab graph

craft
draft craft drift

stuff
stiff staff stuff

Support the child to read the words one by one.
For each word support the child to think whether the word is a real word that makes sense or is a nonsense word.
Have the child put a ring around or highlight just the real words.
Break this task into a number of shorter tasks over a number of lessons if necessary.

Activity 36 Word detective f

niff	fit	flip	stuff	flag
heff	rough	draph	fluff	from
staff	flink	flash	graph	left
frost	sniff	zaff	fan	flop
tough	saff	shift	kift	suff

How many real words did you find? ________

Visual sequential memory is the ability to remember sequences of figures, symbols, pictures and shapes. Children with poor visual sequencing struggle to remember a sequence of letters and follow visual patterns. They may have difficulties writing a sequence of letters to form a word and a sequence of words to form a sentence.

Ask the child to look at the words in the yellow box for at least five seconds, covering the white box underneath. Then cover the yellow box so that the words cannot be seen and reveal the sequence of words in the white box below. Ask the child to remember the missing word from the sequence in the yellow box and write it in the space.

Break this task into a number of shorter tasks over a number of lessons if necessary.

Activity 37 Remembering lots of words f

fed fit
______ fit

fox fin
fox ______

fang fast flat
______ fast flat

from felt fled
from ______ fled

lift left raft
lift left ______

flap flop flip
flap ______ flip

off stuff cliff
off ______ cliff

Print out on card and cut out the sound spelling and picture cards for each word.
Read though the instructions in the 'Working through the programme' section at the start of this book prior to working with a child.

Activity 38 Word build f

l	i	f	t	
f	r	o	m	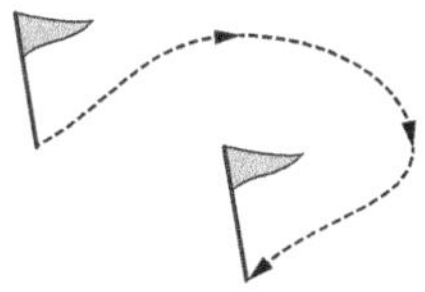
f	l	a	g	
o	ff			

s	n	i	ff	
c	l	i	ff	
g	r	a	ph	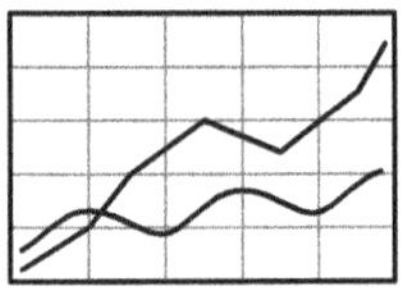

Support the child to read the words on the list one by one.
For each word support the child to think about each of the sounds in the word and their matching sound spellings.
Have the child put a ring around or highlight the sound spelling for each sound.
Break this task into a number of shorter tasks over a number of lessons if necessary.

Activity 39 Word tech f

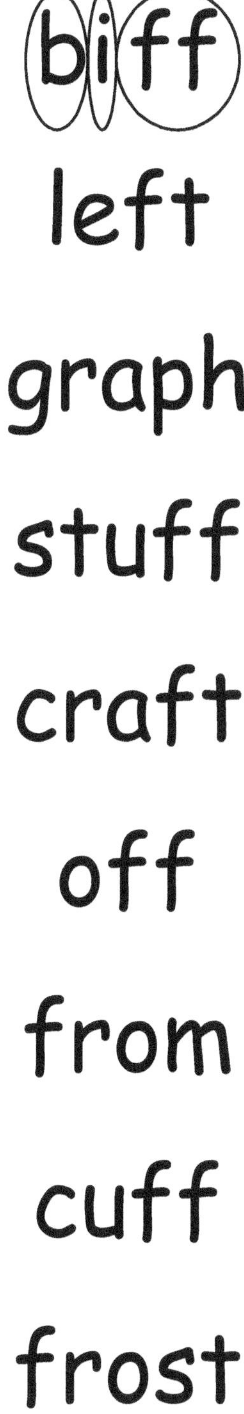

biff
left
graph
stuff
craft
off
from
cuff
frost

Read the clue on the left for the child.
For each clue support the child to work out what the answer word is.
The sound spellings for the answer word are given to help, but they are mixed up – an anagram.
Have the child use the sound spellings to write the answer word on the line on the right.
Encourage the child to say the associated sound as he writes each sound spelling.
Break this task into a number of shorter tasks over a number of lessons if necessary.

Activity 40 Word scramble f

Clue	Sound spellings	Word
Green pond animal	g f r o	______________
Not right	t e f l	______________
Not on	**ff** o	______________
Sharp tooth	a f ng	______________
Information picture	g **ph** a r	______________
Do this to smell	s i n **ff**	______________
Cold and icy	f o s t r	______________
Can take you upstairs	f t l i	______________
Something true	f c a t	______________
Workers	s a **ff** t	______________
Lightning	**sh** a l f	______________

Activity 42 Spelling challenge

felt	f e l t	f e l t	___ ___ ___ ___	______________
from	f r o m	f r o m	___ ___ ___ ___	______________
left	l e f t	l e f t	___ ___ ___ ___	______________
off	o ff	o ff	___ ___	______________
sniff	s n i ff	s n i ff	___ ___ ___ ___	______________
stuff	s t u ff	s t u ff	___ ___ ___ ___	______________
graph	g r a ph	g r a ph	___ ___ ___ ___	______________

Support the child to read the sentences.
Explain that the sentences are OK but that they are very short and could be a bit more interesting!
Then support the child to read the phrases at the bottom of the page and decide which could be used to make each sentence 'better' or 'more interesting'.
Ask the child to write out the sentence, adding the new phrase from the list. Encourage the child to say the sounds at the same time as writing the associated sound spelling when writing each word.
Note that the sentences include high frequency words which contain sounds that the child has not yet encountered in the programme. Support the child to decode these words by supplying information about any unfamiliar sounds and sound spellings and encourage the child to blend for reading. Some sound spellings are highlighted to support this.
Break this task into a number of shorter tasks over a number of lessons if necessary

Activity 45 Making better sentences f

1. The frog sat on the raft.

____

____

2. Sam felt unfit.

____

____

3. Scruff, the dog, ran fast.

____

____

4. Fran's fish can flip and flop.

____

____

5. Tom fled from the fox.

____

____

but sto**pped** to sniff the twigs	so he went to 'fit club'
and drifted from the bank	and flash his red fin
and ran to the top of the cliff	

Support the child to read each sentence one by one.
Ask the child to re-read the sentence, several times if necessary, and try to remember it.
Then cover the sentence and ask the child to recall the sentence verbally.
Once they can do this confidently, ask the child to write out the sentence from memory.

When writing a word, encourage the child to say the sound as they write each associated sound spelling.
When the word is complete then they are to say the whole word.
When the sentence is complete the child reads out their sentence and then compares it to the original.
Note that the sentences may include high frequency words which contain sounds that the child has not yet encountered in the programme. Support the child to decode these words by supplying information about any unfamiliar sounds and their sound spellings and encouraging the child to blend for reading. Some of these sound spellings are highlighted to help the child when writing the words later.

Alternatively, using text to speech software, the child could type the sentence, with the computer reading back each word and then the completed sentence.

Activity 46 Writing challenge f

The fat frog jumps fast.

Fran can fe**tch** the fox.

The staff fed Fluff, the cat.

Dad ran to the cliff top.

Answers f

Page 289
Activity 8 Investigating the sound 'f'

f
from frog left flat flash frost

ff
off sniff stuff cliff cuff

ph
phlox graph

gh
rough tough

Page 306
Activity 25 Sound boxes

f a n
f i b
f e d
f i n
s t a ff
g r a ph
l e f t
s n i ff
f r o g

Page 307
Activity 26 How many sounds?

2 o ff
4 l e f t
3 f a n
4 f l u ff
5 f r o s t
4 s n i ff
4 g r a ph
4 f l a t

Page 310
Activity 30 Sound exchange

fin – fit
from – frog
left – lift
act – fact
stuff – staff
flips – lips
rift – drift
fan – fin
craft – raft

Page 315
Activity 34 Word tracker

frog left stuff
from graph sniff flap
fun lift off
draft fluff tough Phil
rough fan flash raft

18

Page 318
Activity 36 Word detective

fit flip stuff flag
rough fluff from
staff flash graph left
frost sniff fan flop
tough shift

17

Page 323
Activity 39 Word tech

l e f t
g r a ph
s t u ff
c r a f t
o ff
f r o m
c u ff
f r o s t

Page 324
Activity 40 Word scramble

frog
left
off
fang
graph
sniff
frost
lift
fact
staff
flash

Page 326
Activity 45 Making better sentences

1. The frog sat on the raft and drifted from the bank.
2. Sam felt unfit so he went to 'fit club'.
3. Scruff, the dog, ran fast but stopped to sniff the twigs.
4. Fran's fish can flip and flop and flash his red fin.
5. Tom fled from the fox and ran to the top of the cliff.

SECTION 8

I

l leg

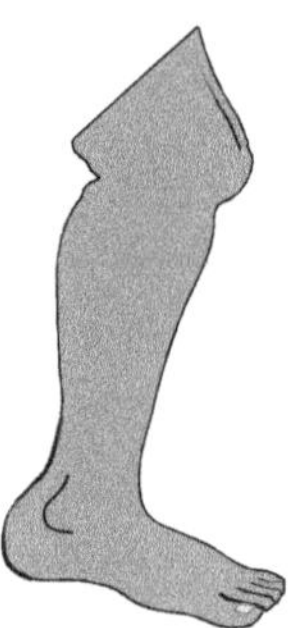

ll hill

Words with an 'l' sound – word list of 1 syllable words

l					ll	
3 sounds	4 sounds	4 sounds	4 sounds	5 sounds	3 sounds	4 sounds
lab	belt	flog	plot	bland	bell	drill
lack	black	flop	plug	blank	bill	frill
lad	blag	glad	plum	blast*	bull	grill
lag	bled	glug	silk	blink	chill	skill
lap	bling	glum	silt	clamp	dell	skull
led	blob	glut	slack	clasp*	dill	smell
leg	blog	held	slam	flank	doll	spell
let	blot	help	slap	flask*	dull	spill
lick	bolt	hulk	slat	lunch	fell	still
lid	bulb	kiln	sled	plank	fill	swill
lip	bulk	lamp	slid	plant*	full	thrill
lit	clad	land	sling	slink	hell	trill
lob	clam	lank	slip	plump	hill	
lock	clan	last*	slit	slant*	kill	
log	clap	left	slob	slump	mill	
long	clash	lend	slog	splash	mull	
lop	cling	lent	slop	splat	pill	
lot	clip	lift	slot		pull	
luck	clod	lilt	slum	6 sounds	sell	
lung	clog	link	sulk	splint	shall	
	clop	lint	tilt		shell	
	clot	list	weld		sill	
	felt	lost	wilt		tell	
	flag	lots			till	
	flan	lump			well	
	flap	melt			will	
	flash	milk			yell	
	flat	pelt				
	fling	plan				
	flip					
	flit					

* for some accents where the a is an 'a' sound rather than an 'ar' sound

Auditory discrimination is the ability to hear differences between sounds. Good auditory discrimination helps us to recognise and identify the sounds in words and so interpret them correctly. Children with poor auditory discrimination may confuse sounds and misinterpret things they have heard. Their spelling and writing may reflect their confusion over which sounds they heard in a word. **Auditory attention and tracking** is the ability to actively listen and follow auditory information from beginning to end. Good auditory attention and tracking helps us to follow a conversation, a story read out loud or a set of instructions, and enables us to focus on key information. Children with poor auditory attention and tracking may find it difficult to follow and respond appropriately to what is being said to them.

This story contains lots of words that contain the sound 'l', which is the 'target' sound.
Read the story out loud to the child or group of children. Encourage the child to listen carefully and spot any word that contains the target sound. Note that there are many ways that 'l' can be represented: **l, ll, le, il, el, al** and **ol,** but the 'l' sound is the same for all of them. At this stage of the programme the child will not meet all these sound spellings but will still hear the 'l' sound when it appears in a word. When a target word has been read, the child indicates that they have heard and spotted it by tapping the table, putting up a hand or any other agreed signal, but without shouting out. Stop reading and discuss the word, making any error correction necessary. If a word is missed, re-read the sentence.
Do not show the written story to the child. The target words are highlighted below for you.

Activity 1 Sound target story l

I went to my friend's house and rang the door bell. He pulled open the lace curtains to see who was there. He couldn't come down because he had been ill and had to stay in bed. I decided to climb on the window sill because I couldn't hear what he was saying. I began to wobble and of course I slipped and fell.

Now I am in bed. I have to rest because I broke my leg. I have to take a pill three times a day to stop the pain. The doctor at the hospital said I had been very silly and should have known better.

My friend is well now and he comes to visit me. He brings me books to read and keeps me company. Lying around all day is not very exciting. I can't wait to be well again and out playing with my friends.

Auditory discrimination is the ability to hear differences between sounds. Good auditory discrimination helps us to recognise and identify the sounds in words and so interpret them correctly. Children with poor auditory discrimination may confuse sounds and misinterpret things they have heard. Their spelling and writing may reflect their confusion over what sounds they heard in a word. **Auditory sequential memory** is the ability to remember and recall a series of things that they have heard. Children with poor auditory sequential memory may find it difficult to remember information given earlier in a conversation or set of instructions and may struggle to recall the sequence of sounds in a word.

The silly sentences contain lots of words containing the sound 'l'.
Read the sentence to the child several times, invite them to join in as you say it and gradually recall it on their own.
Do not show the words to the child.
Ask them to say it as quickly as they can and have some fun with it. Perhaps they can make up their own?
The sentences gradually get longer and more complex.
Break this task into a number of shorter tasks over a number of lessons if necessary.

Activity 2 Tongue twister fun l

Lost lazy lions.

Lots of lads love lego.

Lizzie likes little llamas.

Large lizards live on lumpy logs.

Auditory discrimination is the ability to hear differences between sounds. Good auditory discrimination helps us to recognise and identify the sounds in words and so interpret them correctly. Children with poor auditory discrimination may confuse sounds and misinterpret things they have heard. Their spelling and writing may reflect their confusion over which sounds they heard in a word. **Auditory attention and tracking** is the ability to actively listen and follow auditory information from beginning to end. Good auditory attention and tracking helps us to follow a conversation, a story read out loud or a set of instructions, and enables us to focus on key information. Children with poor auditory attention and tracking may find it difficult to follow and respond appropriately to what is being said to them.

Read out the words and ask the child to identify the odd one out. In 1–10 the child focuses on the sound at the **beginning** of the words and in 11–20 the child focuses on the sound at the **end** of the words.
Do not show the words to the child. The odd one out is highlighted for you.
Break this task into a number of shorter tasks over a number of lessons if necessary.

Activity 3 Odd one out

1.	leg	let	win	2.	lit	met	man
3.	song	long	sing	4.	sack	sock	lock
5.	fell	fill	lot	6.	lent	sent	lend
7.	slip	lamp	left	8.	plug	plan	lost
9.	smell	clap	spill	10.	blast	blink	plant
11.	sell	pull	lad	12.	let	lid	lot
13.	slip	slap	dull	14.	lend	bell	bill
15.	felt	left	help	16.	flag	lost	plug
17.	well	link	lock	18.	spell	still	blink
19.	splash	black	clash	20.	smell	plant	blast

Auditory discrimination is the ability to hear differences between sounds. Good auditory discrimination helps us to recognise and identify the sounds in words and so interpret them correctly. Children with poor auditory discrimination may confuse sounds and misinterpret things they have heard. Their spelling and writing may reflect their confusion over which sounds they heard in a word. **Auditory recall memory** is the ability to remember and recall something that they have just heard. Children with poor auditory recall memory may find it difficult to remember sounds and words and respond appropriately.

Read the list of words below clearly, asking the child to listen carefully. At random points tap the table and stop reading, asking the child to remember and say the last word you said. Then ask them to tell you what the **first** or the **last** sound in the word is.

Break this task into a number of shorter tasks over a number of lessons if necessary.

Activity 4 What sound am I?

1.	lip	bell	hill	leg	sell	lot
2.	tell	lap	full	let	mill	lick
3.	lit	pull	lock	fell	long	will
4.	yell	log	shall	led	well	let
5.	luck	fill	lad	bill	lamp	dull
6.	skill	left	grill	lend	smell	lift
7.	land	spell	lots	thrill	lump	spill
8.	belt	lost	help	list	milk	lung
9.	flag	slip	clap	flat	plug	glad
10.	blast	plant	lunch	blink	clamp	slant

Auditory discrimination is the ability to hear differences between sounds. Good auditory discrimination helps us to recognise and identify the sounds in words and so interpret them correctly. Children with poor auditory discrimination may confuse sounds and misinterpret things they have heard. Their spelling and writing may reflect their confusion over what sounds they heard in a word.

Read out the pairs of words. For 1–12 ask the child to tell you whether or not they start with the same sound and for 13–24 ask whether or not they end with the same sounds. The words get increasingly complex.

Break this task into a number of shorter tasks over a number of lessons if necessary.

Activity 5 Same or different? I

1. lad - lid
2. lit - sit
3. fog - log
4. leg - pet
5. lock - long
6. lift - land
7. held - left
8. list - lamp
9. slip - last
10. sick - lick
11. plant - lunch
12. blink - blast

13. let - mat
14. leg - mug
15. lip - mop
16. will - mum
17. lock - pink
18. lost - lots
19. help - lamp
20. lend - hand
21. lump - felt
22. lift - soft
23. smell - grill
24. skill - thrill

Auditory fusion is the ability to hear the subtle gaps between sounds and words. Children with poor auditory fusion may get lost in conversations and when following a list of instructions given verbally.

Say the sounds or read the words in the list one after another at a brisk pace so that there are no obvious gaps between the sounds or the words. Ask the child to listen carefully and then tell you how many sounds or words you have said. Many of the words contain the sound 'l' (represented by the sound spellings **l** and **ll**) and get increasingly complex.

Break this task into a number of shorter tasks over a number of lessons if necessary.

Activity 6 How many did you hear? l

1. r - l - v
2. l - v - r - l
3. s - l - v - m
4. **th** - l - r - **sh**
5. r - **th** - l
6. **th** - v - r - l - l
7. v - r - l - **th**
8. l - r - l - **th** - l
9. bell - lad - lot
10. let - pull - tell - leg
11. fill - lit - sell - lap
12. well - will - lad
13. lock - long
14. shall - chill - shell
15. last - left - hill - lump
16. lift - grill
17. lend - land - spell
18. lost - lots - lot
19. slip - flag - clap - glad - plug
20. blank - blink - blast
21. spill - still - thrill
22. lunch - smell - skull - slant
23. drill - skill - splint
24. splash - splat

Auditory attention and tracking is the ability to actively listen and follow auditory information from beginning to end. Good auditory attention and tracking helps us to follow a conversation, a story read out loud or a set of instructions, and enables us to focus on key information. Children with poor auditory attention and tracking may find it difficult to follow and respond appropriately to what is being said to them. **Auditory sequential memory** is the ability to remember and recall a series of things that they have heard. Children with poor auditory sequential memory may find it difficult to remember information given earlier in a conversation or set of instructions and may struggle to recall the sequence of sounds in a word.

In this activity the child has to process the auditory information but also respond by working out the pattern and stating the next sound in the sequence. Read out the list of sounds with a clear space between each. Ask the child to listen and work out what sound would come next. The answers follow in red.

Break this task into a number of shorter tasks over a number of lessons if necessary.

Activity 7 What comes next? l

1. r l r l r l r l
2. l n l n l n l ...... n
3. v l v l v l v l
4. j l j l j l j l ...... j
5. s r l s r l s r l ...... s
6. l l r l l r l l r l
7. v v l v v l v v l v
8. **th** l **th th** l **th th** l
9. v l l r v l l r v l l r v
10. r r l n r r l n r r l n ...... r
11. l **th th** n l **th th** n l ...... th
12. **sh th** l r **sh th** l r **sh** ... th
13. l l **th** r l l **th** r l l **th** r l
14. l r l v l r l v l r l v l
15. **th** l l n **th** l l n **th** l l ...... n
16. **th sh** l v **th sh** l v **th** ... sh
17. s l v n s l v n s l
18. **th th** l l n **th th** l l n ...... th
19. r l l v r l l v r l l v ...... r
20. n l v l m l n l v l m l ...... m

This activity results in the child discovering all the sound spellings for the sound and sorting the words into corresponding lists.
Support the child to read the words one by one.
For each word support the child to work out the sound spelling corresponding to the sound 'l' and highlight it.
There are two sound spellings to find at this stage: **l** and **ll**.
In the boxes underneath write the sound spelling, **l** or **ll,** as the heading on the small line at the top of the box, as the child discovers it.
Then work through the word list and sort the words into lists according to the sound spelling.
Encourage the child to say each sound as they write each sound spelling in sequence,
e.g. say 'b' 'e' 'l' as they write **b e ll**.

Break this task into a number of shorter tasks over a number of lessons if necessary.

Activity 8 Investigating the sound l

bell	leg	belt
flat	hill	spill
grill	lamp	link
pull	claps	still

______	______
______________	______________
______________	______________
______________	______________
______________	______________
______________	______________
______________	______________

Activity 10 Sound spelling cards l

l	ll

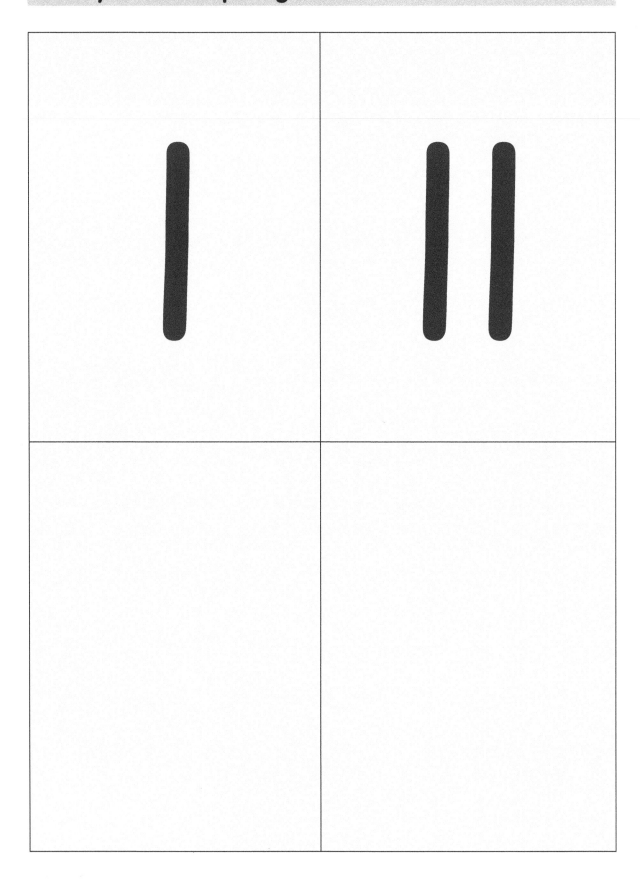

Visual discrimination is the ability to see differences between objects and figures that are similar. Good visual discrimination helps keep us from getting confused when looking at shapes and forms in the environment. Children with poor visual discrimination may find it difficult to recognise letters, may confuse letters such as b and d and may find it difficult to identify mathematical symbols.

Ask the child to look at the sound spelling in the yellow box then track along the row looking at the other sound spellings.
The child indicates or puts a ring around the sound spelling that is the same as the one in the yellow box.
This includes some sound spellings which represent other sounds but are visually similar.

Break this task into a number of shorter tasks over a number of lessons if necessary.

Activity 11 Sound spelling tracker l

ll	l	ll	t	f
l	ll	t	l	f
t	f	l	ll	t
l	ll	l	t	f
ll	l	t	ll	f
f	f	t	ll	l
l	f	ll	l	t
ll	l	ll	t	f

Visual memory is the ability to remember and identify a shape or picture that we have previously seen. Children with poor visual memory may struggle to remember pictures, figures, shapes, letters and numbers and may have difficulties with reading, writing and number work.

Ask the child to look at the sound spelling in the yellow box for at least five seconds, covering the white box underneath. Then cover the yellow box so that the sound spelling cannot be seen and reveal the choice of sound spellings in the white box below. Ask the child to select the matching sound spelling from the white box.

Break this task into a number of shorter tasks over a number of lessons if necessary.

Activity 12 Remembering sound spellings l

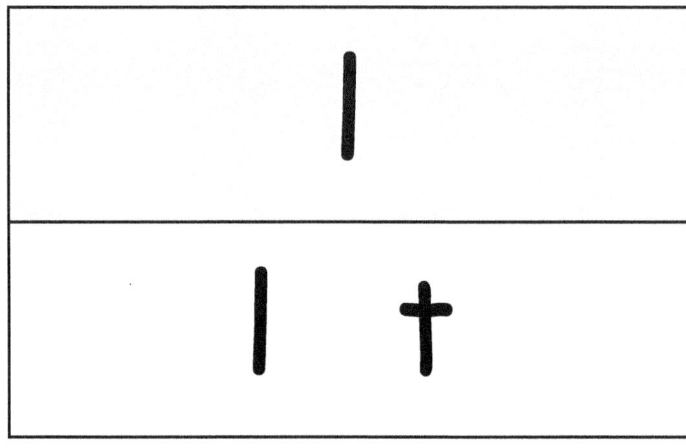

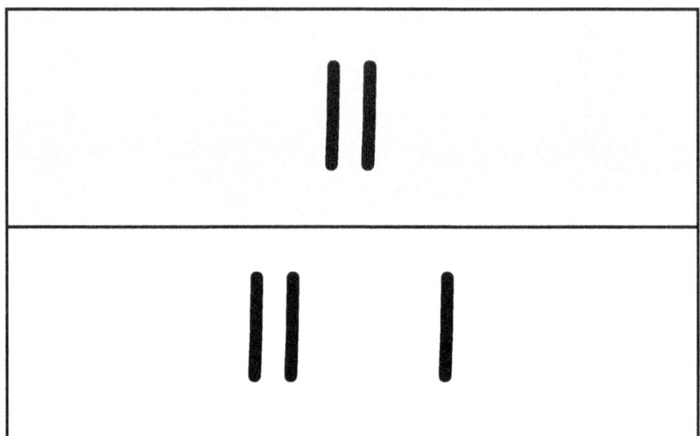

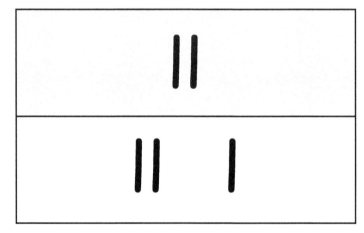

ll
l ll

l
f l

ll
l t ll

l
t l ll

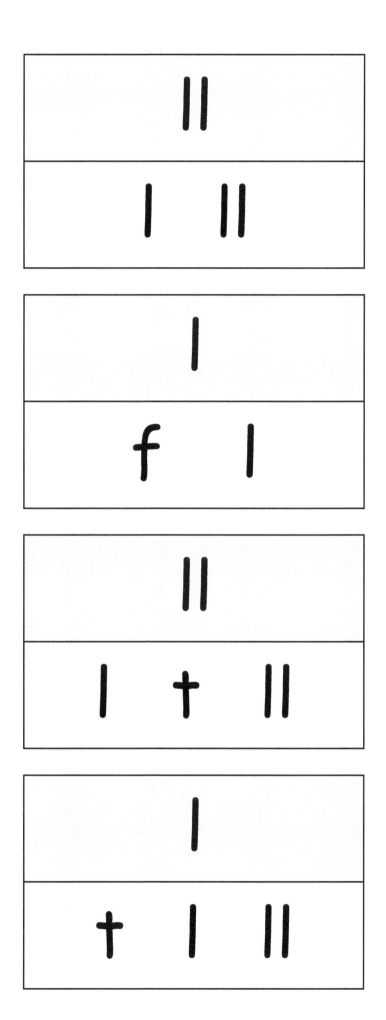

Visual discrimination is the ability to see differences between objects and figures that are similar. Good visual discrimination helps keep us from getting confused when looking at shapes and forms in the environment. Children with poor visual discrimination may find it difficult to recognise letters, may confuse letters such as b and d and may find it difficult to identify mathematical symbols.

Focus on one of the sound spellings featured on this sheet, e.g. **ll** (say the sound 'l' and point to an example rather than using the letter names to identify the sound spelling). Ask the child to look at all the sound spellings and indicate or put a ring round all the sound spellings which match the target. Repeat for another sound spelling featured on the sheet.

Break this task into a number of shorter tasks over a number of lessons if necessary.

Activity 13 Spot the sound spelling l

l t ll ll

l

ll l ll t

ll l

t ll ll

ll t

l

Spatial relations is the ability to perceive the position of objects in relation to ourselves and to each other. This skill helps children to understand relationships between symbols and letters. Children with poor spatial relations may find it difficult to write letters in the correct orientation, write consistently starting at the margin and write letters of the same size.

In the first part, ask the child to copy the sound spellings on the lines below in exactly the same places as they appear above.
In the second part, ask the child to copy the words on the lines below in exactly the same places, saying the matching sound as they write each sound spelling.

Break this task into a number of shorter tasks over a number of lessons if necessary.

Activity 17 Where am I? l

ll l ll

l ll l

let hill

well last

Visual sequential memory is the ability to remember sequences of figures, symbols and shapes. Children with poor visual sequencing struggle to remember a sequence of letters and follow visual patterns. They may have difficulties writing a sequence of letters to form a word and a sequence of words to form a sentence.

Ask the child to look at the sound spellings in the yellow box for at least five seconds, covering the white box underneath. Then cover the yellow box so that the sound spellings cannot be seen and reveal the sequence of sound spellings in the white box below. Ask the child to remember the missing sound spelling and write it in the space.

Break this task into a number of shorter tasks over a number of lessons if necessary.

Activity 18 Remembering lots of sound spellings l

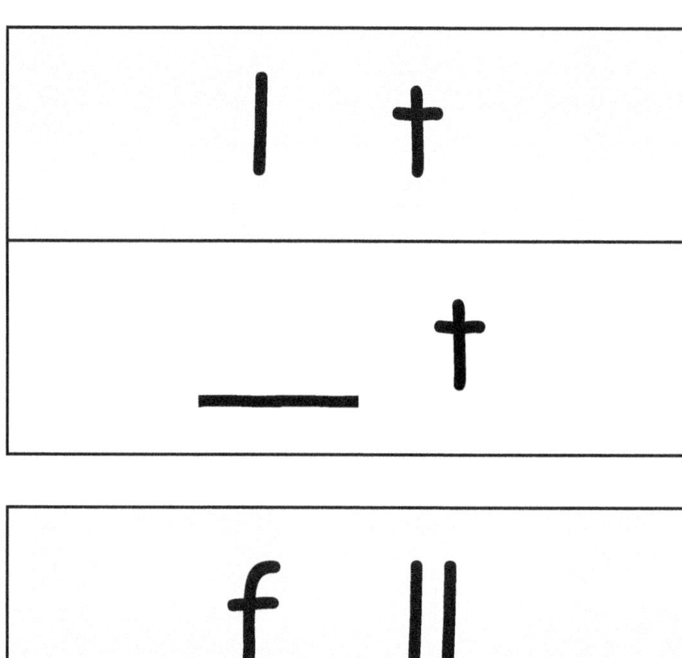

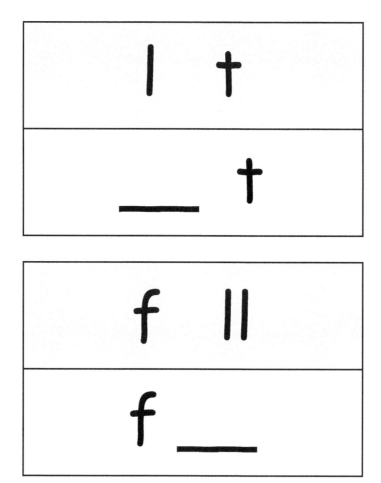

ll l
___ l

l f
l ___

t l ll
t l ___

ll t l
ll ___ l

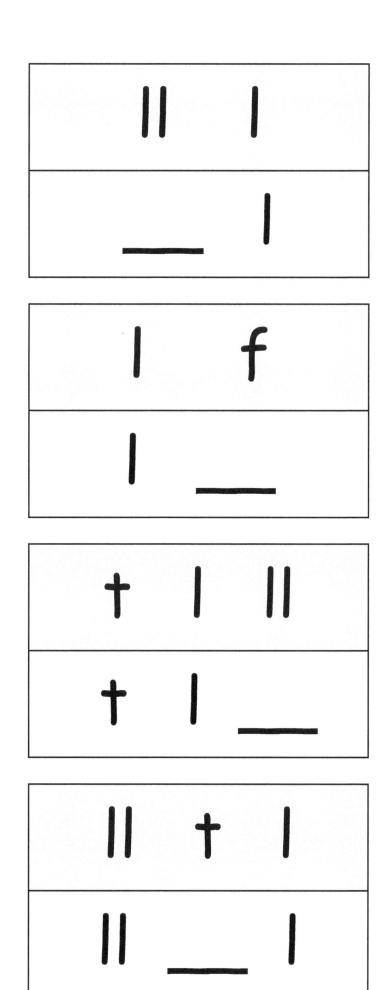

Having introduced the sound and its corresponding sound spellings, it is important that the child is given the opportunity to practise writing them.
In this activity the child can practise forming the sound spellings in a number of ways:

- copying over the grey letters which act as a guide to accurate letter formation,
- writing individual sound spellings within small boxes (with shading to act as a guide), which develops visual-spatial awareness of the letters and
- writing words with a sound spelling in each box.

Encourage the child to say the sound at the same time as writing the sound spelling.

Activity 19 Writing sound spellings l

l l l l l l l

l l l l l l l

ll ll ll ll ll ll ll

ll ll ll ll ll ll ll

l e g

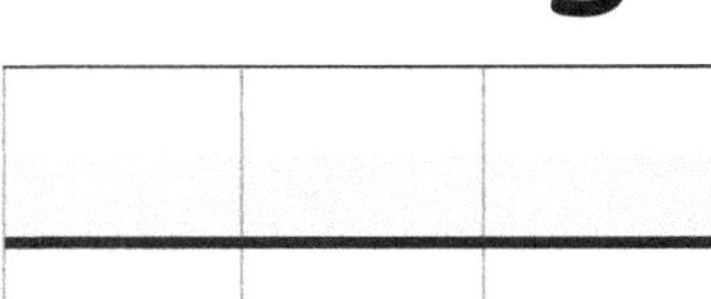

t e ll

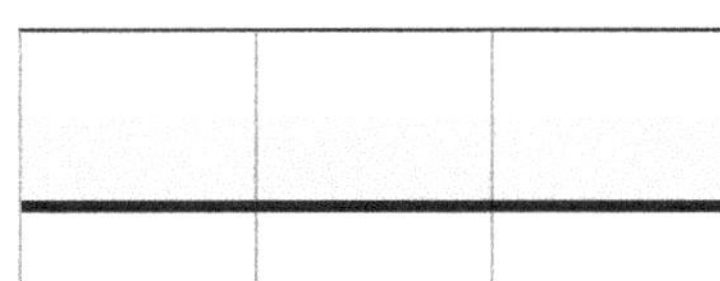

l i d

h i ll

e l f

sh a ll

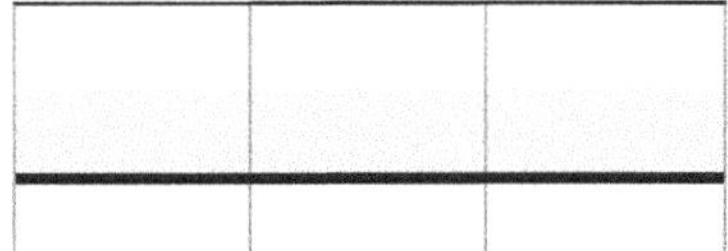

s t i ll

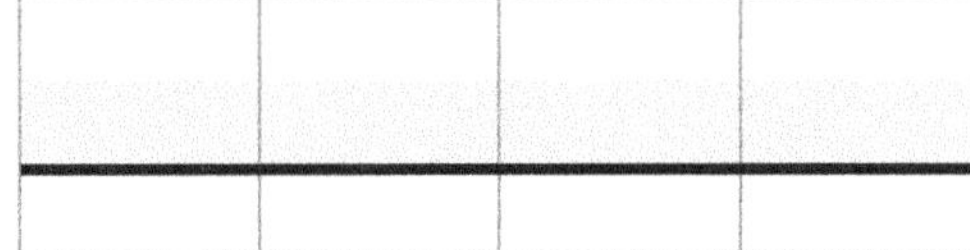

This set of cards is made of up words containing the sound 'l'. The sound spelling for the target sound in each word is highlighted. Copy onto card and cut out.
Practise dynamic blending for reading, as described in the 'Working through the programme' section, using these cards. Model this process for the child if necessary.

Activity 20 Dynamic blending – word cards l

lip	lad
lost	lamp
clap	flat
belt	milk
hill	doll
pull	fell
spell	drill

This set of cards is made of up words containing the sound 'l'. Copy onto card and cut out.
Practise dynamic blending for reading, as described in the 'Working through the programme' section, using these cards. Model this process for the child if necessary.

Activity 20 Dynamic blending – word cards l

lit	lot
list	long
plug	flop
melt	silk
blank	bell
tell	sell
spill	grill

Print out onto card and cut out.
Stack them with the biggest (the complete word) on the bottom and in decreasing size so that the smallest is on the top.
Make sure the left-hand edge of the cards are flush. Staple the cards together on the left-hand side.
When the child runs a finger over the cards the sound spellings flip up. Ask the child to say the sounds and match to the flips.

staple

Activity 24 Flippies for the sound 'l'

l	l o	l o s	l o s t
w	w i	w i ll	
t	t e	t e ll	
f	f e	f e ll	
s	s t	s t i	s t i ll

Read the clue on the left for the child.
Use the clue to work out what the answer word is.
Encourage the child to think about the sounds in that word and write a sound spelling for each sound in the boxes on the right, one by one.
The first two are done for you as an example.
Explain to the child that they may not need to use all the boxes and so some are shaded in.
Break this task into a number of shorter tasks over a number of lessons if necessary.

Activity 25 Sound boxes l

Clue	Sound boxes			
Not well	i	ll		
On top of a pan	l	i	d	
Makes a 'ding dong' sound				
Wood for the fire				
Alight				
Drink cows give us				
Sniff				
Part of the mouth				
Ice turns to water				
Can't find my way home				
Witch's magic				

Support the child to read the words on the left.
For each word, support the child to work out how many sounds there are in it and write that number in the grey box.
Then ask the child to count out the number of white boxes needed to write the word, so that there is one box for each sound, and colour in any boxes that are not needed.
Next ask the child to say the sounds in the word, one by one, and at the same time write the matching sound spelling in the boxes one by one.
The first one is done for you as an example.
Break this task into a number of shorter tasks over a number of lessons if necessary.

Activity 26 How many sounds? I

Word	Number	Writing the sound spellings				
well	3	w	e	ll		
milk						
lots						
smell						
let						
lists						
still						
claps						
flag						

During this activity the child will be asked to slide sounds in and out of words, i.e. practise phoneme manipulation.
A sound might be swapped, added or taken away.
Print the sound spelling cards onto card and cut out.
Activity:

- Spread out all the sound spelling cards so that the child can see them.
- Build a starting word from the prompt list, demonstrating how to dynamically blend the sounds together as you move the sound spelling cards into place.
- Repeat the word, running your finger under the cards so that it corresponds to the sounds within the word.
- Ask the child to change the word to the next word on the prompt list. As you say the new word run your finger under the cards so that it corresponds with the sound you are saying and the matching sound spelling card.

This gives the child the chance to hear and see what is different.

- The child can then swap the appropriate sounds spelling cards.
- Repeat this technique with the next word on the list.

Activity 29 Sound swap

I

Sound swap I

List 1	List 2	List 3
slap	bell	well
lap	tell	will
lab	till	swill
lad	still	spill
land	spill	spell
lend	pill	sell
blend	pull	smell

l	ll	a	e
i	u	s	p
b	d	n	t
w	m		

Support the child to read the words on the left, one by one.
For each word read the clue to the child and then work out what the answer word is.
Explain to the child that they will need to either: add a sound, take away a sound or change a sound to the word on the left to make the answer word, e.g. cot > cost list > lit mat > rat.
Have the child write out the answer word on the right, saying each sound as they write each sound spelling.
An example is done for you
Break this task into a number of shorter tasks over a number of lessons if necessary

Activity 30 Sound exchange

Starting Word	Clue	New word
lad	On top of a pan	lid
milk	Soft, shiny material	________
bell	Had a tumble or trip	________
clash	Money	________
link	Under the taps	________
sell	Witch's magic	________
lend	Mix a fruit smoothie	________
still	Knock over paints	________
pan	Decide what to do	________
splat	Make waves in water	________

Place a whiteboard in front of the child.
Choose a word from the list below. Randomise the words you choose so that you are choosing words with a variety of number of sounds.
Draw dots on the whiteboard to match the number of sounds in the word, one dot for each sound. Do not write the word or show the word to the child as this is a purely auditory activity.
Say the word to the child and as you do so run your finger under the dots so that your finger matches the appropriate sound dot and its corresponding sound as you say it.
Then cover the dot that corresponds to the sound you are going to take away – use the list below. There are lots more words you could use for this activity – refer to the teacher word list at the start of this chapter.
Ask the child to tell you what is left if you take that sound away
Take away another sound or choose a new word.
Remember to time limit this activity.

Activity 31 Sound sums I

No. of sounds in starting word	Word	Take away the sound	What is left?
3	lit	l	it
3	will	w	ill
4	belt	l	bet
4	black	b	lack
4	black	l	back
4	clap	k (c)	lap
4	clap	l	cap
4	clash	l	cash
4	clot	k (c)	lot
4	clot	l	cot
4	flan	l	fan
4	flip	f	lip
4	glum	l	gum
4	land	l	and
4	land	n	lad
4	left	f	let

No. of sounds in starting word	Word	Take away the sound	What is left?
4	lend	l	end
4	lend	n	led
4	melt	l	met
4	plan	l	pan
4	slid	s	lid
4	sling	l	sing
4	slip	l	sip
4	slip	s	lip
4	drill	r	dill
4	smell	m	sell
5	blank	l	bank
5	clamp	k (c)	lamp
5	clamp	l	camp
5	clamp	p	clam
5	clamp	m	clap
5	plank	k	plan
5	splash	p	slash
5	splat	l	spat

This set of cards is made up of high frequency words containing the sound 'l'. Copy onto card and cut out. Practise dynamic blending for reading, as described in the 'Working through the programme' section, using these cards. Model this process for the child if necessary.

Activity 32 Reading high frequency words l

will	fell
tell	still

Starting at 'still', have the child read each of the words on the shapes as quickly as possible.
Support the child to read the words by giving information about sounds and supporting blending but do not supply the whole word.
Time how long it takes to read all the words to 'flag' and record the time in the box.
Repeat at a later point and see if the child can beat his own time.

Activity 33 Reading race: wave the flag! I

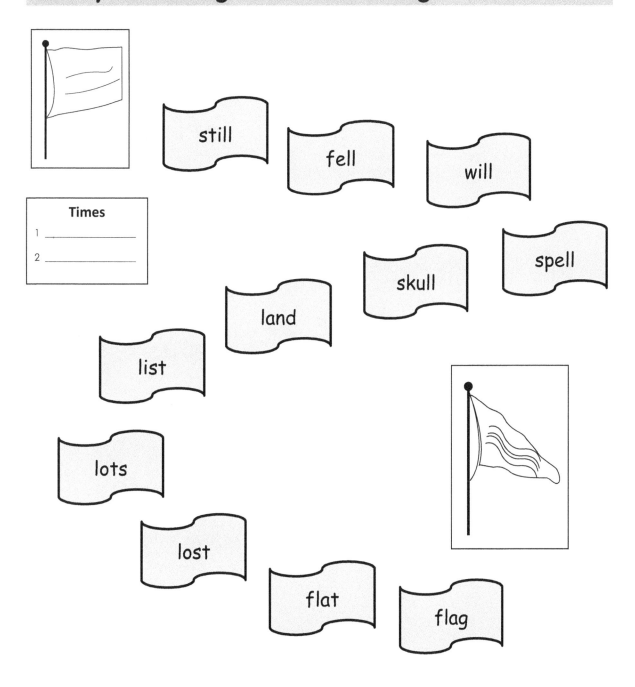

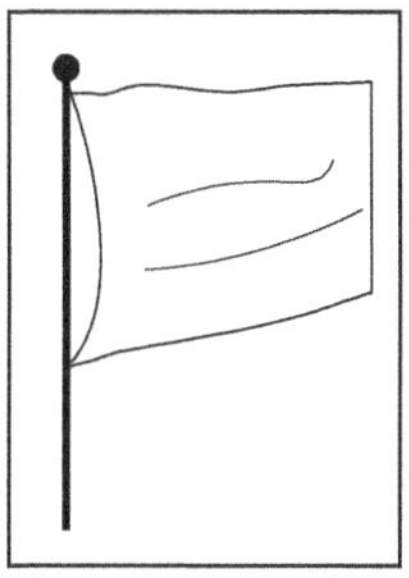

Times

1 ____________

2 ____________

still

fell

will

spell

skull

land

list

lots

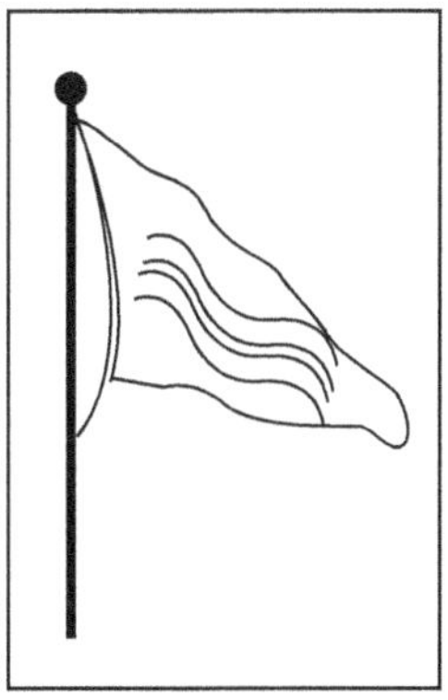

lost

flat

flag

Support the child to read the words one by one.
For each word support the child to think whether there is an 'l' sound in the word.
Have the child put a ring around or highlight just the words that have an 'l' sound.
Remind the child that 'l' can be represented by two sound spellings: **l** and **ll**.
Break this task into a number of shorter tasks over a number of lessons if necessary.

Activity 34 Word tracker **l**

taps	lost	pull	hot	melt
claps	stop	milk	left	still
lots	tell	trap	leg	hat
cost	will	grill	must	land
lump	flat	shall	shop	shelf

How many 'l' words did you find? ________

Visual memory is the ability to remember and identify a shape, figure or picture that we have previously seen. Children with poor visual memory may struggle to remember pictures, figures, shapes, letters and numbers and may have difficulties with reading, writing and number work.

Ask the child to look at the word in the yellow box for at least five seconds, covering the white box underneath. Then cover the yellow box so that the word cannot be seen and reveal a choice of words in the white box below. Ask the child to select the word in the white box that matches the one they saw in the yellow box.

Break this task into a number of shorter tasks over a number of lessons if necessary.

Activity 35 Remembering words l

lap
lad lap

lost
lots lost

land
land lend

held
held help

bell
bell fell tell

spell
spill smell spell

fling
sling fling cling

Support the child to read the words one by one.
For each word support the child to think whether the word is a real word that makes sense or is a nonsense word.
Have the child put a ring around or highlight just the real words.
Break this task into a number of shorter tasks over a number of lessons if necessary.

Activity 36 Word detective

lep	pull	left	will	stull
list	flag	rilt	belt	lots
still	pell	plan	luft	spell
drull	glad	lask	milk	kell
lunk	lunch	snell	shall	lamp

How many real words did you find? ________

Visual sequential memory is the ability to remember sequences of figures, symbols, pictures and shapes. Children with poor visual sequencing struggle to remember a sequence of letters and follow visual patterns. They may have difficulties writing a sequence of letters to form a word and a sequence of words to form a sentence.

Ask the child to look at the words in the yellow box for at least five seconds, covering the white box underneath. Then cover the yellow box so that the words cannot be seen and reveal the sequence of words in the white box below. Ask the child to remember the missing word from the sequence in the yellow box and write it in the space.

Break this task into a number of shorter tasks over a number of lessons if necessary.

Activity 37 Remembering lots of words I

lid let
______ let

bell will
bell ______

last lots lift
______ lots lift

sell full hill
sell ______ hill

flag glad plan
flag glad ______

held milk sulk
held ______ sulk

doll fill shall
doll fill ______

shall flop lend
shall ______ lend

Print out on card and cut out the sound spelling and picture cards for each word.
Read though the instructions in the 'Working through the programme' section at the start of this book prior to working with a child.

Activity 38 Word build l

l	a	m	p	
f	l	a	g	
m	e	l	t	
p	l	u	g	

b	e	ll		
h	i	ll		
s	m	e	ll	

Support the child to read the words on the list one by one.
For each word support the child to think about each of the sounds in the word and their matching sound spellings.
Have the child put a ring around or highlight the sound spelling for each sound.
Break this task into a number of shorter tasks over a number of lessons if necessary.

Activity 39 Word tech

will
left
clap
tell
milk
lost
doll
grill
blink

smell
lots
lunch
shell
pull
shelf
splash
thrill
slack

Read the clue on the left for the child.
For each clue support the child to work out what the answer word is.
The sound spellings for the answer word are given to help, but they are mixed up – an anagram.
Have the child use the sound spellings to write the answer word on the line on the right.
Encourage the child to say the associated sound as he writes each sound spelling.
Break this task into a number of shorter tasks over a number of lessons if necessary.

Activity 40 Word scramble

I

Clue	Sound spellings	Word
Not right	t e f l	______
Not well	ll i	______
Holds up trousers	l b e t	______
Cook outside on this	g ll i r	______
Sniff	s e m ll	______
Where am I?	o l s t	______
Can take you upstairs	f t l i	______
Cast magic	p e s ll	______
Lights a room	m a l p	______
Holds books	**sh** f e l	______
Small mountain	ll h i	______

Activity 42 Spelling challenge

let	l e t	l e t	___ ___ ___	______________
let's	l e t' s	l e t' s	___ ___ ___ ___	______________
lost	l o s t	l o s t	___ ___ ___ ___	______________
will	w i ll	w i ll	___ ___ ___	______________
tell	t e ll	t e ll	___ ___ ___	______________
fell	f e ll	f e ll	___ ___ ___	______________
still	s t i ll	s t i ll	___ ___ ___ ___	______________

Support the child to read the sentences.
Explain that the sentences are OK but that they are very short and could be a bit more interesting!
Then support the child to read the phrases at the bottom of the page and decide which could be used to make each sentence 'better' or 'more interesting'.
Ask the child to write out the sentence, adding the new phrase from the list. Encourage the child to say the sounds at the same time as writing the associated sound spelling when writing each word.
Note that the sentences include high frequency words which contain sounds that the child has not yet encountered in the programme. Support the child to decode these words by supplying information about any unfamiliar sounds and sound spellings and encourage the child to blend for reading. Some sound spellings are highlighted to support this.
Break this task into a number of shorter tasks over a number of lessons if necessary.

Activity 45 Making better sentences

1. I shall pull the plug.

____

____

2. Mum was glad.

____

____

3. I can spell.

____

____

4. Sam had a flask.

____

____

5. Tom rang the bell.

____

____

to get in Rav's h**ou**se	lots of long w**or**ds
so the wat**er** does not spill	full of milk
that the lad was well	

Support the child to read each sentence one by one.
Ask the child to re-read the sentence, several times if necessary, and try to remember it.
Then cover the sentence and ask the child to recall the sentence verbally.
Once they can do this confidently, ask the child to write out the sentence from memory.

When writing a word, encourage the child to say the sound as they write each associated sound spelling.
When the word is complete then they are to say the whole word.
When the sentence is complete the child reads out their sentence and then compares it to the original.
Note that the sentences may include high frequency words which contain sounds that the child has not yet encountered in the programme. Support the child to decode these words by supplying information about any unfamiliar sounds and their sound spellings and encouraging the child to blend for reading. Some of these sound spellings are highlighted to help the child when writing the words later.

Alternatively, using text to speech software, the child could type the sentence, with the computer reading back each word and then the completed sentence.

Activity 46 Writing challenge l

The lad left the lid on the jam.

I lost the last list.

Jack went up the hill with Jill.

I will fill the cup with ink.

Answers

Page 339
Activity 8 Investigating the sound 'l'

l
leg belt flat lamp link claps

ll
bell hill spill grill pull still

Page 353
Activity 25 Sound boxes

b e ll
l o g
l i t
m i l k
s m e ll
l i p s
m e l t
l o s t
s p e ll

Page 354
Activity 26 How many sounds?

4 m i l k
4 l o t s
4 s m e ll
3 l e t
5 l i s t s
4 s t i ll
5 c l a p s
4 f l a g

Page 357
Activity 30 Sound exchange

milk – silk
bell – fell
clash – cash
link – sink
sell – spell
lend – blend
still – spill
pan – plan
splat – splash

Page 362
Activity 34 Word tracker

lost pull melt
claps milk left still
lots tell leg
will grill land
lump flat shall shelf

17

Page 365
Activity 36 Word detective

pull left will
list flag belt lots
still plan spell
glad milk
lunch shall lamp

15

Page 370
Activity 39 Word tech

w i ll s m e ll
l e f t l o t s
c l a p l u n ch
t e ll sh e ll
m i l k p u ll
l o s t sh e l f
d o ll s p l a sh
g r i ll th r i ll
b l i n k s l a ck

Page 371
Activity 40 Word scramble

left
ill
belt
grill
smell
lost
lift
spell
lamp
shelf
hill

Page 373
Activity 45 Making better sentences

1. I shall pull the plug so the water does not spill.
2. Mum was glad that the lad was well.
3. I can spell lots of long words.
4. Sam had a flask full of milk.
5. Tom rang the bell to get in Rav's house.

SECTION 9

S

s sun

ss glass

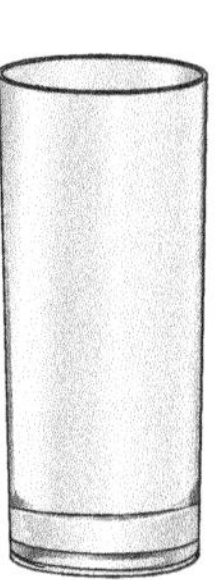

Words with an 's' sound – word list of 1 syllable words

s

3 sounds

ask*
asp
bus
gas
sad
sag
sang
sap
sat
set
sing
sip
sit
song
sun
sung
sup
this

4 sounds

best
cask*
cast*
fast*
gasp*
last*
list
lost
mask*
mast*
must
nest
past*
pest
rest
sand
sank
send
sent
sink
skin
skip
slack
slam
slip
snag
soft
spat
spin
spit
spot
stem
sting
stop
swam
swim
vast*
vest

+ plurals & verbs e.g.

cats
sits

5 sounds

brisk
clasp*
crust
scrap
scrum
slump
splash
splat
split
spring
stamp
stand
stink
string
trust

6 sounds

splint
sprint

ss

3 sounds

chess
fuss
hiss
kiss
less
loss
mass
mess
miss
moss
pass*
toss

4 sounds

bless
brass*
class*
cress
cross
dress
floss
glass*
gloss
grass*
press

5 sounds

stress

* for some accents where the a is an 'a' sound rather than an 'ar' sound

Auditory discrimination is the ability to hear differences between sounds. Good auditory discrimination helps us to recognise and identify the sounds in words and so interpret them correctly. Children with poor auditory discrimination may confuse sounds and misinterpret things they have heard. Their spelling and writing may reflect their confusion over which sounds they heard in a word. **Auditory attention and tracking** is the ability to actively listen and follow auditory information from beginning to end. Good auditory attention and tracking helps us to follow a conversation, a story read out loud or a set of instructions, and enables us to focus on key information. Children with poor auditory attention and tracking may find it difficult to follow and respond appropriately to what is being said to them.

This story contains lots of words that contain the sound 's', which is the 'target' sound.
Read the story out loud to the child or group of children. Encourage the child to listen carefully and spot any word that contains the target sound. Note that there are two ways that 's' can be represented: **s** and **ss**, but the 's' sound is the same for both. When a target word has been read, the child indicates that they have heard and spotted it by tapping the table, putting up a hand or any other agreed signal, but without shouting out. Stop reading and discuss the word, making any error correction necessary. If a word is missed, re-read the sentence.
Do not show the written story to the child. The target words are highlighted below for you.

Activity 1 Sound target story s

Sam always wanted to be a singer. He sang all the time, wherever he was.

He would sing when he woke at the start of the day, when he was washing, when he was snacking and when he was sleepy!

Sam also made up his own songs.

He would sing about the sun shining and the raindrops splashing on the pavement.

He would sing about happy people smiling and sad people crying.

He would sing about snowdrops in spring and roses in summer.

He would sing about fish swimming and mice scratching.

Sam would sing about anything.

There was only one snag. Sam was a cat.

When Sam sang, all his human family heard was rasping and spitting and shrieking.

'Shut up, Sam, ' they would say crossly. Poor misunderstood Sam.

Auditory discrimination is the ability to hear differences between sounds. Good auditory discrimination helps us to recognise and identify the sounds in words and so interpret them correctly. Children with poor auditory discrimination may confuse sounds and misinterpret things they have heard. Their spelling and writing may reflect their confusion over what sounds they heard in a word. **Auditory sequential memory** is the ability to remember and recall a series of things that they have heard. Children with poor auditory sequential memory may find it difficult to remember information given earlier in a conversation or set of instructions and may struggle to recall the sequence of sounds in a word.

The silly sentences contain lots of words containing the sound 's'.
Read the sentence to the child several times, invite them to join in as you say it and gradually recall it on their own.
Do not show the words to the child.
Ask them to say it as quickly as they can and have some fun with it. Perhaps they can make up their own?
The sentences gradually get longer and more complex.
Break this task into a number of shorter tasks over a number of lessons if necessary.

Activity 2 Tongue twister fun — s

Sophie sings softly.

See the sun in summer.

Six salty sausages sizzling slowly.

Some smart snails search for salad.

Auditory discrimination is the ability to hear differences between sounds. Good auditory discrimination helps us to recognise and identify the sounds in words and so interpret them correctly. Children with poor auditory discrimination may confuse sounds and misinterpret things they have heard. Their spelling and writing may reflect their confusion over which sounds they heard in a word. **Auditory attention and tracking** is the ability to actively listen and follow auditory information from beginning to end. Good auditory attention and tracking helps us to follow a conversation, a story read out loud or a set of instructions, and enables us to focus on key information. Children with poor auditory attention and tracking may find it difficult to follow and respond appropriately to what is being said to them.

Read out the words and ask the child to identify the odd one out. In 1–10 the child focuses on the sound at the **beginning** of the words and in 11–20 the child focuses on the sound at the **end** of the words.
Do not show the words to the child. The odd one out is highlighted for you.
Break this task into a number of shorter tasks over a number of lessons if necessary.

Activity 3 Odd one out s

1.	set	sip	lad	2.	this	fog	fan
3.	net	song	nap	4.	sit	sad	this
5.	hiss	less	loss	6.	miss	fuss	mess
7.	list	lost	soft	8.	send	best	sand
9.	cross	skip	swim	10.	spot	stop	press
11.	bus	gas	sat	12.	miss	bell	kiss
13.	spin	skin	fuss	14.	mess	rest	sent
15.	stem	hiss	slam	16.	dress	stick	cross
17.	smell	floss	press	18.	blink	thank	stamp
19.	split	stress	splat	20.	trust	class	glass

Auditory discrimination is the ability to hear differences between sounds. Good auditory discrimination helps us to recognise and identify the sounds in words and so interpret them correctly. Children with poor auditory discrimination may confuse sounds and misinterpret things they have heard. Their spelling and writing may reflect their confusion over which sounds they heard in a word. **Auditory recall memory** is the ability to remember and recall something that they have just heard. Children with poor auditory recall memory may find it difficult to remember sounds and words and respond appropriately.

Read the list of words below clearly, asking the child to listen carefully. At random points tap the table and stop reading, asking the child to remember and say the last word you said. Then ask them to tell you what the **first** or the **last** sound in the word is.

Break this task into a number of shorter tasks over a number of lessons if necessary.

Activity 4 What sound am I? s

1.	gas	sun	bus	hiss	set	pass
2.	sad	sat	less	sip	kiss	fuss
3.	mess	sing	loss	this	sang	hiss
4.	best	sand	list	sent	rest	vest
5.	spot	class	stop	chess	press	swam
6.	skip	dress	spin	floss	bless	slip
7.	class	swim	cross	skin	spit	glass
8.	stick	swish	stand	still	spell	switch
9.	splash	stress	trust	stamp	string	splint

Auditory discrimination is the ability to hear differences between sounds. Good auditory discrimination helps us to recognise and identify the sounds in words and so interpret them correctly. Children with poor auditory discrimination may confuse sounds and misinterpret things they have heard. Their spelling and writing may reflect their confusion over what sounds they heard in a word.

Read out the pairs of words. For 1–12 ask the child to tell you whether or not they start with the same sound and for 13–24 ask whether or not they end with the same sounds. The words get increasingly complex.

Break this task into a number of shorter tasks over a number of lessons if necessary.

Activity 5 Same or different? s

1. bus - kiss
2. sip - set
3. sun - gas
4. sad - sit
5. song - wing
6. best - last
7. sent - soft
8. skin - this
9. must - sand
10. mess - miss
11. dress - cross
12. glass - grass
13. sit - set
14. bus - gas
15. this - sing
16. swim - slam
17. stop - spot
18. lost - lots
19. less - loss
20. dress - press
21. must - sink
22. glass - glad
23. stress - smell
24. splat - split

Auditory fusion is the ability to hear the subtle gaps between sounds and words. Children with poor auditory fusion may get lost in conversations and when following a list of instructions given verbally.

Say the sounds or read the words in the list one after another at a brisk pace so that there are no obvious gaps between the sounds or the words. Ask the child to listen carefully and then tell you how many sounds or words you have said. Many of the words contain the sound 's' (represented by the sound spellings **s** and **ss**) and get increasingly complex.

Break this task into a number of shorter tasks over a number of lessons if necessary.

Activity 6 How many did you hear? s

1. m - s - f - h
2. v - s - f
3. m - v - s - l - h
4. s - h - m - n
5. s - f - h
6. v - s - v - s
7. v - **sh** - s - **th** - v
8. **sh** - s - **th** - v - s - s
9. gas - sit - sad
10. fuss - set - bus - sun
11. hiss - mess - sip
12. kiss - sat - loss
13. best - soft - chess - spin
14. sand - class
15. sank - list - dress
16. press - nest - skip - sent
17. glass - slam - cross
18. pest - floss - spit
19. this - grass - swim - less
20. sink - stress
21. vest - sand - must
22. sock - sell - wish
23. trust - stand - splash
24. splat - spin - stack
25. stink - crust - split - splint
26. glass - smash - stuck

Auditory attention and tracking is the ability to actively listen and follow auditory information from beginning to end. Good auditory attention and tracking helps us to follow a conversation, a story read out loud or a set of instructions, and enables us to focus on key information. Children with poor auditory attention and tracking may find it difficult to follow and respond appropriately to what is being said to them. **Auditory sequential memory** is the ability to remember and recall a series of things that they have heard. Children with poor auditory sequential memory may find it difficult to remember information given earlier in a conversation or set of instructions and may struggle to recall the sequence of sounds in a word.

In this activity the child has to process the auditory information but also respond by working out the pattern and stating the next sound in the sequence. Read out the list of sounds with a clear space between each. Ask the child to listen and work out what sound would come next. The answers follow in red.

Break this task into a number of shorter tasks over a number of lessons if necessary.

Activity 7 What comes next? s

1. s v s v s v ...... s
2. **sh** s **sh** s **sh** s ...... sh
3. f s f s f s ...... f
4. h s h s h s ...... h
5. s v h s v h s v h ...... s
6. f s **th** f s **th** f s **th** ...... f
7. **sh** s h **sh** s h **sh** ...... s
8. **th** **sh** s **th** **sh** s ...... th
9. v s s v s s v s s v
10. **sh** **sh** s **sh** **sh** s **sh** **sh** ..... s
11. s **th** s s **th** s s **th** ...... s
12. **sh** **th** s **sh** **th** s **sh** ...... th
13. s s **sh** **sh** s s **sh** **sh** ...... s
14. s s **th** **th** s s **th** **th** s s ...... th
15. s v f h s v f h ...... s
16. v **sh** s f v **sh** s f v
17. s l v n s l v n s l
18. **sh** **sh** s s f **sh** **sh** s s f ...... sh
19. **th** s s v **th** s s v **th** s ...... s
20. s f v m s f v m s f v m ...... s

This activity results in the child discovering all the sound spellings for the sound and sorting the words into corresponding lists.
Support the child to read the words one by one.
For each word support the child to work out the sound spelling corresponding to the sound 's' and highlight it.
There are two sound spellings to find at this stage: **s** and **ss**.
In the boxes underneath write the sound spelling, **s** or **ss,** as the heading on the small line at the top of the box, as the child discovers it.
Then work through the word list and sort the words into lists according to the sound spelling. Encourage the child to say each sound as they write each sound spelling in sequence, Encourage the child to say each sound as they write each sound spelling in sequence, e.g. say 'd' 'r' 'e' 's' as they write **d r e ss**.

Break this task into a number of shorter tasks over a number of lessons if necessary.

Activity 8 Investigating the sound s

dress	stand	mess
nest	cross	spot
miss	swim	list
sent	press	kiss

______	______
______	______
______	______
______	______
______	______
______	______
______	______
______	______

Activity 10 Sound spelling cards s

s
ss

Visual discrimination is the ability to see differences between objects and figures that are similar. Good visual discrimination helps keep us from getting confused when looking at shapes and forms in the environment. Children with poor visual discrimination may find it difficult to recognise letters, may confuse letters such as b and d and may find it difficult to identify mathematical symbols.

Ask the child to look at the sound spelling in the yellow box then track along the row looking at the other sound spellings.
The child indicates or puts a ring around the sound spelling that is the same as the one in the yellow box.
This includes some sound spellings which represent other sounds but are visually similar.

Break this task into a number of shorter tasks over a number of lessons if necessary.

Activity 11 Sound spelling tracker s

ss	s	ss	z	x
s	z	ss	s	z
c	c	o	a	e
s	ss	s	z	x
ss	x	z	s	ss
z	ss	x	s	z
ss	z	s	ss	x
s	ss	s	z	x

Visual memory is the ability to remember and identify a shape or picture that we have previously seen. Children with poor visual memory may struggle to remember pictures, figures, shapes, letters and numbers and may have difficulties with reading, writing and number work.

Ask the child to look at the sound spelling in the yellow box for at least five seconds, covering the white box underneath. Then cover the yellow box so that the sound spelling cannot be seen and reveal the choice of sound spellings in the white box below. Ask the child to select the matching sound spelling from the white box.

Break this task into a number of shorter tasks over a number of lessons if necessary.

Activity 12 Remembering sound spellings s

s
z s

ss
ss ll

ss
s ss

s
s z

ss
s ss z

s
z ss s

Visual discrimination is the ability to see differences between objects and figures that are similar. Good visual discrimination helps keep us from getting confused when looking at shapes and forms in the environment. Children with poor visual discrimination may find it difficult to recognise letters, may confuse letters such as b and d and may find it difficult to identify mathematical symbols.

Focus on one of the sound spellings featured on this sheet, e.g. **ss** (say the sound 's' and point to an example rather than using the letter names to identify the sound spelling). Ask the child to look at all the sound spellings and indicate or put a ring round all the sound spellings which match the target. Repeat for another sound spelling featured on the sheet.

Break this task into a number of shorter tasks over a number of lessons if necessary.

Activity 13 Spot the sound spelling s

z s ss ss

s

ss s

ss

z

z ss

ss

ss z z s

Spatial relations is the ability to perceive the position of objects in relation to ourselves and to each other. This skill helps children to understand relationships between symbols and letters. Children with poor spatial relations may find it difficult to write letters in the correct orientation, write consistently starting at the margin and write letters of the same size.

In the first part, ask the child to copy the sound spellings on the lines below in exactly the same places as they appear above.
In the second part, ask the child to copy the words on the lines below in exactly the same places, saying the matching sound as they write each sound spelling.

Break this task into a number of shorter tasks over a number of lessons if necessary.

Activity 17 Where am I? s

ss s s

s ss s

sad less

stop dress

Visual sequential memory is the ability to remember sequences of figures, symbols and shapes. Children with poor visual sequencing struggle to remember a sequence of letters and follow visual patterns. They may have difficulties writing a sequence of letters to form a word and a sequence of words to form a sentence.

Ask the child to look at the sound spellings in the yellow box for at least five seconds, covering the white box underneath. Then cover the yellow box so that the sound spellings cannot be seen and reveal the sequence of sound spellings in the white box below. Ask the child to remember the missing sound spelling and write it in the space.

Break this task into a number of shorter tasks over a number of lessons if necessary.

Activity 18 Remembering lots of sound spellings s

s z
___ z

ss s
ss ___

ss z
___ z

ss s
ss ___

ss s z
ss s ___

z s ss
z ___ ss

Having introduced the sound and its corresponding sound spellings, it is important that the child is given the opportunity to practise writing them.
In this activity the child can practise forming the sound spellings in a number of ways:

- copying over the grey letters which act as a guide to accurate letter formation,
- writing individual sound spellings within small boxes (with shading to act as a guide), which develops visual-spatial awareness of the letters and
- writing words with a sound spelling in each box.

Encourage the child to say the sound at the same time as writing the sound spelling.

Activity 19 Writing sound spellings s

s s s s s s s

s s s s s s s

s						

ss ss ss ss ss

ss ss ss ss ss ss ss

ss						

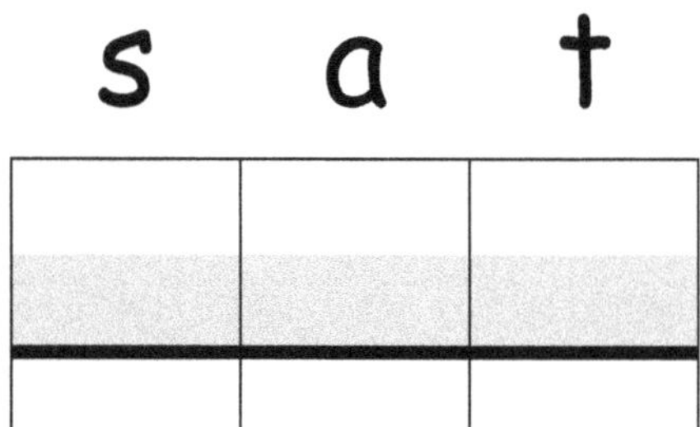

s i p

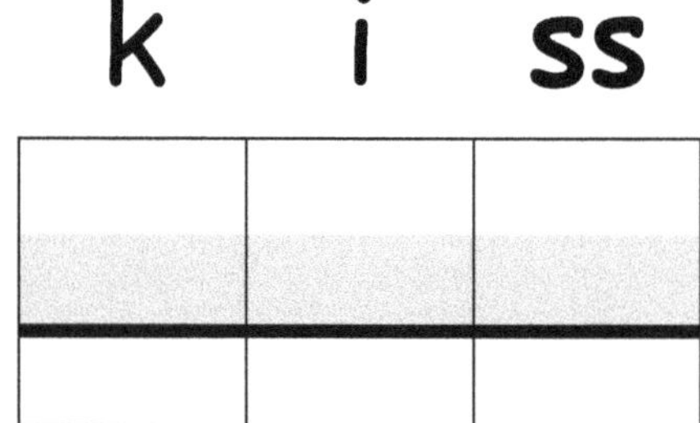

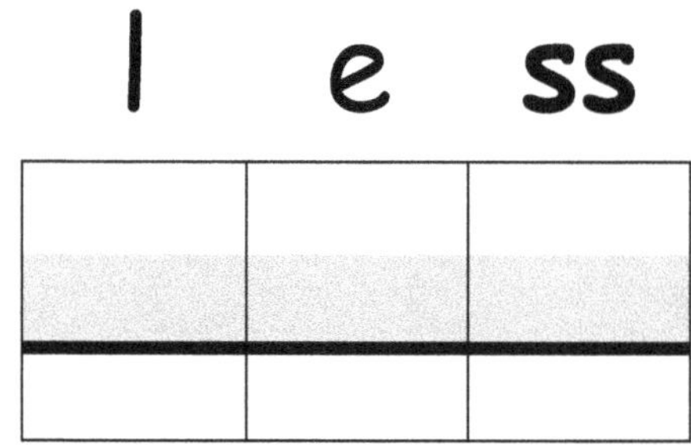

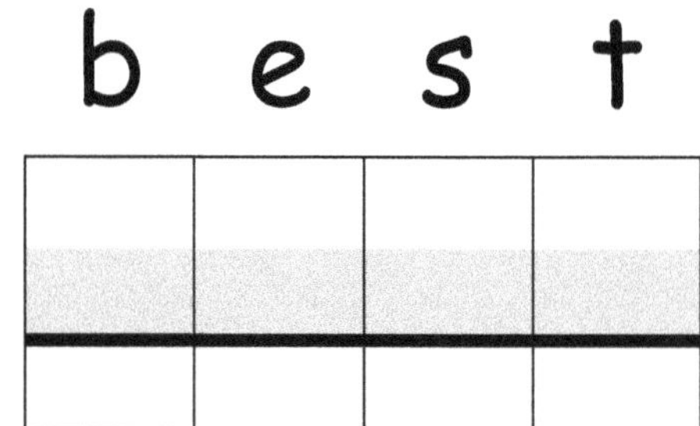

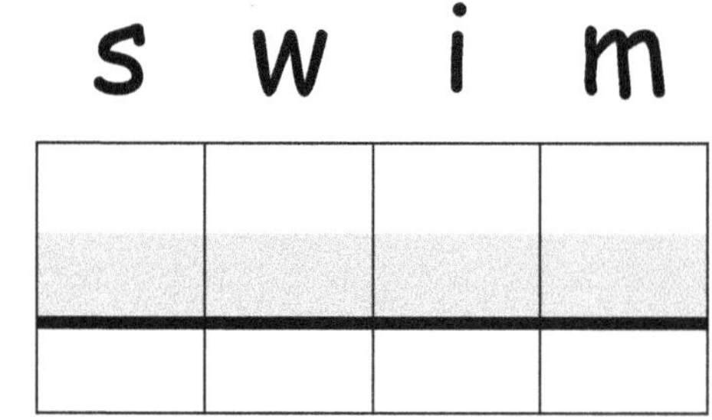

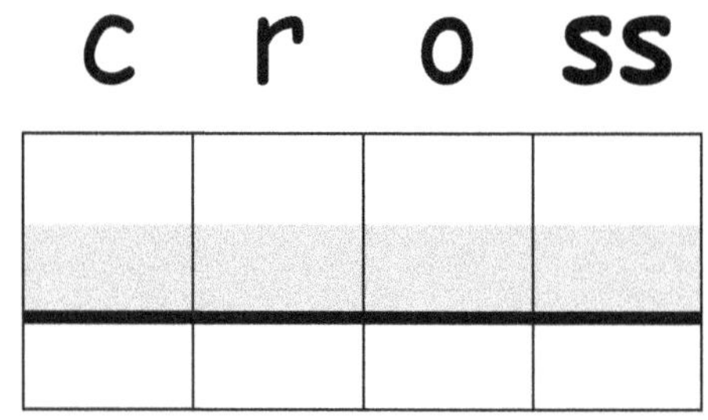

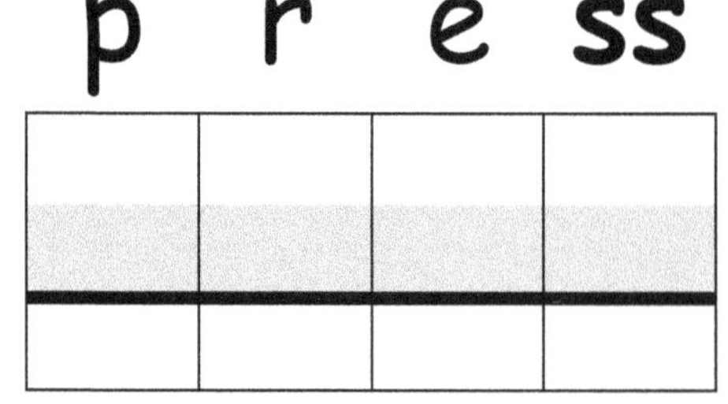

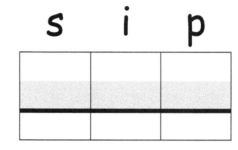

This set of cards is made of up words containing the sound 's'. The sound spelling for the target sound in each word is highlighted. Copy onto card and cut out.
Practise dynamic blending for reading, as described in the 'Working through the programme' section, using these cards. Model this process for the child if necessary.

Activity 20 Dynamic blending – word cards s

sent	vest
list	split
crust	stamp
splash	sprint
less	miss
kiss	dress
cross	stress

This set of cards is made of up words containing the sound 's'. Copy onto card and cut out.Practise dynamic blending for reading, as described in the 'Working through the programme' section, using these cards. Model this process for the child if necessary.

Activity 20 Dynamic blending – word cards s

sat	send
desk	trust
stamp	stand
spend	string
less	mess
fuss	miss
dress	press

Print out onto card and cut out.
Stack them with the biggest (the complete word) on the bottom and in decreasing size so that the smallest is on the top.
Make sure the left-hand edge of the cards are flush. Staple the cards together on the left-hand side.
When the child runs a finger over the cards the sound spellings flip up. Ask the child to say the sounds and match to the flips.

staple

Activity 24 Flippies for the sound 's'

s	s	w	s	w	i	s	w	i	m
s	s	e	s	e	n	s	e	n	d
m	m	i	m	i	ss				
c	c	r	c	r	o	c	r	o	ss
p	p	r	p	r	e	p	r	e	ss

Read the clue on the left for the child.
Use the clue to work out what the answer word is.
Encourage the child to think about the sounds in that word and write a sound spelling for each sound in the boxes on the right, one by one.
The first one is done for you as an example.
Explain to the child that they may not need to use all the boxes and so some are shaded in.
Break this task into a number of shorter tasks over a number of lessons if necessary.

Activity 25 Sound boxes s

Clue	Sound boxes			
Untidy	m	e	ss	
Not hit the target				
Shines in the sky				
Some ladies wear this				
Push a button				
Take a break. Have a ...				
Part of your mouth				
Shiny paint surface				
Covers the body				
Move through water				
Lots of this at the beach				

Support the child to read the words on the left.
For each word, support the child to work out how many sounds there are in it and write that number in the grey box.
Then ask the child to count out the number of white boxes needed to write the word, so that there is one box for each sound, and colour in any boxes that are not needed.
Next ask the child to say the sounds in the word, one by one, and at the same time write the matching sound spelling in the boxes one by one.
The first one is done for you as an example.
Break this task into a number of shorter tasks over a number of lessons if necessary.

Activity 26 How many sounds? s

Word	Number	Writing the sound spellings				
miss	3	m	i	ss		
sad						
mess						
rest						
stand						
press						
crust						
stress						
kiss						

During this activity the child will be asked to slide sounds in and out of words, i.e. practise phoneme manipulation.
A sound might be swapped, added or taken away.
Print the sound spelling cards onto card and cut out.
Activity:

- Spread out all the sound spelling cards so that the child can see them.
- Build a starting word from the prompt list, demonstrating how to dynamically blend the sounds together as you move the sound spelling cards into place.
- Repeat the word, running your finger under the cards so that it corresponds to the sounds within the word.
- Ask the child to change the word to the next word on the prompt list. As you say the new word run your finger under the cards so that it corresponds with the sound you are saying and the matching sound spelling card.

This gives the child the chance to hear and see what is different.

- The child can then swap the appropriate sounds spelling cards.
- Repeat this technique with the next word on the list.

Activity 29 Sound swap s

Sound swap s

List 1	List 2	List 3
slap	lots	bless
slip	lot	less
sip	lost	loss
sit	list	moss
set	lit	miss
sent	lip	kiss
send	clip	
sand	clips	
stand	claps	
	clap	

s	ss	a	e
i	o	l	p
t	n	d	c
b	m	k	

Support the child to read the words on the left, one by one.
For each word read the clue to the child and then work out what the answer word is.
Explain to the child that they will need to either: add a sound, take away a sound or change a sound to the word on the left to make the answer word, e.g. cot > cost list > lit mat > rat.
Have the child write out the answer word on the right, saying each sound as they write each sound spelling.
An example is done for you.
Break this task into a number of shorter tasks over a number of lessons if necessary.

Activity 30 Sound exchange s

Starting word	Clue	New word
list	Has light	lit
miss	Untidy	______
sip	Skid on wet surface	______
sung	Shines in the sky	______
cress	×	______
spit	Dot or round mark	______
press	Some women wear this	______
snap	Short sleep	______
trust	Corrosion on metal	______
string	First season	______

Place a whiteboard in front of the child.
Choose a word from the list below. Randomise the words you choose so that you are choosing words with a variety of number of sounds.
Draw dots on the whiteboard to match the number of sounds in the word, one dot for each sound. Do not write the word or show the word to the child as this is a purely auditory activity.
Say the word to the child and as you do so run your finger under the dots so that your finger matches the appropriate sound dot and its corresponding sound as you say it.
Then cover the dot that corresponds to the sound you are going to take away – use the list below. There are lots more words you could use for this activity – refer to the teacher word list at the start of this chapter.
Ask the child to tell you what is left if you take that sound away.
Remember to time limit this activity.

Activity 31 Sound sums s

No. of sounds in starting word	Word	Take away the sound	What is left?
3	sit	s	it
4	best	s	bet
4	list	s	lit
4	lost	s	lot
4	nest	s	net
4	pest	s	pet
4	sand	s	and
4	sand	n	sad
4	sent	n	set
4	slip	s	lip
4	slip	l	sip
4	spat	p	sat
4	spat	s	pat
4	spin	s	pin
4	spit	s	pit

No. of sounds in starting word	Word	Take away the sound	What is left?
4	spit	p	sit
4	spot	s	pot
4	sting	t	sing
4	stop	s	top
4	vest	s	vet
4	bless	b	less
4	floss	f	loss
5	crust	k (c)	rust
5	slump	s	lump
5	splash	p	slash
5	splat	l	spat
5	splat	p	slat
5	split	l	spit
5	split	p	slit
5	stand	t	sand
5	stink	t	sink
5	string	r	sting
5	trust	t	rust
6	splint	n	split

This set of cards is made up of high frequency words containing the sound 's'. Copy onto card and cut out. Practise dynamic blending for reading, as described in the 'Working through the programme' section, using these cards. Model this process for the child if necessary.

Activity 32 Reading high frequency words s

miss	across

Starting at 'spring', have the child read each of the words on the shapes as quickly as possible.
Support the child to read the words by giving information about sounds and supporting blending but do not supply the whole word.
Time how long it takes to read all the words to 'splash' and record the time in the box.
Repeat at a later point and see if the child can beat his own time.

Activity 33 Reading race: spring is sprung! s

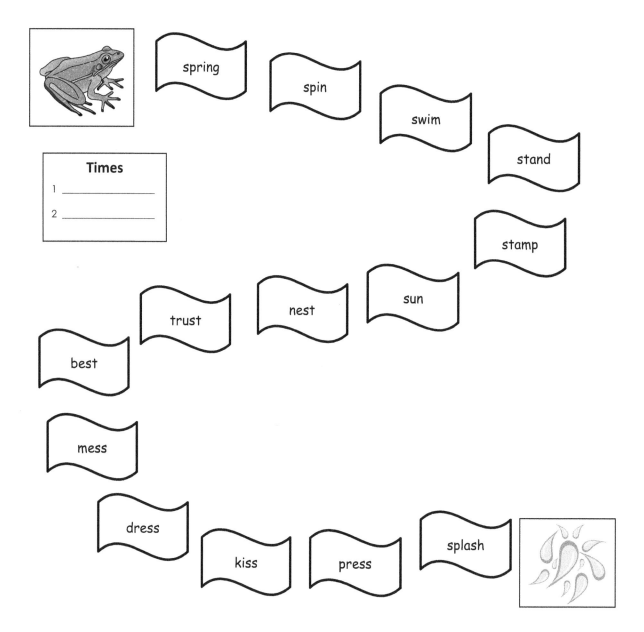

spring

spin

swim

stand

Times

1 ____________

2 ____________

stamp

sun

nest

trust

best

mess

dress

kiss

press

splash

Support the child to read the words one by one.
For each word support the child to think whether there is an 's' sound in the word.
Have the child put a ring around or highlight just the words that have an 's' sound.
Remind the child that 's' can be represented by two sound spellings: **s** and **ss**.
Break this task into a number of shorter tasks over a number of lessons if necessary.

Activity 34 Word tracker **s**

belt	mess	sent	swam	ship
kiss	caps	mint	press	ink
shift	cross	chips	trust	land
sting	fish	less	pram	slip
traps	splash	crash	dress	shop

How many 's' words did you find? ________

Visual memory is the ability to remember and identify a shape, figure or picture that we have previously seen. Children with poor visual memory may struggle to remember pictures, figures, shapes, letters and numbers and may have difficulties with reading, writing and number work.

Ask the child to look at the word in the yellow box for at least five seconds, covering the white box underneath. Then cover the yellow box so that the word cannot be seen and reveal a choice of words in the white box below. Ask the child to select the word in the white box that matches the one they saw in the yellow box.

Break this task into a number of shorter tasks over a number of lessons if necessary.

Activity 35 Remembering words s

set
sat set

slip
slip slap

sand
send sand

mess
mess mass

dress
press dress

stamp
slump stamp

string
sting spring string

Support the child to read the words one by one.
For each word support the child to think whether the word is a real word that makes sense or is a nonsense word.
Have the child put a ring around or highlight just the real words.
Break this task into a number of shorter tasks over a number of lessons if necessary.

Activity 36 Word detective s

miss	wess	nest	spot	slen
sliss	cross	swim	fless	lots
vest	priss	trust	dress	gluss
kiss	sent	fets	must	press
cless	stand	hunts	list	stamp

How many real words did you find? ________

Visual sequential memory is the ability to remember sequences of figures, symbols, pictures and shapes. Children with poor visual sequencing struggle to remember a sequence of letters and follow visual patterns. They may have difficulties writing a sequence of letters to form a word and a sequence of words to form a sentence.

Ask the child to look at the words in the yellow box for at least five seconds, covering the white box underneath. Then cover the yellow box so that the words cannot be seen and reveal the sequence of words in the white box below. Ask the child to remember the missing word from the sequence in the yellow box and write it in the space.

Break this task into a number of shorter tasks over a number of lessons if necessary.

Activity 37 Remembering lots of words s

sit sad
______ sad

mess hiss
mess ______

must nest best
______ nest best

kiss less moss
kiss ______ moss

spin swim skip
spin swim ______

lost lots stop
lost ______ stop

fuss miss less
fuss miss ______

trust stand brisk
trust ______ brisk

Print out on card and cut out the sound spelling and picture cards for each word.
Read though the instructions in the 'Working through the programme' section at the start of this book prior to working with a child.

Activity 38 Word build s

s	a	n	d	
s	p	i	n	
n	e	s	t	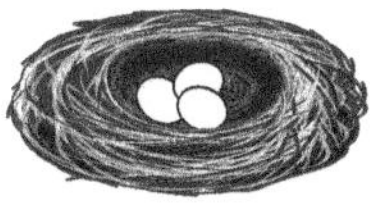
l	o	s	t	

k	i	ss		
d	r	e	ss	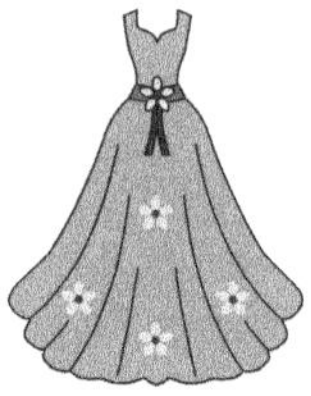
c	r	o	ss	

Support the child to read the words on the list one by one.
For each word support the child to think about each of the sounds in the word and their matching sound spellings.
Have the child put a ring around or highlight the sound spelling for each sound.
Break this task into a number of shorter tasks over a number of lessons if necessary.

Activity 39 Word tech s

dress

best

splash

hiss

skin

crust

spring

stand

desks

snack

bless

cross

stink

press

stress

spent

slack

Read the clue on the left for the child.
For each clue support the child to work out what the answer word is.
The sound spellings for the answer word are given to help, but they are mixed up – an anagram.
Have the child use the sound spellings to write the answer word on the line on the right.
Encourage the child to say the associated sound as he writes each sound spelling.
Break this task into a number of shorter tasks over a number of lessons if necessary.

Activity 40 Word scramble s

Clue	Sound spellings	Word
On the beach	s n d a	__________
Drink carefully	p s i	__________
Bird's house of twigs	t n s e	__________
Lady's clothes	d **ss** r e	__________
A hug and...	i k **ss**	__________
Have to do something	s m t u	__________
Push a button	r p e **ss**	__________
Turn around quickly	p s i n	__________
Snake noise	**ss** i h	__________
Edge of bread	t s c u r	__________
Put this on a letter	t a s p m	__________

Activity 42 Spelling challenge s

sat	s a t	s a t	___ ___ ___	________
let's	l e t' s	l e t' s	___ ___ ___ ___	________
nest	n e s t	n e s t	___ ___ ___ ___	________
send	s e n d	s e n d	___ ___ ___ ___	________
miss	m i ss	m i ss	___ ___ ___	________
cross	c r o ss	c r o ss	___ ___ ___ ___	________
press	p r e ss	p r e ss	___ ___ ___ ___	________

Support the child to read the sentences.
Explain that the sentences are OK but that they are very short and could be a bit more interesting!
Then support the child to re-read the phrases at the bottom of the page and decide which could be used to make each sentence 'better' or 'more interesting'.
Ask the child to write out the sentence, adding the new phrase from the list. Encourage the child to say the sounds at the same time as writing the associated sound spelling when writing each word.
Note that the sentences include high frequency words which contain sounds that the child has not yet encountered in the programme. Support the child to decode these words by supplying information about any unfamiliar sounds and sound spellings and encourage the child to blend for reading. Some sound spellings are highlighted to support this.
Break this task into a number of shorter tasks over a number of lessons if necessary.

Activity 45 Making better sentences s

1. Sam will sprint.

____

____

2. Mum got a n**ew** dress.

____

____

3. I **ea**t crusts.

____

____

4. Let's jump.

____

____

5. We must rush.

____

____

and rush past Tom	with spots on
in the p**oo**l and swim	on br**ea**d and t**oa**st
to the bus stop or we will miss the bus	

Support the child to read each sentence one by one.
Ask the child to re-read the sentence, several times if necessary, and try to remember it.
Then cover the sentence and ask the child to recall the sentence verbally.
Once they can do this confidently, ask the child to write out the sentence from memory.

When writing a word, encourage the child to say the sound as they write each associated sound spelling.
When the word is complete then they are to say the whole word.
When the sentence is complete the child reads out their sentence and then compares it to the original.
Note that the sentences may include high frequency words which contain sounds that the child has not yet encountered in the programme. Support the child to decode these words by supplying information about any unfamiliar sounds and their sound spellings and encouraging the child to blend for reading. Some of these sound spellings are highlighted to help the child when writing the words later.

Alternatively, using text to speech software, the child could type the sentence, with the computer reading back each word and then the completed sentence.

Activity 46 Writing challenge s

Sam stops and sits on the mat.

I can sing a song on the bus.

Miss Ross had a chess set.

Dad put a cross in the box.

Answers s

Page 388
Activity 8 Investigating the sound 's'

s
stand nest spot swim list sent

ss
dress mess cross miss press kiss

Page 402
Activity 25 Sound boxes

m i ss
s u n
d r e ss
p r e ss
r e s t
l i p s
g l o ss
s k i n
s w i m
s a n d

Page 403
Activity 26 How many sounds?

3 sad
3 m e ss
4 r e s t
5 s t a n d
4 p r e ss
5 c r u s t
5 s t r e ss
3 k i ss

Page 406
Activity 30 Sound exchange

miss – mess
sip – slip
sung – sun
cress – cross
spit – spot
press – dress
snap – nap
trust – rust
string – spring

Page 411
Activity 34 Word tracker

mess sent swan
kiss caps press
cross chips trust
sting less slip
traps splash dress

15

Page 414
Activity 36 Word detective

miss nest spot
cross swim lots
vest trust dress
kiss sent must press
stand hunts list stamp

17

Page 419
Activity 39 Word tech

l e ss	d r e ss
b e s t	s p l a sh
h i ss	s k i n
c r u s t	s p r i ng
s t a n d	d e s k s
s n a ck	b l e ss
c r o ss	s t i n k
p r e ss	s t r e ss
s p e n t	s l a ck

Page 420
Activity 40 Word scramble

sand
sip
nest
dress
kiss
must
press
spin
hiss
crust
stamp

Page 422
Activity 45 Making better sentences

1. Sam will sprint and rush past Tom.
2. Mum got a new dress with spots on.
3. I eat crusts on bread and toast.
4. Let's jump in the pool and swim.
5. We must rush to the bus stop or we will miss the bus.